'The author shines a light on the less well-understood or more complex presentations of autism, including pathological demand avoidance, in this insightful, compassionate and practical book. Combining the latest research, years of direct clinical experience and detailed individual stories, this much-needed book will be invaluable for families and professionals.'

– Trustees of the PDA Society

'An excellent book by a knowledgeable author. It is easy to read and understand, and answered many of the questions I had about autism spectrum disorders. I recommend this book to anyone who is interested in learning more about this topic.'

– Dr Olumide Kuti, consultant forensic psychiatrist,
The Huntercombe Hospital Norwich

of related interest

Women and Girls with Autism Spectrum Disorder
Understanding Life Experiences from Early Childhood to Old Age
Sarah Hendrickx
ISBN 978 1 84905 547 5
eISBN 978 0 85700 982 1

A Practical Guide to Mental Health Problems in
Children with Autistic Spectrum Disorder
It's not just their autism!
Khalid Karim, Alvina Ali and Michelle O'Reilly
ISBN 978 1 84905 323 5
eISBN 978 0 85700 697 4

Understanding Pathological Demand Avoidance Syndrome in Children
A Guide for Parents, Teachers and Other Professionals
Phil Christie, Margaret Duncan, Ruth Fidler and Zara Healy
ISBN 978 1 84905 074 6
eISBN 978 0 85700 253 2

Attacking Anxiety
A Step-by-Step Guide to an Engaging Approach to Treating Anxiety and
Phobias in Children with Autism and Other Developmental Disabilities
Karen Levine and Naomi Chedd
ISBN 978 1 84905 788 2
eISBN 978 1 78450 044 3

Understanding and Treating Self-Injurious Behavior in Autism
A Multi-Disciplinary Perspective
Edited by Stephen M. Edelson and Jane Botsford Johnson
Foreword by Temple Grandin
ISBN 978 1 84905 741 7
eISBN 978 1 78450 189 1

A GUIDE TO MENTAL HEALTH ISSUES IN GIRLS AND YOUNG WOMEN ON THE AUTISM SPECTRUM

Diagnosis, Intervention and Family Support

Dr Judy Eaton

Jessica Kingsley *Publishers*
London and Philadelphia

First published in 2018
by Jessica Kingsley Publishers
73 Collier Street
London N1 9BE, UK
and
400 Market Street, Suite 400
Philadelphia, PA 19106, USA

www.jkp.com

Library of Congress Cataloging in Publication Data
Names: Eaton, Judy, author.
Title: A guide to mental health issues in girls and young women on the autism
spectrum : diagnosis, intervention and family support / Dr. Judy Eaton.
Description: London ; Philadelphia : Jessica Kingsley Publishers, 2018. |
Includes bibliographical references and index.
Identifiers: LCCN 2017017079 | ISBN 9781785920929 (alk. paper)
Subjects: | MESH: Autism Spectrum Disorder--diagnosis | Women | Autism
Spectrum Disorder--complications | Child | Adolescent | Family Relations |
Professional-Patient Relations | United Kingdom | Case Reports
Classification: LCC RC553.A88 | NLM WS 350.8.P4 | DDC 616.85/882--dc23 LC
record available at https://lccn.loc.gov/2017017079

British Library Cataloguing in Publication Data
A CIP catalogue record for this book is available from the British Library

ISBN 978 1 78592 092 9
eISBN 978 1 78450 355 0

Printed and bound in Great Britain

MIX
Paper from
responsible sources
FSC® C013056
www.fsc.org

This book is dedicated to all the girls and young women with autism, and their families

Acknowledgements

With grateful thanks to all the brave young women and their families who were kind enough to share their stories of diagnosis and coming to terms with diagnosis.

My very special thanks go to those who were able to talk about their struggles with mental health difficulties.

Contents

Preface

The motivation to write this book came about as a result of many years of working clinically with individuals who have autism, both in a diagnostic capacity and therapeutically.

Many girls and women did not (and still do not) get a diagnosis of their difficulties, and there is growing evidence that they will have an increased risk of experiencing issues with friendships and relationships, be prone to bullying and harassment, and may well experience significant mental health problems.

It is hoped that this book will further raise awareness of this important area and provide guidance for both families and those working professionally with this group.

List of Abbreviations

3Di	Developmental, Dimensional and Diagnostic Interview
ABA	applied behavioural analysis
ADHD	attention deficit hyperactivity disorder
ADI-R	Autism Diagnostic Interview – Revised
ADOS	Autism Diagnostic Observation Schedule
AQ	autism-spectrum quotient
ARFID	avoidant and restrictive food intake disorder
ASD	autism spectrum disorder
BMI	body mass index
BVAQ	Bermond-Vorst Alexithymia Questionnaire
CAMHS	Child and Adolescent Mental Health Services
CAT	cognitive analytic therapy
CBT	cognitive behavioural therapy
CDC	Centers for Disease Control and Prevention
CGAS	Children's Global Assessment Scale
CRT	cognitive remediation therapy
CTO	community treatment order
DID	dissociative identity disorder
DISCO	Diagnostic Interview for Social and Communication Disorders
DBD	disruptive behaviour disorders
DBT	dialectical behavioural therapy
DDP	dyadic developmental psychotherapy

DSM-5	*Diagnostic and Statistical Manual of Mental Disorders, 5th Edition*
ECT	electroconvulsive therapy
EDA-Q	Extreme Demand Avoidance Questionnaire
EQ	empathy quotient
FII	fabricated and induced illness
GP	general practitioner
ICD-10	*International Classification of Diseases and Related Health Problems, Version 10*
IRI	Interpersonal Reactivity Index
IU	intolerance of uncertainty
MCDD	multiple complex developmental disorder
NICE	National Institute for Health and Care Excellence
NLD	non-verbal learning disability
OCD	obsessive compulsive disorder
ODD	oppositional defiance disorder
PBS	positive behaviour support
PDA	pathological demand avoidance
PDD-NOS	pervasive developmental disorder not otherwise specified
PTSD	post-traumatic stress disorder
RBS-R	Repetitive Behaviour Scale – Revised
SCID-IV	Structured Clinical Interview for DSM-IV Axis I Disorders
SQ	systemising quotient
WISC-IV	Wechsler Intelligence Scale for Children, Version IV

Chapter 1

Accessing a Diagnosis

This chapter explores the issues that face families trying to access a diagnosis from their local autism/neurodevelopmental team.

It also examines the NICE (National Institute for Health and Care Excellence) guidelines for assessment and diagnosis and the ICD-10 and DSM-5 criteria, and explores both autism and pathological demand avoidance in girls.

This chapter also looks at the types of assessment tools (including 'gold standard' assessments such as the Autism Diagnostic Observation Schedule (ADOS)) commonly used in diagnosis and examines how these tools can often fail to identify the difficulties experienced by girls on the autism spectrum.

The idea for writing this book started when I began working in a newly opened Tier 4 CAMHS (Child and Adolescent Mental Health Services) inpatient unit in the United Kingdom, for adolescents between the ages of 12 and 18. The unit opened in 2013 and plans were in place, at that time, to expand the age range up to 25. This came about following the report by Austen (2009) which referred to the transition from child to adult mental health services as like 'falling off a cliff'. Many of the patients admitted to the unit were female and it quickly became apparent that a high number of these young women either came into hospital with a diagnosis of autism or were subsequently assessed and given a diagnosis. Presenting difficulties ranged from eating disorders through to extreme self-harm and suicidal ideation. Most also presented with extremely challenging, and often violent, behaviour. A number were (wrongly) diagnosed as having emerging borderline personality disorder or schizo-affective disorder. Some seemed to meet diagnostic criteria for bipolar affective disorder. All were extremely troubled and distressed young women, who were often many miles away from family and friends and placed in an environment which, although every effort had been made to make the hospital as welcoming and friendly as possible, was often very noisy and brightly lit.

It was then decided to carry out an informal audit of all the patients admitted. This revealed that some 36 per cent of all of the girls admitted to the hospital were somewhere on the autism spectrum. Some, initially diagnosed with autism (usually 'atypical' autism), quite clearly met the criteria for pathological demand avoidance (PDA). Pathological demand avoidance was first described by Elizabeth Newson in the 1980s and is now widely accepted as being part of the broader autism spectrum. However, very little research evidence is available regarding the behavioural outcomes of children diagnosed with pathological demand avoidance when they reach adolescence and beyond. Many professionals dislike the use of the term 'pathological' when describing the degree of anxiety and demand avoidance, as they feel it is 'judgemental' and 'derogatory' to the young person. Others object to its use in diagnostic terms, because it does not appear in the current versions of the diagnostic manuals used in clinical practice. However, there is no doubt that there is a (albeit small) group of young people (both males and females) who present with a consistent pattern of extremely high levels of anxiety and rigid thinking, which leads to avoidance of everyday demands (such as dressing, going to school, holding down a job), including everyday boundaries and instructions. Some clinicians attribute this to trauma and early attachment difficulties, others to parenting issues, and there are currently no clear guidelines for supporting this group of young people, and little research about the impact of these difficulties over a person's lifetime.

Research evidence regarding the mental health issues experienced by young people on the autism spectrum (Skokausus and

Gallagher 2012) noted that around 46.2 per cent are likely to suffer from significant anxiety. This is probably an under-estimation. Clinical experience of working with this client group would suggest that the percentage is likely to be much higher. Siegel *et al.* (2011) noted in a study of 33,000 children in the United States that young people with autism were 11.9 times more likely to need admission to a psychiatric hospital than typically developing children. A study by Ghaziuddin *et al.* (2002) suggested that 40 per cent of males with a diagnosis of autism show evidence of psychiatric co-morbidity (depression, anxiety, obsessive compulsive disorder (OCD), episodes of psychosis). It was also reported that the Lorna Wing Centre for Autism (which is one of a handful of centres across the United Kingdom that assess the more complex cases where autism is suspected) revealed that the co-morbidity of autism for psychiatric conditions in women was very high, with diagnoses of eating disorders, personality disorder and selective mutism being common.

A study carried out in 2006 (Crocombe *et al.* 2006) for the National Autistic Society examined cases of women who were detained in high secure hospitals in the United Kingdom (by definition these would have been women presenting with very significant levels of challenging behaviour). The study found that, out of 51 patients, six had an existing diagnosis of autism and a further five could be diagnosed as 'probable autism'.

A further, cross-sectional study, looking at adult females in a psychiatric unit diagnosed with borderline personality disorder (Ryden, Ryden and Jecker 2008), concluded that 15 per cent of these patients would also meet criteria for a diagnosis of autism. The study also found that these patients were presenting with significantly higher levels of self-harm than those who only received a diagnosis of borderline personality disorder.

Finally, a paper presented by Chithiramohan *et al.* (2013) at the 2013 Royal College of Psychiatrists Annual Meeting analysed inpatient admissions to a Midlands CAMHS Tier 4 service. Their particular interest was in girls who were presenting with eating disorders. It was reported that of the girls admitted primarily for eating difficulties, 36 per cent were subsequently diagnosed with autism, and an interesting article by Simmons (2016) entitled 'Women with autism: Do they really suffer less than men?' describes the case of a girl called Lucy who was ultimately diagnosed with autism at the age of 17, following her admission to an eating disorders unit with episodes of self-harm.

All of these studies would suggest that it is entirely possible that there are a significant number of young women with (possibly undiagnosed) autism in the psychiatric system in the United Kingdom. It may be helpful, therefore, to explore the reasons why it appears that so many young women are 'missed' or overlooked in terms of a diagnosis.

Autism is a lifelong developmental condition, with overall prevalence rates believed to be around the 1 per cent mark, although the study published by Christensen et al. in 2012 for the Centers for Disease Control and Prevention (CDC) in the United States discussed an overall prevalence rate for autism in the United States of 1:68 (1:45 for boys and 1:189 for girls). Evidence currently suggests (Tantam 2012) that autism, although a lifelong condition, may present challenges for some individuals at different stages in their lives. For many, times of transition (from infant to junior school, junior to senior school, and school to adult life) can present significant issues, for others their difficulties may abate as they approach adulthood. It is now acknowledged that for many young people, their difficulties do not become apparent until the social and academic demands upon them increase during the middle school years.

Brugha (2009), in the most recent and comprehensive study of adults, estimated an overall population prevalence rate in the United Kingdom of 1 per cent (1.8% of males, 0.2% of females).

An earlier study carried out by Lorna Wing in 1981 cited ratios of 15:1 male to female prevalence of autism. The ratio for those children at the more severe end of the spectrum, where the children often presented with severe learning difficulties in addition to behaviours that could be attributed to autism, was cited as 2:1 male to female. More recent studies (Attwood 2000; Ehlers and Gillberg 1993) have revised the 15:1 ratio to a more realistic 4:1 boys to girls.

However, there is significant evidence to suggest that females with autism are likely to be under- or misdiagnosed. The Somerset Asperger's team, a specialist team based at Somerset Partnership NHS Foundation Trust, who were commissioned to carry out assessments of adults and young people over the age of 18, carried out a small-scale (unpublished) study between 2008 and 2010. Of the 40 diagnoses made during this time, 33 per cent were female.

The paper by Gould and Ashton-Smith (2011) entitled 'Missed diagnosis or misdiagnosis' explores the reasons why so many girls may not initially receive an appropriate diagnosis, and the ways in which autism may present differently in boys and girls. In order to further explore the reasons why this might be the case, it is necessary to examine how a diagnosis of an autism spectrum disorder (ASD) is made.

Diagnosis of children

Quite often, one of the biggest challenges that parents in the United Kingdom face is timely access to a diagnostic assessment when they suspect their child may be on the autism spectrum.

The National Autism Plan for Children was developed by the National Autistic Society and published in 2003, in collaboration with the Royal College of Paediatrics and Child Health and the Royal College of Psychiatrists. The National Autism Plan for Children was the first set of guidelines in the United Kingdom that were designed to address identification, assessment, diagnosis and access to early interventions for pre-school and primary school age children who were suspected of having autism.

NICE (2011) have produced a pathway to aid clinicians in assessing for possible autism in the United Kingdom. It includes guidelines for recognition, referral and diagnosis, as follows:

» Each geographical area should have a dedicated multi-disciplinary team which should include:

– a paediatrician and/or a child and adolescent psychiatrist

- a clinical and/or educational psychologist

- a speech and language therapist.

» Each team should also have access to (if not included in the core team) the expertise of the following group of professionals:

- a paediatric neurologist/paediatrician

- a child and adolescent psychiatrist

- an educational psychologist

- a clinical psychologist

- an occupational therapist.

The NICE guidelines also highlight the importance of including other key professionals who are likely to make a valuable contribution to any assessment. These include, for example, a specialist health visitor or nurse, a specialist teacher and a social worker.

It was also recommended that each area has a dedicated single point of referral to the autism team.

The process for assessment and diagnosis appears to be similar across the English-speaking world. In the United States, assessment of autism may be conducted by a range of professionals including psychiatrists, psychologists, neurologists and paediatricians. However, in order for the child to be eligible for a range of support in school, federal law dictates that a 'multi-disciplinary' approach is required, which usually involves a psychologist and a speech and language pathologist. In Australia and Canada, the process is similar. However, in Australia, concerned parents are able to access intervention programmes prior to receiving a formal diagnosis.

In the United Kingdom, most areas now have a dedicated team for the assessment and diagnosis of autism. The NICE guidelines also state that assessment for autism should be started within three months of a referral being made. In reality, the experience of many parents in the United Kingdom is very different. In 2015 a group of researchers (Crane *et al.* 2015) recruited parents through the National Autistic Society. The National Autistic Society is a British charity for people with autism spectrum disorders, the purpose of which is to improve the lives of those living with autism in the United Kingdom. The National Autistic Society invited parents to contact them via their website and answer questions about their experiences of getting a diagnosis for their child. Ninety-five per cent of respondents were from a white Caucasian background, with few responses from black and minority ethnic backgrounds. The study revealed that, on the whole, parents are very good at identifying difficulties in their own children. Most had noticed problems before the age of five. On average, parents waited 'around one year' before contacting a health professional with their concerns. The average delay between first contact with a professional and final diagnosis was 3.6 years, with delays of four years for more able children being quite common. Public Health England, cited in the British Academy of Childhood Disability (BACD) Spring Newsletter, found that in the UK in 2016, waits of between 84 and 95 weeks for an assessment have been reported (BACD 2016). Many parents report experiencing severe stress during this wait period, as they believe (sometimes incorrectly) that access to support and services is dependent upon a diagnosis.

In addition, and perhaps more importantly for families who are often struggling with challenging behaviour or worrying levels of anxiety, the NICE Quality Standards (2014) recommend that all families who are given a diagnosis for their child should have the following:

» a plan, which is personalised for the individual, that is developed in partnership with family and/or carers

» the offer of support from a named keyworker to assist in coordinating the support outlined in their plan

» the opportunity to meet with a member of the autism team post-diagnosis to discuss what interventions might be helpful and appropriate for them.

In reality, the Crane *et al.* (2015) study showed that whilst 85 per cent of respondents received a report outlining their child's difficulties, only 56 per cent were offered a follow-up appointment with professionals. Many parents report (personal correspondence) that it is becoming increasingly difficult to access any kind of follow-on support from local Child and Adolescent Mental Health teams due to increasing pressure on these services. A number reported having been told that their child's difficulties were 'not sufficiently severe' to be able to access intervention and support. As a consequence, many parents feel obliged to source what support they can from social media or (voluntary) parent support groups.

How autism is diagnosed and the implications for girls on the spectrum

Autism and Asperger's syndrome were formerly diagnosed in the United Kingdom and Europe using the ICD-10 (*International Statistical Classification of Diseases and Related Health Problems, 10th Revision*) and DSM-IV (*Diagnostic and Statistical Manual of Mental Disorders, Version IV*) which were based on Wing and Gould's (1979) triad of impairments. The DSM-IV did not include a diagnostic category for Asperger's syndrome until 1994. The DSM was revised recently and many clinicians are now using the DSM-5 (American Psychiatric Association (APA) 2013).

Some of the most important changes from the DSM-IV to the DSM-5 are those made in the diagnostic criteria for autism. The revised criteria were intended to provide greater medical and scientific accuracy in the diagnostic process. The DSM-IV included four separate categories of disorder: autistic disorder, Asperger's disorder, disintegrative disorder, and the somewhat unhelpful diagnosis of pervasive developmental disorder not otherwise specified (PDD-NOS). However, a neurodevelopmental work group, led by Dr Susan Swedo, senior investigator at the National Institute of Mental Health, found that these diagnoses were not being consistently applied and it was felt that the criteria proposed for the DSM-5 should improve the diagnosis of autism.

The ICD-10 is due to be revised by 2018 and it is anticipated that ICD-11 will mirror the changes in DSM-5. The National Autistic Society (2016) has produced a full explanation of how these changes may affect the diagnostic process in future. A summary is included below:

> The previous use of three domains of impairments has been reduced to two domains:
>
> » social communication and interaction
>
> » restricted, repetitive patterns of behaviour, interests or activities.

Sensory difficulties are included in the diagnostic criteria for the first time, under the 'restricted, repetitive patterns of behaviours' descriptors.

The DSM-5 has also introduced 'dimensional elements' which are designed to give an indication of how much someone's condition affects them. It is likely that these 'dimensional elements' will be used to determine how much support an individual is likely to need.

The DSM-5 also includes a new category called 'social communication disorder'. There has always been a group of children who have significant social communication difficulties and who may have fulfilled that element of the diagnostic criteria, but who did not present with particularly rigid and inflexible behaviour. It remains to be seen how useful this category is for parents of young people diagnosed with this condition and the young people themselves, as attempting to define the degree of 'rigid and inflexible behaviour' an individual demonstrates is always going to be subjective.

The DSM-5 no longer has a separate category for Asperger's syndrome. This has caused some concern amongst those with this diagnosis who often identify strongly with being an 'Aspie'. One recent study (Hartley-McAndrew *et al.* 2016) studied the case records of 1552 children previously assessed for autism using the DSM-IV and found significantly fewer would have received a diagnosis using the DSM-5 (39% compared to 50%). It will be interesting to see whether this study is replicated, and to examine the impact of the new 'social communication disorder' diagnosis upon the level of support that children receive.

Wing, Gould and Gillberg (2011) also concluded that the new DSM-5 criteria might make it even more difficult for girls on the spectrum to get a diagnosis.

In addition, and most importantly, the criteria outlined above were initially devised for assisting in the diagnosis of young children. They do not always easily fit an adolescent or adult diagnostic assessment. Haskins and Silva (2006) discussed how sometimes obtaining accurate and objective information about a young person's early developmental history can be difficult, if not impossible. This is especially pertinent if the young person has been adopted or is in the care system as a 'looked after child', particularly if there have been multiple caregivers and/or placement moves.

In terms of the assessment and diagnosis of girls, autism is a neurodevelopmental disorder and there tends to be higher numbers of males diagnosed with all neurodevelopmental disorders. As a consequence, it is likely that the diagnostic criteria, which have evolved for autism and conditions such as attention deficit hyperactivity disorder (ADHD), are biased towards a 'male' presentation of the disorders. The work of Professor Simon Baron-Cohen from the Cambridge-based Autism Research Centre in the United Kingdom is well known. In 2002, Baron-Cohen published the article 'Extreme male brain theory of autism' which examined gender differences in systemising and empathising. Most clinicians are more familiar with the 'male' version of autism. There is now some evidence to suggest that the way in which autism presents in girls is less well documented.

Going right back to the work of Leo Kanner in the 1940s (Kanner 1943), when autism was in the early stages of identification, ratios such as four boys for every one girl diagnosed were cited. This remains true for the relatively small percentage of children who are identified at a very young age with the classic 'Kanner's' autism. These girls tend to be those who have been diagnosed with an additional learning difficulty, are often non-verbal and display the typical autistic stereotyped movements and repetitive behaviours.

However, for girls at the higher end of the IQ spectrum, getting a diagnosis can be extremely difficult. A paper examining sex differences in autism spectrum disorders by Halladay *et al.* (2015) mirrors Gould and Ashton-Smith (2011) in describing the different ways in which girls on the spectrum present. Both papers point towards girls having better verbal ability and fewer restricted interests and repetitive behaviours compared to boys. Gould and Ashton-Smith (2011) state that 'unenlightened clinicians perceive someone who is superficially "able" and who has reciprocal social communication, may not meet criteria using ICD 10 or DSM-5' (p.37). Play is often perceived to be better in girls on the autism spectrum compared to boys, and they often appear to make reciprocal friendships so it is not surprising if they are initially missed. It could be argued that, because of the inherent sex differences between boys and girls, separate criteria for the diagnosis of girls should be included in the guidelines.

It also appears that girls generally tend to be diagnosed later. Hiller, Young and Weber (2016) noted that, in the absence of intellectual impairment, girls tend not to be assessed until late childhood.

This trend was reflected in my clinical experience working in a United Kingdom National Health Service autism diagnostic team in the Midlands during the 2000s. Between 2003 and 2006, researchers from Durham University on behalf of the Department of Health carried out annual mapping of the national CAMHS in the United Kingdom. This mapping exercise required all CAMHS teams to submit demographic data about the children they had involvement with. As the autism team I worked in was set up specifically to receive referrals for autism assessments, the data generated provided an insight into the age at which children were referred. In line with expectations, the gender split in the early years was around 4:1 boys to girls. However, it was noted that there was a significant increase in the number of girls referred between the ages of 10 and 16. This is the age when social relationships in general, and friendships in particular, become much more complex and cracks may start to appear in terms of social interaction for girls, particularly as they approach puberty. The differences observed between girls on the autism spectrum and their neuro-typical peers become slowly more apparent. Although they may have a strong desire to 'fit in', very often they will get things slightly wrong – the clothes they wear may be slightly odd or their make-up (if they choose to wear it) may be somewhat garish and 'over the top'. Alternatively, they may not be remotely interested in fitting in with others, and may develop their own slightly 'quirky' style, and be more interested in animals or a fantasy world than fitting in with peers. Personal hygiene may also become an issue.

Pathological demand avoidance

Although pathological demand avoidance does not appear in the current versions of either the DSM-5 or the ICD-10 (World Health Organization 2016), no discussion of the diagnosis of autism in girls would be complete without consideration of this complex disorder, as current thinking suggests that there are roughly equal numbers of boys and girls diagnosed with the pathological demand avoidance behavioural profile.

The concept of pathological demand avoidance, as a separate diagnostic category, was first proposed by Elizabeth Newson some 20 years ago, and since then a large number of children have been assessed and found to fit the clinical picture she described (Newson, LeMarechal and David 2003). Initial figures for the gender ratio for children with pathological demand avoidance was 50:50 boys to girls. The overriding feature of these children was that, although they often did not quite fit the classical presentation of an autism spectrum disorder, they were very similar to *each other*. The National Autistic Society now views pathological demand avoidance as part of the broader autism spectrum. In the United Kingdom, the degree to which pathological demand avoidance is accepted as a diagnosis, or as a behavioural description, varies. It is not currently as well known or accepted in other parts of the world.

Children with pathological demand avoidance have an inability to tolerate demands imposed upon them and an overwhelming need to control their environment. This need for control is fuelled by huge levels of anxiety, leading to the child engaging in increasingly challenging, and often outrageous, behaviour. These children may exhibit superficial sociability, but tend to lack responsibility and awareness of acceptable boundaries (social or otherwise). They also tend to be extremely impulsive and demonstrate lability of mood with frequent temper tantrums and 'meltdowns'. These difficulties often become more apparent when the child begins to attend school, when demands on them tend to become greater. Behaviour can deteriorate quickly and the child may resort to manipulation, or even violence, to avoid demands. More often the child will resort to this type of behaviour across all settings, causing huge disruption within the classroom. However, it is not uncommon for children to 'hold it together' and remain compliant whilst they are at school, and display extremely challenging and distressed behaviour when out of school. This can include hitting, biting and kicking and distressed behaviour which can last for many hours.

Avoidance tactics can include repetitive questioning, ignoring, changing the subject, talking over people, or other extreme behaviour, such as removing clothing. Their behaviour can be humiliating and distressing to parents. They can find it difficult to negotiate with peers and can become bossy and domineering during play.

Diagnostic criteria for pathological demand avoidance are still in development. The Extreme Demand Avoidance Questionnaire (EDA-Q) described in O'Nions *et al.* (2014) is currently in the process of validation. O'Nions *et al.* (2016) discusses identifying features of pathological demand avoidance using the Diagnostic Interview for Social and Communication Disorders (DISCO), which is one of the better-known structured instruments for assessing autism. Gillberg *et al.* (2015) conducted a screen for autism of the total population of 15–24-year-olds in the Faroe Islands. They identified

67 young people who would meet diagnostic criteria for autism (in line with a 1% prevalence rate). However, interestingly, of those 67 children, nine children (13%) were found to meet the criteria for pathological demand avoidance.

There has been much debate about how pathological demand avoidance differs from an attachment disorder or oppositional defiance disorder (ODD). There are superficially significant overlaps between the two. However, there are significant differences, which can often be missed in a standard diagnostic assessment appointment. Girls who have autism and, in particular, those who have pathological demand avoidance, are often very good at masking their difficulties. They often have an inherent desire to please and to fit in with social norms for behaviour, and try very hard to maintain a 'persona' whilst in public. (See Chapter 10 for some examples of this in women reflecting upon their own journey towards a diagnosis of autism.)

Clinical experience has also shown that many parents, when they present with their child for assessment, are faced with the suggestion that their child may have attachment difficulties, or even be given a diagnosis of attachment disorder. Listed below are a number of behaviours frequently seen in children with attachment disorders:

» superficially charming in order to get what he/she wants

» indiscriminately affectionate with unfamiliar adults

» lacks genuine affection with primary caregivers (especially mother)

» controlling, bossy, manipulative, defiant, argumentative, demanding, impulsive

» preoccupied with fire, death, blood or gore

» cruel to animals, destroys property, aggressive toward others or self

» destructive, accident-prone

» has rages or long temper tantrums, especially in response to adult authority

» gives poor eye contact, except when lying

» blames others for his or her problems

» lacks self-control

» lacks cause-and-effect thinking

» lies, steals, shows no remorse, has no conscience, is defiant

» hoards or sneaks food, has strange eating habits

» has poor hygiene: wets or soils him- or herself

» has difficulty maintaining friendships

» is an underachiever

» asks persistent nonsense questions and chatters incessantly

» has a grandiose sense of self

» lacks trust in others to care for him/her.

As can be seen, the overlap with pathological demand avoidance is extensive and it can sometimes be difficult to unpick the two. However, it does highlight the need for a full and comprehensive assessment, as when the child with suspected pathological demand avoidance is assessed, subtle autistic difficulties almost always become apparent within a relatively short time. Children with a pathological demand avoidance profile are also likely to have difficulties with the social (or pragmatic) use of language. They tend not to be very 'streetwise' and may behave in ways that make them quite vulnerable or appear naive. The majority will often have sensory or motor processing difficulties and most will demonstrate very high levels of anxiety, often when things they want to do don't go to plan, or they cannot have something that they want. The issue of missed or inappropriate diagnosis is explored more fully in the next chapter, along with a more detailed description of the differences and similarities between autism and other diagnoses (such as attachment disorder, conduct disorder and oppositional defiance disorder).

Assessing for autism

It is important to note that there is no one process which is either recommended or followed by health professionals in either the United Kingdom or elsewhere in terms of referral or diagnosis. The NICE guidelines provide just that – a guideline. Experiences vary across the country. For some, the assessment process takes place over a period of time. If concerns are raised when a child is young, the first appointment might be with a paediatrician or specialist health visitor, who may then refer on for further assessment. For older children, especially those whose difficulties may not become apparent until the early years at school, the first person to raise concerns may be a teacher. Diagnostic assessments may be carried out at a variety of locations or at a specialist clinic. Some teams collect information and operate a diagnostic 'panel' system whereby assessments from several professionals are considered, sometimes without actually meeting the child. Parents are often confused and anxious about the process, and about the delays that often occur between appointments.

Diagnosis in childhood in the United Kingdom, as stated in the 2011 NICE guidelines, recommends that assessment is carried out by a multi-disciplinary team that includes paediatrics/psychiatry (to rule out any medical conditions/syndromes), psychology (to assess cognitive ability) and speech and language therapy (to distinguish between autism and language disorders). The input of a paediatric occupational therapist (to examine and advise upon sensory processing issues) is also recommended.

Certain standardised diagnostic instruments such as the DISCO, the Autism Diagnostic Interview – Revised (ADI-R) and the Developmental, Dimensional and Diagnostic Interview (3Di) alongside the ADOS are often considered as the 'gold standard' for assessment and diagnosis. However, the NICE guidelines also acknowledge that whilst standardised assessment tools allow for greater confidence in any diagnosis given, much of the diagnostic decision making will still need to rely on strong clinical experience and judgement. This is unfortunately where the diagnostic process often falls short. Many autism teams find that they are stretched to capacity, due to the rate at which children are referred to them.

Some teams can be over-reliant upon the results of certain standardised assessments. I and other colleagues involved in the diagnostic process frequently hear, 'I was told that although there were some features of autism she didn't score above the cut-off in the ADOS, so they ruled out autism.' This is most definitely *not* what the ADOS is designed for. Instructions for using the ADOS explicitly state that it is to be used as *part of* a comprehensive assessment and that it is *not* a stand-alone assessment for autism. The ADOS is an excellent assessment tool, consisting of four modules that provide a standardised mixture of play-based activities and interview-type questions which can be used to assess very young children, right through to adults. It is scored by appropriately trained assessors, who will be looking at the quality of play and interaction demonstrated during the assessment along with the use of gesture, facial expression and the overall rapport built with the examiner. However, it is a subjective judgement based upon the behaviour seen on that day, in that context. It is a snapshot of the child. It is not always good at picking up girls on the autism spectrum. A recent study by Rynkiewicz *et al.* (2016) investigated the 'camouflage' effect for girls in autism using the ADOS. They found that girls with autism tended to be more verbally able and, more importantly, used more 'vivid' gestures than boys. Their eye contact also tended to be better. In addition, it is well documented that girls on the autism spectrum tend to engage in more imaginative play than boys on the spectrum. Again, this might lead assessors to miss features of autism in girls when using certain assessments.

Watching a girl on the autism spectrum playing during a play-based assessment such as the ADOS can be fascinating. What may initially feel like perfectly normal pretend play with miniature figures is, upon close observation, quickly revealed to be very different. Girls with autism often like to organise toys. Dolls' houses are beautifully arranged with everything in its place. When asked to play with the toys, they will often re-enact a sequence, and frequently this will be something they have experienced during their day. However, when watched for a period of time, it becomes apparent that these girls do not move on or extend the play sequence in any way. When the examiner joins in with the play (which is also part of the ADOS assessment), any attempt to move the game on or take the play off in a different direction is often met with refusal. Usually this is done quite gently but firmly, but at other times it can be apparent that the child is becoming anxious or even quite cross. Sometimes, the reaction can be total bemusement or, if asked to carry on playing the game alone, the girl may simply freeze and look lost.

The ADOS also contains a number of questions that examine the understanding of everyday relationships, such as friendship. Many girls can, and do, give a perfectly acceptable answer for these types of questions. Very often though, this is a learned response. Many girls spend hours watching TV programmes and YouTube videos, quite literally learning how to behave socially.

There are four modules in the ADOS, which aim to cover both the age range and language level of the child/adult. All three of the modules that are intended for children who have reasonably good verbal skills contain an element of unstructured conversation. This allows the examiner to look at the degree of reciprocity and the back-and-forth nature of the child or young person's conversation. This is probably the most revealing part of the whole assessment. It allows the examiner to evaluate whether the child can follow a conversational lead, and demonstrate an interest in what the other person is saying. Quite often, when I have been carrying out such an assessment, and the conversation has turned, for example, to a liking of animals, I will say, 'Oh, I love animals. We often go to see the baby seals on the beach near our house…' Most children would follow that up with a supplementary question like, 'Where is the beach?', 'Can you touch the baby seals?' or something similar. Almost without exception, the girls who have been assessed who subsequently receive a diagnosis will either completely ignore this type of 'conversational lead', or will continue the conversation on a totally different topic. Girls on the autism spectrum will also quite often start talking about something they have been thinking about without providing the examiner with the slightest clue about the topic. As a result, conversation with these girls tends not to flow and can contribute to what becomes a slightly stilted, or unnatural, conversation.

Impairment in the pragmatic or social use of language is often the first clue to social communication difficulties in girls. This can include interrupting others, taking the conversation off at a tangent on a topic of interest to themselves, and talking over people. Many girls find it a challenge to know what to say in unstructured situations and to 'read' the emotion in the room.

Girls on the autism spectrum also have significant difficulties with what is referred to as 'social imagination'. Difficulties with social imagination mean that girls with autism may find it hard to:

>> understand and interpret other people's thoughts, feelings and actions

>> predict what will happen next, or what could happen next

>> prepare for change and plan for the future

>> cope in new or unfamiliar situations.

Difficulties with social imagination should not be confused with a lack of imagination.

Very often, in girls on the autism spectrum, difficulties in social imagination are demonstrated by their poor skills of inference and prediction when answering questions. They may also struggle to problem solve in a situation, or to think creatively when playing a game. In the ADOS assessment there is also a storytelling task, in which they are shown a series of pictures and are asked to describe what is happening. Girls with autism assessed using the ADOS often find this very difficult, as they struggle to see how the clues in the pictures are linked from one page to another. Their narrative often becomes more a list of events than a story. Even when the theme is actually pointed out to them, this can still be a struggle.

A further example of where a lack of social imagination can be picked up during an assessment, is a tendency to expect other people to know what is being talked about without providing context or content. This, in combination with difficulty in answering questions that require her to use her own knowledge to make basic predictions, problem solve or create an explanation, is indicative of a weak theory of mind. Girls on the autism spectrum can find it hard to draw on their own experiences and think about the impact of their actions on others.

There are also issues with regard to the assessment of girls with some of the standardised developmental history tools. The ADI-R, for example, includes questions designed to explore the level of repetitive or obsessive behaviour displayed by the child. The questions ask about 'special interests' which may be 'all encompassing' in terms of intensity. Other questions explore whether the child lines up toys or sorts them in some way. These questions are more in line with the 'systemising' theory of autism put forward by Baron-Cohen and his colleagues, which tends to reflect a more 'male' presentation of the disorder. Girls on the autism spectrum tend to have fewer obsessive and all-encompassing interests than boys.

In addition, girls on the autism spectrum do tend to fare somewhat better in terms of friendships, at least in the primary school years. Therefore, questions which examine social approaches, group play with peers, or friendships are often answered positively. Many girls will have a 'best friend' and they may, at least superficially, play quite well with others. Again, it is necessary to dig beneath the surface and examine in detail the nature of these friendships. A girl with autism may jealously guard her 'best friend' and become distressed and angry if she wishes to play with someone else. Friendships in groups may be superficial and short-lived. Very often the girl on the autism spectrum will be too bossy or insistent upon playing games her way, and will quickly lose friends.

The NICE guidelines also recommend that the child is seen in different contexts (or at least that information about the child is gathered from someone outside of the family, such as a school teacher or support worker who knows the child well). This can also present a difficulty when attempting to assess a girl for autism. To the untrained eye, she may appear perfectly 'normal' in terms of her interaction with others. She may well be able to 'hold it all together' whilst she is at school and work really hard at not drawing attention to herself. Sadly, this takes its toll and many parents report huge meltdowns and behavioural difficulties as soon as the child gets home (or sometimes as soon as they exit the school gates). In these cases, it can be really hard for a diagnostic team to justify a diagnosis. Sometimes, unfortunately, this can result in the spotlight being turned in the direction of the parents, and more specifically their parenting style. Prior to being accepted for a diagnostic assessment, many parents have to effectively jump through hoops and attend parenting courses before their concerns are taken seriously. In some extremely sad cases, parents have reported involvement by children's services, including having their child placed on the Child Protection Register, or even being subject to care proceedings and removal of their child from their care. Other parents have been accused of fabricating their child's difficulties. These cases are thankfully rare but the pain and distress caused by this should not be underestimated (Chapter 10 includes accounts of this).

In addition, it is not unusual, once a diagnosis is given, for this to be challenged or overlooked when young people develop more serious mental health problems.

JS, a mother of a young adult with autism and PDA, described the difficulties she and her daughter have experienced:

> It wasn't difficult to get a diagnosis but it was impossible to get any help or support, as girls with autism can mimic normality, so it was seen that she didn't need any help. Even with a diagnosis, girls are not the same as boys, so the diagnosis isn't helpful as no one believes it, so they confront the issues caused by the autism rather than supporting them [the young person].

When questioned specifically about who questioned the diagnosis, JS replied:

Everyone, teachers, family, other parents, those in university, those in school – even people who were responsible for the care of children with special needs, almost any professional really. Also, there's no way of informing people about the diagnosis anyway, as the message is often not passed on.

Finally, and this is by no means an isolated case, when JS's daughter got older, her mental health deteriorated and she was ultimately seen by adult psychiatric services. As her daughter was an adult, JS was not automatically entitled to be part of any assessment. She also found that the paperwork confirming her daughter's diagnosis was archived and no record of it was made on her computerised general practitioner (GP) file. Her daughter was subsequently treated by her local mental health team, and her presentation deteriorated. Eventually JS 'gate-crashed' a session and her daughter was eventually re-diagnosed with autism. However, the daughter chose not to share this diagnosis when she was ultimately admitted to an inpatient psychiatric unit under a Mental Health Section. Again, it took her mother's intervention to clarify her diagnosis with her treating team.

Finally, in summary, it seems vital that the work done by Judith Gould and Jacqui Ashton-Smith through the Lorna Wing Centre for Autism in the United Kingdom, which outlines clearly the differences in the ways boys and girls with autism present, is shared widely and used as a starting point to develop separate diagnostic criteria for girls on the autism spectrum.

These differences are summarised below:

» In terms of social interaction, girls appear more able to copy their peers and imitate ways of behaving. This often masks their underlying autism.

» Girls tend to be more socially motivated and have a strong desire for friendship. However, they may have a tendency to become possessive of their friends and can become distressed if these friendships fail.

» Girls with autism tend to be more socially competent than boys with autism but they do struggle with social communication, will find small talk difficult and may struggle to appreciate social hierarchies.

» Girls with autism generally have an active imagination, particularly with regard to fantasy. They may also engage in more superficially imaginative play with dolls and miniature figures than boys.

» Girls with autism tend to have fewer special interests than boys on the autism spectrum. They can, however, become obsessed by people or fixated upon certain TV programmes, often imitating the sayings or mannerisms of the girls on these programmes.

» It is not uncommon for girls on the autism spectrum to be able to mask their difficulties at school and outside of the home environment. They may not be able to hold things together at home and angry outbursts and emotional meltdowns can be common.

(Gould and Ashton-Smith 2011)

References

American Psychiatric Association (2013) *Diagnostic and Statistical Manual of Mental Disorders, 5th Edition: DSM-5.* Arlington, VA: American Psychiatric Association.

Attwood, T. (2000) Asperger Syndrome: Some Common Questions: Do Girls have a Different Expression of the Syndrome? Accessed on 1 June 2017 at www.aspergerfoundation.org.uk/faq.htm#10.

Austen, B. (2009) The Development of Guidance for Commissioning and Delivery of Services for People Aged 16+ with Asperger Syndrome. A literature search for the South West Development Centre Regional Oversight Group.

BACD (2016) *British Academy of Childhood Disability Newsletter, Spring 2016.* London: BACD. Accessed on 17 August 2017 at www.bacdis.org.uk/publications/documents/BACDSpring2016.pdf.

Baron-Cohen, S. (2002) Extreme male brain theory of autism. *Trends in Cognitive Sciences 6,* 6, 248–254.

Brugha, T. (2009) *Autism Spectrum Disorders in Adults Living in Households throughout England: Report from the Adult Psychiatric Morbidity Survey 2007.* The NHS Information Centre for Health and Social Care. Accessed on 2 May 2017 at http://content.digital.nhs.uk/catalogue/PUB01131/aut-sp-dis-adu-liv-ho-a-p-m-sur-eng-2007-rep.pdf.

Chithiramohan, A., Silvasubramanian, K., Wardakhan, M. *et al.* (2013) 'Eating Disorders and Autism.' Presented at Royal College of Psychiatrists Faculty of Child and Adolescent Psychiatry Annual Residential Meeting, Edinburgh, 18–20 September.

Christensen, D.L., Baio, J., Braun, K.V. *et al.* (2012) Prevalence and characteristics of autism spectrum disorder among children aged 8 years. Autism and Developmental Disabilities Monitoring Network, 11 Sites, United States. *MMWR Surveillance Summary* 65 (No SS-3), 1–23.

Crane, L., Chester, J.W., Goddard, L. *et al.* (2015) Experiences of autism diagnosis: A survey of over 1000 parents in the United Kingdom. *Autism 20*, 2, 153–162.

Crocombe, J., Mills, R., Wing, L. *et al.* (2006) *ASD in the High Security Hospitals of the UK: A Summary of Two Studies*. London: National Autistic Society.

Ehlers, S. and Gillberg, C. (1993) The epidemiology of Asperger syndrome: A total population study. *Journal of Child Psychology and Psychiatry 34*, 8, 1327–1350.

Ghaziuddin, M., Ghaziuddin, N. and Greden, G. (2002) Depression in persons with autism: Implications for research and clinical care. *Journal of Autism and Developmental Disorders 32*, 4, 299–306.

Gillberg, C., Gillberg, I.C., Thompson, L. *et al.* (2015) Extreme (pathological) demand avoidance in autism: a general population study in the Faroe Islands. *European Journal of Child Adolescent Psychiatry 24*, 8, 979–984.

Gould, J. and Ashton-Smith, J. (2011) Missed diagnosis or misdiagnosis: Girls and women on the autism spectrum. *Good Autism Practice 12*, 1, 34–41.

Halladay, A.K., Bishop, S., Constantino, J.N. *et al.* (2015) Sex and gender differences in ASD: Summarising evidence gaps and identifying emerging areas of priority. *Molecular Autism*, doi 10.1186/s13229-015-0019-y.

Hartley-McAndrew, M., Mertz, J., Hoffman, M. *et al.* (2016) Rates of autism spectrum disorder diagnosis under the DSM-5 criteria compared to DSM-IV-TR criteria in a hospital-based clinic. *Paediatric Neurology 57*, 34–38.

Haskins, B.G. and Silva, J.A. (2006) Asperger's disorder and criminal behaviour: Forensic-psychiatric considerations. *Journal of the American Academy of Psychiatry Law 34*, 3, 374–384.

Hiller, R.M., Young, R.L, and Weber, N. (2016) Sex differences in pre-diagnosis concerns for children later diagnosed with autism spectrum disorders. *International Journal of Research and Practice 20*, 1, 75–84.

Kanner, L. (1943) Autistic disturbances of affective contact. *Nervous Child 2*, 217–250. National Initiative for Autism (2003) *National Autism Plan for Children (NAPC)*. London: National Autistic Society.

National Autistic Society (2016) Autism Profiles and Diagnostic Criteria. Accessed on 1 June 2017 at www.autism.org.uk/about/diagnosis/criteria-changes.aspx#criteria

Newson, E., LeMarechal, K. and David, C. (2003) Pathological demand avoidance syndrome: A necessary distinction within the pervasive developmental disorders. *Archives of Diseases in Childhood 88*, 7, 595–600.

NICE (2011) *Autism Spectrum Disorder in Under 19s: Recognition, Referral and Diagnosis (Clinical guideline CG128)*. London: NICE.

NICE (2014) *Autism Quality Standard (QS51)*. London: NICE.

O'Nions, E., Christie, P., Gould, J. *et al.* (2014) Development of the 'Extreme Demand Avoidance Questionnaire' (EDA-Q): Preliminary observations of a trait measurement for PDA. *Journal of Child Psychology and Psychiatry 55*, 7, 758–768.

O'Nions, E., Gould, J., Christie, P. *et al.* (2016) Identifying features of 'pathological demand avoidance' using the Diagnostic Interview for Social and Communication Disorders (DISCO). *European Journal of Child and Adolescent Psychiatry 25*, 407–419.

Ryden, G., Ryden, E. and Jecker, H. (2008) Borderline personality disorder and autism spectrum disorder in females – a cross-sectional study. *Clinical Neuropsychiatry 5*, 1, 22–30.

Rynkiewicz, A., Schuller, B., March, E. *et al.* (2016) An investigation of the female 'camouflage' effect in autism using a computerised ADOS-2 and a test of sex/gender differences. *Molecular Autism*, doi 10.1186/s13229-016-0073-0.

Siegel, M., Doyle, K., Chemelski, B. *et al.* (2011) Specialised inpatient psychiatry units for children with autism and developmental disorders: A United States survey. *Journal of Autism and Developmental Disorders 42*, 9, 1863–1869.

Simmons, E. (2016) Women with autism: Do they really suffer less than men? *New Statesman*, 29 February. Accessed on 2 May 2017 at www.newstatesman.com/politics/health/2016/02/women-autism-do-they-really-suffer-less-men.

Skokausus, N. and Gallagher, L. (2012) Mental health aspects of autistic spectrum disorders in children. *Journal of Intellectual Disability Research 56*, 3, 248–257.

Tantam, D. (2012) *Autism Spectrum Disorders through the Lifespan*. London: Jessica Kingsley Publishers.

Wing, L. (1981) Sex ratios in early childhood autism and related conditions. *Psychiatry Research 5*, 2, 129–137.

Wing, L. and Gould, J. (1979) Severe impairments of social interaction and associated abnormalities in children: Epidemiology and classification. *Journal of Autism and Developmental Disorders 9*, 1, 11–29.

Wing, L., Gould, J. and Gillberg, C. (2011) Autism spectrum disorders in the DSM-V: Better or worse than the DSM-IV? *Research in Developmental Disability 32*, 2, 768-773.

World Health Organization (2016) *International Statistical Classification of Diseases and Related Health Problems, 10th Revision*. Geneva: World Health Organization.

Chapter 2

Misdiagnosis

> This chapter explores, using case studies, occasions when girls on the autism spectrum are wrongly diagnosed with emerging personality disorder, oppositional defiance disorder or conduct disorder. The differences between autism and PDA, personality disorder, conduct disorder and oppositional defiance disorder are examined in addition to how girls on the spectrum present when they have co-morbid ADHD.
>
> Finally, this chapter will examine the difficulties that parents of girls on the autism spectrum have experienced in accessing appropriate support at home and at school, particularly if the child is able to mask her difficulties in school.

The previous chapter described the issues faced by many parents and carers in initially accessing an assessment for possible autism; but what happens if, after all that waiting, parents finally get an assessment only to be told that the team conducting the assessment do not feel that there is sufficient evidence to confirm a diagnosis of autism? Worse still, how do parents feel, after struggling for years to make sense of their daughter's behaviour, if they are told that the difficulties are due to an attachment disorder, oppositional defiance disorder or poor parenting, or even that they are fabricating or exaggerating their child's symptoms?

Two distinct areas of misdiagnosis will be discussed in this chapter. The first is that of 'primary misdiagnosis' and will explore the potential for mistakenly attributing a child's behaviour to either attachment disorder, oppositional defiance disorder/ conduct disorder or poor parenting. The second explores the issue of 'secondary misdiagnosis'. This term is used to describe the experiences of many young women on the autism spectrum who may or may not have had a diagnosis of autism at some time during their childhood and who go on to come in contact with adult mental health services. Quite often these young women and their families report that the paperwork for their initial diagnostic assessment is 'lost' or unavailable, leading to delays in accessing the most appropriate type of support or even to them receiving completely inappropriate treatment.

The case described in the paper by Von Schalkwyk *et al.* (2015) is fairly typical. The study describes the experiences of a 19-year-old woman, who was seen in an adult mental health outpatient clinic when she reported experiencing auditory hallucinations. These were most often reported after she had behaved aggressively. She had been assessed for and received a diagnosis of autism at the age of 11 but, somehow, the results from this assessment were 'not available' to the clinicians who were treating her. Consequently, this young woman was given a diagnosis of schizo-affective disorder and put on anti-psychotics. Even though it was noted that this young woman had high levels of anxiety associated with her mother's (and primary caregiver's) ill health, significant social communication difficulties and an apparent lack of empathy, it took some time before it became clear to those working with her that she had autism. Consequently, it was found that the 'voices' she reported waxed and waned depending upon her anxiety level at any given time. Her anti-psychotic medication was reduced and she was put on anti-anxiety medication instead. This particular case had a good outcome. Unfortunately, this is not the case for many young women on the autism spectrum, who often continue to receive inappropriate support and care for many years.

Another label given to young women on the autism spectrum is that of 'borderline personality disorder'. Interestingly, although borderline personality disorder should not be used as a formal diagnosis before the age of 18, it is surprising how many young women are being diagnosed as having an 'emerging borderline personality disorder' as young as 13.

This chapter aims to clarify the key features of attachment disorder, oppositional defiance disorder, conduct disorder and personality disorder and how autism presents in girls with co-morbid ADHD, and, more importantly, how the features of these disorders differ from those seen in girls with autism. In addition to the case studies found in the research literature, many parents kindly shared their experiences of their daughters being misdiagnosed and described how this has impacted upon their family, and the young person involved. Their stories are included throughout the chapter, and in more detail in Chapter 10.

Finally, this chapter examines the issues faced by many families in accessing appropriate support, including ongoing support for mental health issues from local CAMHS, particularly for those girls who have the ability to mask their difficulties in school (particularly common in girls with pathological demand avoidance).

Distinguishing attachment disorders from autism

According to the diagnostic criteria (DSM-5, APA 2013 and ICD-10, World Health Organization 2016) both attachment disorder and autism affect social skills and relationships. In addition, children with attachment disorders can, and do, display some rigid and inflexible behaviour. Secure attachments develop through patterns of behaviour by, and interaction with, parents/caregivers who are able to meet the physical and emotional needs of the child. It is well documented in an extensive literature base that disruption to the attachment process can occur even in cases where children have not experienced a hugely traumatic early start (Moran 2010). These children are often referred to as having 'attachment difficulties' even if they do not fully meet the criteria for an attachment disorder (see below for full criteria). The criteria for a diagnosis of reactive attachment disorder as outlined in full in the DSM-5 are:

A. The child demonstrates a pattern of withdrawn or inhibited behaviour towards parents/caregivers which is often seen as:

    a. the child failing to seek comfort when he or she is upset

    b. the child failing to be comforted by parents or caregivers.

B. The child appears to be both socially and emotionally withdrawn, which is seen as:

    a. little response to either social or emotional overtures

    b. little evidence of being happy

    c. periods of appearing irritable, sad or scared that are observed during everyday and non-threatening interactions with parents or caregivers.

C. The child has experienced a longstanding pattern of inadequate or inconsistent care as outlined below:

    a. a persistent lack of comfort, support, stimulation or affection from parents or caregivers

    b. frequent changes of caregiver which impacts upon the child's ability to form meaningful attachments

    c. being brought up in an institution where there is a high child:caregiver ratio which limits opportunities to form stable attachments.

D. There is evidence to suggest that the care in criterion C is responsible for the behaviour observed according to criterion A.

E. The child does not have an autism spectrum disorder.

F. The behaviours are evident before the age of five.

G. The child has a developmental age of at least nine months.

In addition, clinicians involved in any assessment are asked to comment upon whether the observed difficulties are persistent (i.e. have been present for at least twelve months) and the severity of any difficulties. A diagnosis of Reactive Attachment Disorder is described as 'severe' if all features of the disorder are observed with every feature being classified as severe.

An article by Giltaij, Sterkenberg and Schwengel (2015), which explores the psychiatric diagnostic screening of social maladaptive behaviour (including autism), outlines that if, after screening, a child is *not* felt to meet the diagnostic criteria for autism, then a diagnosis of reactive attachment disorder should be given. This is highly controversial. When discussing the diagnostic criteria for reactive attachment disorder, Zeanah and Gleason (2015) noted that children with both autism and intellectual disability (ID) can, and do, form normal attachment relationships.

Newborn babies have an inborn tendency to cry, cling and orient towards their caregiver when distressed. When these behaviours lead to a soothing response, secure attachment develops. Consistently low sensitivity towards the need of the child leads to reduced attachment behaviour, whereas inconsistent parenting can result in hypervigilance, particularly in cases where the primary attachment figure is either very available or completely unavailable (as in cases where there is significant alcohol or substance abuse). This is regardless of whether the child has autism.

The diagnosis of disorders such as autism and reactive attachment disorders do not (and cannot) rely upon specific neurological or biological tests and are often based upon observations of behaviour. When carried out in the context of a diagnostic assessment process, these observations will often only represent a snapshot of how the child presents. In diagnostic teams where the process of assessment is based upon a 'panel' model (where a group of experienced professionals meet to discuss information gathered about a child and decide upon a diagnosis), a diagnosis of autism (or not) could be given solely on the basis of the subjective opinion of others involved in the child's care. So, in cases where the child masks her difficulties and presents very differently away from her parents, this could easily lead to the team deciding against a diagnosis of autism. There is often a misconception amongst professionals that features of autism are (or should be) apparent across all contexts in order for a diagnosis to be appropriate. This most definitely is not the case, particularly with girls. As outlined in the previous chapter, Gould and Ashton-Smith (2011) clearly outline the ability of girls on the autism spectrum to mimic and imitate the behaviour of their peers. The ability to mask can perhaps be best described in terms of 'social energy'. Working so hard to cover up difficulties and appear normal can be draining and can lead to outbursts and meltdowns at the end of the day which, unsurprisingly, are often directed at, or in the presence of, their loved ones. This often leads to speculation about attachment and parenting. When considering an alternative diagnosis of reactive attachment disorder, a diagnosis should, in theory, only be made on the basis of observed behaviour when certain adverse environmental conditions are either observed or reported, and not because a child is complex and nothing else appears to fit.

Kendall-Jones (2014) highlights a number of 'threats' with regard to potential diagnostic errors which include lack of skill and knowledge on the part of the diagnostic team.

The paper by Heather Moran, published in *Good Autism Practice* in 2010, was the first attempt at distinguishing between autism and attachment disorders in young children. She highlighted the challenge that this poses for clinicians, particularly in cases where the child has had a difficult start in life. Moran observes that the key feature of both children and young adults with attachment difficulties is the repeated use of behaviour patterns that push other people into responding or reacting in some way. It may appear that they are seeking attention or pushing boundaries. Children with attachment disorders can be hypervigilant to percieved criticism, often as a result of their experiences, which can lead to them complaining that adults or other children are picking on them.

As stated in the previous chapter, there is no one, definitive, assessment process for autism. Any assessment, however carefully carried out, will to some extent be subjective (even the NICE guidelines acknowledge this) and dependent upon individual clinical experience. Moran states in her paper that the clinicians she approached all reported a different 'emotional feel' when interacting with children with attachment disorders. This intuitive feeling resonates with me but is very difficult to capture and quantify in an autism assessment. Moran argues that the most sensible approach would be to assess children over a period of time and at the same time offer appropriate interventions such as Theraplay® or dyadic developmental psychotherapy.[1]

Very often when clinical teams have the opportunity to work with families for an extended period of time, underlying developmental issues become more apparent. Unfortunately many assessment teams in the United Kingdom do not have the luxury of working with families (particularly those with school-age children) over an extended period. This can result in children, particularly girls, being misdiagnosed or missed altogether, leaving them and their families without access to appropriate support and advice.

The ICD-10 (World Health Organization 2016) highlights five clear features of how reactive attachment disorder differs from autism spectrum disorders:

> » Children who have a reactive attachment disorder will have the underlying ability to react and respond socially.

> » When abnormal social reciprocity is noted in children with reactive attachment disorder, it will tend to improve significantly when the child is placed in a more nurturing environment.

> » Children with reactive attachment disorder do not display the types of unusual communication seen in children with autism.

---

1   Theraplay® is a treatment programme for children who have been adopted or fostered but is also used in families where relationships are strained. It addresses attachment issues and can work well with resistant or oppositional children. Dyadic developmental psychotherapy (DDP) has been developed as a treatment programme for families with adopted or fostered children who have experienced neglect or abuse in their early years.

» Children with reactive attachment disorder do not have the unusual cognitive profile often observed in children with autism.

» Children with reactive attachment disorder do not display the types of restricted interests or repetitive behaviours seen in children with autism.

However, none of the information cited above is helpful if you are a parent who has taken your child for a diagnostic assessment and come away without a diagnosis or with a strong suggestion that your child has an attachment disorder. Parents often report that they feel they are in an 'us and them' situation with nowhere to turn for support. However, there are some interesting findings emerging from research with regard to how it is possible to discriminate between the two conditions.

First, as Schopler, Short and Mesibov (1989) report, when children who are suspected of having an attachment disorder are placed in a more 'favourable environment' they can, to all intents and purposes, 'recover'.

Second, it is estimated that a relatively high percentage of the population will experience less than optimal attachment experiences in life. Fearon *et al.* (2010) and Groh *et al.* (2012) both report that insecure and disorganised patterns are not inherently pathological and are only modestly associated with elevated risks of developing behavioural problems. In other words, not every child who experiences some disruption to their attachments will develop the types of behavioural problems reported by many parents of children suspected of having autism. The two do not necessarily go together. It would appear to be dangerously over-simplistic to make the assumption that every child presenting with behavioural difficulties who does not immediately appear to fit the diagnostic criteria for autism must have attachment difficulties. Giltaij *et al.* (2015) estimated that 14 per cent of their sample would meet criteria for both autism and a reactive attachment disorder. This is not surprising given the level of difficulty some parents report. Giltaij *et al.* go on to report that in their study, caregivers who have a child with autism were likely to have experienced poor support, problematic interactions with their child, and the psychological difficulties associated with attempting to parent a child with a difficult temperament.

Distinguishing autism from oppositional defiance disorder and conduct disorder

Children with autism, particularly those who do not present with classic or Kanner's autism (Kanner 1943), also frequently receive a diagnosis of oppositional defiance disorder and/or conduct disorder alongside (or sometimes instead of) a diagnosis of autism. Oppositional defiance disorder is a highly prevalent disorder, frequently co-diagnosed with conduct disorder. Ezpeleta *et al.* (2015), in their paper exploring oppositional defiance disorder and callous-unemotional traits in pre-school children, report that research often combines the two conditions under the general heading of disruptive behaviour disorders (DBD). However, they consider that the two conditions should be viewed separately, as they have different developmental trajectories and are associated with different long-term risks and outcomes.

Conduct disorder is characterised by a pattern of behaviour that includes the violation of the rights of others, violation of age-appropriate rules and aggressive behaviour towards teachers, peers and caregivers. Children with conduct disorder tend to have high levels of callous and unemotional traits. These include lack of empathy, lack of remorse or guilt, and restricted emotional expression. These children tend to display higher levels of impulsive and sensation-seeking behaviour, show higher levels of aggression with earlier onset, and display reduced responsiveness to fear and emotional distress. These traits have been linked to anomalies in the amygdala and occipito-frontal cortex, and are believed to be highly heritable (between 40% and 78%).

Callous and unemotional traits can appear very early in childhood and are not always associated with anti-social behaviour and are not necessarily linked to future psychopathic tendencies (which is often the concern of many parents).

Children with the pathological demand avoidance profile of autism are often diagnosed with conduct disorder. Pathological demand avoidance is now believed to be a presentation seen in some children with autism and is characterised by behavioural meltdowns which are often extremely challenging and frequently include high levels of aggression.

However, there is a clear, and highly significant, difference between children with conduct disorder and children with the pathological demand avoidance profile, namely their anxiety levels. According to Ezpeleta *et al.* (2015) children with high levels of callous and unemotional traits present with *low* levels of fear and anxiety. This is supported by the findings of Dolan and Rennie (2007), Frick and Ellis (1999) and Pardini, Lochman and Powell (2007).

Pathological demand avoidance is very strongly linked with high anxiety levels. Indeed, this is now believed to be the single underpinning factor in the challenging behaviour reported by parents of children presenting with this profile. It is also explained quite eloquently below by a young adult with pathological demand avoidance:

> If doing the demand without any complaints was so easy then wouldn't most people do that? No one wants an argument over having to do a simple task such as getting dressed or taking the bin out, and the energy expended avoiding these can be exhausting for everyone involved. So why do PDA people go to such great lengths to avoid demands? There must be something that is so bad that it is worth a two hour fight to avoid it.
>
> The answer: anxiety.
>
> They say anxiety can be crippling. Well, for some people it is. It's like a knife tearing into you, a horrible feeling so bad that you'd do anything to reduce or avoid it. Our brains don't work the way they are supposed to. Anxiety is supposed to keep us alive, help us avoid deadly scenarios. See that poisonous berry over there, it's bad, don't eat it. See that ledge, you're now feeling intense anxiety about it so you don't go too near and fall to your death.

For people with PDA it's not a case of what's easier time wise, it's a case of what's easier anxiety wise. It might not make sense to us logically but emotionally it's overwhelming.

Meltdowns can be in the form of shouting, screaming, throwing things, lashing out, excessive crying, hyperventilating, being sick etc. People with PDA have a meltdown usually when they are forced into a situation they have tried to avoid due to high levels of anxiety but have been unsuccessful in avoiding and so the situation and their emotions/anxiety has escalated to a point whereby they have a meltdown. Many people with PDA become completely unaware of what they are doing at this point, they can even forget what led up to the meltdown once they have calmed down, often returning to what they were doing before their anxiety reached critical point. (Taken from Riko's PDA Facebook page; reproduced with permission)

Girls are less likely than boys to be diagnosed with conduct disorder and generally score lower in terms of callous and unemotional traits. They do, however, tend to score higher on an 'internalising' scale (Frick and Nigg 2012; Stadler *et al.* 2007). Those girls who do receive a diagnosis of conduct disorder tend to suffer more from anxiety problems (Lehto-Salo *et al.* 2009) and this anxiety is associated with more severe aggression and anti-social behaviour (Euler *et al.* 2015). Pathological demand avoidance remains a controversial diagnosis in both girls and boys but it would be interesting to explore further how many girls are wrongly diagnosed with conduct disorder based upon the research above.

Oppositional defiance disorder tends to present in response to emotional and threatening stimuli and is often linked to exposure to dysfunctional parenting. Young people with oppositional defiance disorder tend to have more intense reactions to what they perceive as people behaving in a way they feel is hostile or unfair in some way. It is often linked to poor verbal intelligence and poor ability to express oneself. Children and young people with oppositional defiance disorder often do very well in environments designed for children with emotional, social and behavioural difficulties where they are provided with clear, unambiguous boundaries and expectations.

Children with pathological demand avoidance do not respond well to this type of environment, and in fact the demands placed upon them by this type of approach can often make them worse. The behavioural interventions which have been found to be effective for children with pathological demand avoidance tend to focus upon compromise, negotiation and allowing the child or young person to maintain a degree of control, within manageable parameters.

Girls with ADHD and autism

Professor Digby Tantam in his book *Autism Spectrum Disorders through the Lifespan* (2012) reported that studies indicate the high level of overlap between autism and ADHD and strongly predict that the two will ultimately be classified together.

Nyden, Hjelmquist and Gillberg (2000) specifically examined girls on the autism spectrum and found that almost half of the group of young people on the autism spectrum also met diagnostic criteria for ADHD. However, there were differences in the way they presented. Girls (according to Grskovic and Zentall 2010) were more verbally impulsive, engaging in 'faster conversations'. They were also reported as being more easily bored, having greater 'moodiness', stubbornness and anger issues (Grskovic and Zentall 2010). Sciberros, Ohan and Anderson (2012) noted higher levels of bullying and victimisation by peers in adolescent girls.

This vulnerability seen in girls with ADHD and autism is possibly the single biggest contributory factor in terms of mental health issues, especially in those girls who try very hard to mask their difficulties in order to fit in with peers.

Distinguishing autism from borderline personality disorder

A diagnosis of borderline personality disorder is often given to adults (predominantly female) who have had a poor attachment history and ongoing relationship difficulties. In theory, a personality disorder diagnosis should not be given until a young person is at least 18, but frequently diagnoses of 'emerging personality disorder' are given to girls much younger than this.

Many young adult females interviewed whilst writing this book talked about their experiences either as out- or inpatients in adult services where their existing diagnosis of autism (or at that point undiagnosed autism) was overlooked or ignored in favour of a diagnosis of borderline personality disorder. One adult female who presented with extreme anxiety and challenging behaviour as a child of 11 was initially seen by her GP who suggested she may have emerging borderline personality disorder. She was ultimately hospitalised on a children's ward after refusing to return home, and having been picked up by the police. A hospital paediatrician who examined her initially suggested that her mother was deliberately fabricating her difficulties and discharged her after three days. She was subsequently re-admitted for self-harming behaviour and, on this occasion, her mother refused to take her home until she was properly assessed. She ultimately saw a child and adolescent psychiatrist who, for the first time, acknowledged her difficulties and suggested she may have autism and pathological demand avoidance. This was a relatively new diagnosis at that time and seemed to fit her presentation perfectly. Her care was managed by this psychiatrist until she was discharged from CAMHS. Some time later, she was referred to an adult psychiatrist because she was struggling to cope with her high levels of anxiety, was told 'there is no such thing as pathological demand avoidance' and was subsequently diagnosed with borderline emotionally unstable personality disorder. She was later seen by a psychiatric nurse who evaluated her and eventually recognised that she had features of autism. However, she has struggled to have this formally recognised, and reported that she was lucky if she saw the same psychiatrist twice as her local service had been staffed by a series of locum doctors on short-term contracts.

This story is only one of many examples provided and perhaps highlights a potentially significant difficulty with regard to psychiatric training. According to an article by Eminson and Goodyer (2004) entitled 'Time for a change to a developmental perspective in the education and training of psychiatrists', it would appear that the practice of psychiatry in the United Kingdom is predominantly focused upon the needs of adults. Trainees starting psychiatric training begin their clinical careers working with adults. Experience with young people is not included in their first year (of six years) of training. Specific training about child and adolescent development is only included in the specialist training for those who wish to become child and adolescent psychiatrists. The authors of the report argue that all trainee psychiatrists should have training in lifespan developmental disorders such as ADHD and autism because, without this knowledge, there is a danger that these difficulties will be missed or misdiagnosed in adult patients. A recent examination of the Royal College of Psychiatry training website (2017) suggests that in 2016 the training model remains as cited in Eminson and Goodyer's 2004 article. Conditions such as autism and ADHD are lifelong conditions and do not magically disappear when the young person reaches adulthood. Without the psychiatric community adopting a lifespan developmental approach, it is likely that stories like the one cited above will continue, and the transition from child to adult services will remain difficult.

There appear to be similar difficulties in the United States. Von Schalkwyk *et al.* (2015, p.911) attributed difficulties in obtaining a diagnosis for autism in an adult population as being due to the 'combination of adult psychiatrists being relatively inexperienced with this population and the system of care which requires providers to apply diagnostic labels in order to justify inpatient hospitalisation'.

It may therefore be helpful to examine the ways in which girls presenting with autism differ from those who have borderline personality disorder. Using the criteria outlined in the DSM-5 for autism spectrum disorder, below are some of the ways in which adolescent girls with autism may present differently to those whose primary difficulties appear to be based upon poor attachment history (which is a well-documented precursor for borderline personality disorder).

Social and emotional reciprocity and non-verbal communication

As stated in the Coventry Grid (Moran 2010), children with attachment disorders often display lack of attention to the needs of their listener due to poor atunement. Their eye contact can be affected by their emotional state and they can often be over-sensitive to voice tone, due to hypervigilance and fear of rejection. In girls with an emerging personality disorder this remains true. In addition, they frequently use bad or sexualised language with the deliberate intention of shocking or offending others.

In contrast, girls on the autism spectrum struggle with expressing their feelings and in determining appropriate ways of communicating with other people, especially their peers. Their language often appears silly or childish in content and they frequently fail to get it right in terms of jokes or humour. Understanding sarcasm continues to present a difficulty and they often appear to be on the periphery of any social interaction. It is possible to observe them watching others for cues about how to behave. They are often perceived as 'weird' by other girls of their age. They may adopt a babyish tone of voice. If their attempts at interaction are rejected or fail, they may become mute and uncommunicative. Vocal tics can appear when the young person is particularly upset and can cause considerable distress.

Developing, maintaining, and understanding relationships

Girls with an emerging personality disorder are often referred to as manipulative. They can present as charming and will often use this charm in an attempt to get their own way. They understand the feelings and motives of others and are well able to read social cues.

They will deliberately try to 'split' people living or working with them by portraying some people as 'good' and 'kind' and others as 'bad' or 'mean'. This can include parents, teachers, other professionals, and even friends.

In contrast, girls on the autism spectrum are less able to read the social cues and frequently misunderstand the motives and intentions of others. Any apparent attempts to manipulate others (particularly in those girls with pathological demand avoidance) tend to be a way of trying to control and manage their environment. Many use superficially manipulative strategies in order to try to ease the anxiety they feel. Socially, they continue to get things wrong. Friendships are often short-lived and they become increasingly vulnerable and unhappy as their attempts to fit in continue to fail. They can often be over-controlling of their friends (many are accused of being bossy). Girls with emerging personality disorder tend to have 'favourites' and can become overly attached to people even if the relationship is unhelpful or even abusive. Girls on the spectrum have more of a tendency to become obsessed by particular individuals, to the extent that they may engage in stalker-like behaviour, copy someone's look or mannerisms, and try to be as much like them as possible. This often leads to rejection and the girl being labelled as 'weird'. In terms of sexual relationships, girls with emerging personality disorder are often sexually disinhibited and promiscuous and may engage in risky sexual activity. Girls on the spectrum in contrast often present as extremely naive. Their desire to fit in and gain approval from boys can lead to them engaging in sexual activity (which they are not emotionally ready for) and making themselves vulnerable by, for example, posting intimate pictures of themselves on social media sites.

Girls with emerging personality disorder tend to have more awareness of the opinion of others. They can behave in an extreme manner but generally are much more able to control this behaviour, to the extent of being able to 'snap out' of an outburst quite quickly if they choose to. In contrast girls on the spectrum (again more particularly those with the pathological demand avoidance profile) appear to continue to have the type of behavioural meltdowns that are frequently reported in younger children on the spectrum. These meltdowns can last for hours and the young person can appear unaware or disinterested in the impression they are making on others, including their peers. These meltdowns appear to be driven by perceived loss of control, or by demands being made on the young person, and are often underpinned by extreme anxiety. At times, the anxiety can appear so great that the young person effectively goes into a dissociative state and completely shuts down and becomes unresponsive to external stimuli.

Restricted, repetitive patterns of behaviour, interests or activities

This aspect of the diagnostic criteria has always proved more difficult for those involved in the assessment and diagnosis of girls on the autism spectrum. Generally (although this is not always the case) girls tend to display less of the more obvious obsessions and restricted interests seen in boys. Girls on the spectrum can often become fixated upon certain people or celebrities. This type of obsession has a very different feel to the type of emotional over-attachment demonstrated towards particular individuals by young girls with emerging personality disorder. It may result in the girl with autism wanting to collect memorabilia or facts about someone, or wanting to copy their look or mannerisms. Girls on the spectrum will frequently present with extreme anxiety (and anger) when routines or plans have to change, or when events do not happen in the order expected. In contrast, girls with emerging personality disorder tend to become angry when they perceive their needs are not being met. For example, they may become distressed if mealtimes or promised treats fail to happen at a particular time. However, this is more related to feelings of emotional neglect and abandonment, which result from early attachment difficulties.

Can someone have a diagnosis of autism and borderline personality disorder?

The short answer appears to be yes. A diagnosis of personality disorder is made on the basis of the presence of certain behavioural features which can be present in girls with autism too. The reasons why these behaviours have developed might be very different for a girl on the spectrum but may, nonetheless, describe her behaviour very well, as can be seen from the DSM-5 criteria outlined below:

DSM-5 criteria for borderline personality disorder

A longstanding pattern of unstable personal relationships, poor self-image and a tendency towards impulsive behaviour that is apparent by early adulthood and is present across contexts and manifest in the following behaviour:

> » feelings of abandonment

> » unstable and intense personal relationships

> » persistently poor self-image

> » impulsive behaviour in two areas that could be detrimental (e.g spending, sexual behaviour, binge eating or substance abuse)

> » repeated suicidal thoughts and behaviour, or self-harm

> » unstable moods and intense mood swings

> » feelings of emptiness

> » difficulties controlling temper or inappropriate anger outbursts

> » paranoid thoughts or dissociative episodes.

Ryden, Ryden and Jecker (2008), cited in the previous chapter, is a cross-sectional study that aimed to establish, first, if the two conditions can co-exist and, second, if so, how the two groups differ on certain clinical measures such as suicide attempts, self-harm and average length of stay in inpatient units. Ryden *et al.* found that 15 per cent of their sample fulfilled diagnostic criteria for both borderline personality disorder and autism. This group of women made a significantly higher number of suicide attempts than the borderline personality disorder only group. They attributed this to the poorer ability to 'mentalise' (the ability to infer the thoughts, feelings and emotions of others) found in the group with borderline personality disorder and autism (see also Bateman and Fonagy 2004; Fonagy 1998; Frith 2001; Frith and Frith 2003).

In young women with borderline personality disorder, the ability to mentalise tended to fluctuate depending on their current circumstances and mental state, whereas for those young women with borderline personality disorder and autism, this difficulty was pervasive and lifelong (Ryden *et al.* 2008).

Ryden *et al.* felt that the consequence of this lack of ability to mentalise observed in the borderline personality disorder with autism group was a result of poorer social imagination and theory of mind, which lead them to have greater difficulty appreciating the impact of their suicidal actions upon others. They concluded that self-harm and suicide attempts in the patients with autism were less likely to be manipulative or carried out as a means of seeking attention, and should be better understood as a way of managing 'overwhelming feelings' and as the 'fragmentation of self' (Bateman and Fonagy 2003). The young women with borderline personality disorder and autism also reported more negative self-perception. The authors speculated that those young women with borderline personality disorder and autism may prove harder to support, as their difficulties with theory of mind and mentalisation may account for some of the challenges they are reported to face with accepting help and support from others.

Fabricated and induced illness

As part of the research for this book, several parents of children, particularly those with daughters on the autism spectrum, have reported having been accused of deliberately fabricating symptoms or exaggerating the degree of difficulty they were experiencing at home.

Girls, in particular, are very good at masking their difficulties outside of their home environment. A paper by Tierney, Burns and Kilbey (2016) entitled 'Looking behind the mask: Social coping strategies of girls on the autism spectrum' explored the experiences of ten adolescent girls with autism, all of whom reported that they had realised from an early age that they needed to mask their difficulties in order to fit in with their peers. Unfortunately, this degree of masking can often be extremely stressful for the young person and can lead to behavioural meltdowns when in the privacy and safety of their own homes.

Fabricated illness (Lazenbatt 2013) is described as the process of exaggerating, fabricating or inducing physical, psychological and mental health problems. The report by Lazenbatt cites the overall prevalence rate for children under the age of 16 (in the UK and Ireland) as being 0.5 per 100,000. Lazenbatt reported that the cases that prove most difficult for professionals are those where the 'reported symptoms only occur when mother is present or are only observed by mother or carer' (p.67), and therein lies the problem for parents of girls on the autism spectrum, who may be masking their difficulties. A recent conference by the Pathological Demand Avoidance Society in the United Kingdom issued a questionnaire asking parents about their biggest challenges. The responses from this reflected the issues that many parents face. One parent cited 'getting school to understand that it is the way they deal with her that causes the increase in anxiety, and then the challenging behaviour we have at home'. Another said, 'Being believed. Going through a Child Protection investigation for fabricated and induced illness (all found to be totally unfounded).'

Accessing the right support

For many parents, getting a diagnosis of autism for their daughter is only the first step on a long and difficult journey.

When the autism strategy *Fulfilling and Rewarding Lives* (Department of Health 2011) was published in the United Kingdom in 2011 it was hoped that services for both adults and young people who received a diagnosis of autism in the United Kingdom would improve. However, the report focused upon intended outcomes and did not specify how these outcomes were to be implemented. Sadly, even though the economic case for providing specialist intervention services, post-diagnosis, for people with autism was clearly made by the Audit Commission, these do not appear to have materialised, if the experiences reported by the families who reported their experiences at the Pathological Demand Avoidance Society Conference in 2015 are indeed representative. The first issue they raised was the wide variety of diagnoses received following their initial concerns and subsequent assessment. These ranged from autism and 'mixed neurological disorder' through to 'secondary oppositional defiance disorder in relation to anxiety' and 'a unique profile of social, emotional and sensory difficulties that we do not yet understand'. Seventy per cent of the conference participants reported that they had received no ongoing support from CAHMS. Those who did manage to access some support made the following comments and observations:

> Dreadful...practitioners with no knowledge of how to treat our child.

> Well-meaning but could only offer courses on anger management and parenting. Non-involvement with either of these options means no further support despite significant mental health issues.

> CAMHS saw my child once and said there was nothing else they could offer in the way of support or help.

> [My child] was misdiagnosed by Tier 4 [inpatient] services, discharged and referred back to Tier 3 [specialist services]. I am still awaiting confirmation of what support might be available.

> Still waiting for our first appointment, 11 months after our initial appointment.

Professionals were patronising.

There was no consistency, they failed to deliver on agreed support. There were multiple handovers to different team members and a failure to ensure transition to adult services.

The service is failing children all over the country. We saw psychologist after psychologist. We had psychiatrists diagnosing wrongly. I was sent on parenting courses for my 'badly behaved child'.

These issues do not appear to be confined to the United Kingdom. Chiri and Erikson Warfield (2012) described the situation for families in the United States. Families in the United States would appear to be 'significantly more at risk for having unmet needs, specifically support and therapy' (p.1088). These families were also more likely to cite 'provider lack of skills to treat their child' (p.1088) as the barrier to accessing therapy provision.

Warren *et al.* (2013), who also studied the experiences of families in the United States following a diagnosis of autism for their child, reported similar results and stated that many families implemented recommendations from a diagnostic assessment on their own, without access to any professional support.

At the Pathological Demand Avoidance Society Conference, many parents reported their biggest challenges post-diagnosis as being 'loneliness and isolation', 'feeling like I am not a good enough parent', 'grief and anger and dealing with other people's reactions' and 'being misunderstood and judged'. Others cited the huge issues for other members of their family and even, in some cases, their marriages. The majority stated that they had received most support and advice from social media groups (such as Facebook) and other parent support groups. It appeared that most had given up hope of receiving targeted and timely support from professionals.

This does raise a very serious question about the usefulness of a diagnosis if that is all that is available. If parents have to wait for years to even get an assessment of their child's needs, it is hardly surprising if they have clung onto the hope that having a diagnosis will somehow open doors for them and allow them to access support. The disappointment must be immense if, after all the waiting, there is still no support or guidance about just how they are supposed to manage their challenging or distressed child. The longer parents of children with autism are denied access to considered and evidence-based support, the more likely it is that families will become burnt out and suffer significant levels of stress. In addition, it would seem logical that the longer children and young people are left unsupported or inappropriately supported, the more likely they will be to develop mental health problems as they grow up, presenting an even greater potential cost to society in the future.

References

American Psychiatric Association (2013) *Diagnostic and Statistical Manual of Mental Disorders, 5th Edition: DSM-5.* Arlington, VA: American Psychiatric Association.

Bateman, A. and Fonagy, P. (2003) The development of an attachment-based treatment program for borderline personality disorder. *Bulletin of the Meninger Clinic 67,* 3, 187–211.

Bateman, A. and Fonagy, P. (2004) *Psychotherapy for Borderline Personality Disorder: Mentalisation-Based Treatment.* Oxford: Oxford University Press.

Chiri, G. and Erickson Warfield, M. (2012) Unmet need and problems accessing core health services for children with autism spectrum disorders. *Maternal Child Health Journal 16,* 5, 1081–1091.

Department of Health (2011) *Fulfilling and Rewarding Lives: The Strategy for Adults with Autism in England.* London: Department of Health. Accessed on 2 May 2017 at www.gov.uk/government/news/fulfilling-and-rewarding-lives-the-strategy-for-adults-with-autism-in-england.

Dolan, M.C. and Rennie, C.E. (2007) The relationship between psychopathic traits measured by the Youth Psychopathic trait inventory in a UK sample of conduct disordered boys. *Journal of Adolescence 30,* 4, 601–611.

Erinson, D.M. and Goodyer, I.M. (2004) Time for a change to a developmental perspective in the education and training of psychiatrists. *British Journal of Psychiatry Bulletin.* doi 10:1192/pb.28.10.378.

Euler, F., Jenkel, N., Stadler, C. *et al.* (2015) Variants of girls and boys with conduct disorder: Anxiety symptoms and callous-unemotional traits. *Journal of Abnormal Child Psychology 43,* 4, 733–785.

Ezpeleta, L., Granero, R., de la Osa, N. *et al.* (2015) Clinical characteristics of pre-school children with oppositional defiant disorder and callous-unemotional traits. *PLoS One 10,* 9, e0139346.

Fearon, R.P., Bakermans-Kranenburg, M.J., van IJzendoorn, M.H. *et al.* (2010) The significance of insecure attachment and disorganization in the development of children's externalizing behaviour: A meta-analytic study. *Child Development 81,* 2, 435–456.

Fonagy, P. (1998) An attachment theory approach to treatment of the difficult patient. *Bulletin of the Menninger Clinic 62*, 2, 147–169.

Frick, P.J. and Ellis, M. (1999) Callous-unemotional traits and subtypes of conduct disorder. *Clinical Child and Family Psychology Review 2*, 3, 149–168.

Frick, P.J. and Nigg, J.T. (2012) Current issues in the diagnosis of attention deficit hyperactivity disorder, oppositional defiant disorder, and conduct disorder. *Annual Review of Clinical Psychology 8*, 8, 77–107.

Frith, U. (2001) Mindblindness and the brain in autism. *Neuron 32*, 6, 969–979.

Frith, U. and Frith, C.D. (2003) Development and neurophysiology of mentalising. *Philosophical Transactions of the Royal Society of London, Series B, Biological Sciences 358*, 1431, 459–473.

Giltaij, H.P., Sterkenberg, P.S. and Schwengel, C. (2015) Psychiatric diagnostic screening of social maladaptive behaviour. *Journal of Intellectual Disability Research 59*, 2, 138–149.

Gould, J. and Ashton-Smith, J. (2011) Missed diagnosis or misdiagnosis: Girls and women on the autism spectrum. *Good Autism Practice 12*, 1, 34–41.

Groh, A.M., Roisman, G., van IJzendoorn, M.H. *et al.* (2012) The significance of insecure and disorganized attachment for children's internalizing symptoms: A meta-analytic study. *Child Development 83*, 2, 591–610.

Grskovic, J.A. and Zentall, S.S. (2010) Understanding attention deficit hyperactivity disorder in girls: Identification and social characteristics. *International Journal of Special Education 25*, 1, 171–184.

Kanner, L. (1943) Autistic disturbances of affective contact. *Nervous Child 2*, 217–250.

Kendall-Jones, R. (2014) An Investigation into the Differential Diagnosis of Autism Spectrum Disorder and Attachment Difficulties. Doctoral thesis, University of Birmingham. Accessed on 22 May 2017 at http://etheses.bham.ac.uk/4812.

Lazenbatt, A. (2013) Fabricated or induced illness in children: A narrative review of the literature. *Childcare in Practice 19*, 1, 61–67.

Lehto-Salo, P., Narhi, V., Ahonen, T. *et al.* (2009) Psychiatric comorbidity more common among adolescent females with conduct disorder/oppositional defiance disorder than among males. *Nordic Journal of Psychiatry 63*, 4, 308–315.

Moran, H. (2010) Clinical observations of the differences between children on the autistic spectrum and those with attachment problems: The Coventry Grid. *Good Autism Practice 11*, 20, 42–57.

Nyden, A., Hjelmquist, E. and Gillberg, C. (2000) Autism spectrum disorders in girls, some neuropsychological aspects. *European Child and Adolescent Psychiatry 9*, 3, 180–185.

Pardini, D, Lochman, J.E. and Powell, N. (2007) The development of callous and unemotional traits and anti-social behaviour in children: Are there shared and/or unique predictors? *Journal of Clinical Child and Adolescent Psychology 36*, 3, 319–333.

Pardini, D., Stepp, S., Hipwell, A. *et al.* (2012) The clinical utility of the proposed DSM-5 callous-unemotional subtype of conduct disorder in young girls. *Journal of the American Academy of Child and Adolescent Psychiatry 51*, 1, 62–73.

Royal College of Psychiatry (2017) Core and Speciality Training. Accessed on 1 June 2017 at www.rcpsych.ac.uk/traininpsychiatry/corespecialtytraining.aspx.

Ryden, G., Ryden, E. and Jecker, H. (2008) Borderline personality disorder and autism spectrum disorder in females – a cross-sectional study. *Clinical Neuropsychiatry 5*, 1, 22–30.

Schopler, E., Short, A. and Mesibov, G. (1989) Relation of behavioural treatment to normal functioning: Comment on Lovaas. *Journal of Consulting and Clinical Psychology 57*, 1, 162–164.

Sciberros, E., Ohan, J. and Anderson, V. (2012) Bullying and peer victimisation in adolescent girls with attention deficit hyperactivity disorder. *Child Psychiatry Human Development 43, 2,* 254–270.

Stadler, C., Poustka, F. and Sterzer, P. (2010) The heterogeneity of disruptive behavior disorders–implications for neurobiological research and treatment. *Frontiers in Psychiatry 1,* 21, 1–14.

Stadler, C., Rohrmann, S., Knopf, A. *et al.* (2007) Socio-moral reasoning in boys with conduct disorder – the influence of cognitive, educational and psychosocial factors. *Zeitschrift fur Kinder und Jugendpsychiatrie und Psychotherapie 35,* 3, 169–178.

Tantam, D. (2012) *Autism Spectrum Disorders through the Lifespan.* London: Jessica Kingsley Publishers.

Tierney, S., Burns, J. and Kilbey, E. (2016) Looking behind the mask: Social coping strategies of girls on the autistic spectrum. *Research in Autism Spectrum Disorders 23,* 73–83.

Von Schalkwyk, G.I., Peluso, F., Qayyum, Z. *et al.* (2015) Varieties of misdiagnosis in ASD: An illustrative case series. *Journal of Autism and Developmental Disorders 45,* 4, 911–918.

Warren, Z., Veham, A., Dohrmann, E. *et al.* (2013) Brief report: Service implementation and maternal distress surrounding evaluation recommendations for young children diagnosed with autism. *Autism: The International Journal of Research and Practice 17,* 6, 693–706.

World Health Organization (2016) *International Statistical Classification of Diseases and Related Health Problems, 10th Revision.* Geneva: World Health Organization.

Zeanah, C.H. and Gleason, M.M. (2015) Annual research review: Attachment disorders in early childhood – clinical presentation, causes, correlates, and treatment. *Journal of Child Psychology and Psychiatry 56,* 3, 207–222.

Chapter 3

The Mental Health Act

This chapter examines the use of the Mental Health Act (MHA) 2007, what it can mean for young people and their families and what it aims to achieve. The use of both Section 2 and Section 3 of the MHA are explained in terms of assessment and treatment of young people with mental health difficulties. Differences and similarities between the mental health system in the United Kingdom and other parts of the English-speaking world are also discussed.

This chapter focuses on some of the more serious aspects of mental health difficulties experienced by girls on the autism spectrum and the process by which individuals (children and adults) can be 'sectioned' or detained under the Mental Health Act (in the United Kingdom). It also explores similarities and differences between the system used in the United Kingdom and in other parts of the world.

This chapter also discusses the chronic shortage of inpatient beds, particularly for adolescents, in the United Kingdom, and discusses the benefits of autism-specific units.

Many young women on the autism spectrum experience rejection and bullying by their peers. Their socio-sexual knowledge tends to be poor. They struggle to interpret the thoughts, feelings and intentions of others and are consequently very vulnerable to abuse and being drawn into sexual situations they are not comfortable with. Some find themselves becoming involved in 'sexting', which involves sending intimate pictures of oneself to others, and can very easily be 'groomed' by older men. The rise in the popularity of social media sites appears, for some girls, to have proved to be an additional strain – at least in pre-social media times if someone was bullied or having a hard time at school, they could escape from it at home. Now social media is ever-present and, for some, an inescapable pressure.

Some young women on the autism spectrum may use alcohol as a social facilitator – a means of attempting to reduce their anxiety levels around social interaction. They may fail academically in spite of being cognitively able. Those who react aggressively to anxiety-provoking situations can find they alienate friends and family members. Those who do not outwardly express their distress may begin (or increase) self-harming.

L, one of the young women interviewed for this book, received a diagnosis in her early teens. However, she reported that following her diagnosis, she received little explanation of how this might impact upon her. She, and her family, received no specific follow-up support. L talked about her long history of rejection and bullying by her peers. She also reported that she always felt like she was 'doing things wrong' as far as her parents were concerned. She reported never having had friends or anyone to spend time with. She also reported finding her school work either 'pointless' or difficult to understand. She did well in science-based subjects, but found subjects like English almost impossible. She explained this as follows:

> I was always told I needed to look for a deeper level of interpretation, but I just didn't know what they meant by this. As far as I was concerned there was no deeper level of interpretation. It was just words.

She went to university and struggled through her course, finding the social aspects of communal living very difficult. She reported a time when a fellow student stole food from her part of the refrigerator and her subsequently shouting at him in the corridor. She stated, 'I think he was scared of me. He never spoke to me again.' She described herself as feeling lonely, but not really knowing how to make or keep friends. She had issues of trust with people of both sexes, feeling that she had been exploited.

Her story is not uncommon. She subsequently returned home and became extremely depressed and suicidal. She was admitted as a voluntary patient to her local psychiatric hospital where she remained for three months. At 25, although she is now on medication and is no longer suicidal, she still reports that she is lonely and struggles with low self-esteem.

As has been outlined in the previous chapters, the process of accessing an assessment and diagnosis can be lengthy and ongoing support for young people and their families can be patchy or non-existent. Even for those fortunate enough to have had an assessment and those who have been prescribed medication, the transition to adult mental health services can also prove difficult and it is often not possible to ensure continuity of care. Austen (2009) referred to the transition from child (CAMHS) to adult (AMHS) services in the United Kingdom as like 'falling off a cliff'. It is not surprising, therefore, that a proportion of girls on the autism spectrum need more specialist psychiatric care at some point during their lives. Some young adult females on the autism spectrum go on to become 'revolving door' patients, requiring frequent admission to hospital, as unresolved difficulties re-occur throughout their lives.

The process of admission into a psychiatric inpatient service in the United Kingdom, particularly when this is not voluntary, is stressful for anyone, but for those on the autism spectrum it can be particularly hard. It is also extremely upsetting for parents. There are a large number of very dedicated parents of both adolescents and adults on the spectrum who try desperately hard to access support for their children. They often cope with extremely challenging (and sometimes aggressive) behaviour, with many reporting breakages and damage to property, altercations with neighbours, bruising, scratching and other injuries. Some even report having been threatened with knives and, at times, having been in fear of their lives. Others report trying to manage chronically depressed and self-harming individuals and living in constant fear of their children successfully committing suicide.

Some parents interviewed in the course of many years of clinical experience had, in desperation, called the police for support. Most found them very supportive, but unable to offer more than immediate help for a particularly difficult situation.

Most of the parents spoken to reported being fearful of acknowledging these difficulties, and worrying that this would result in their child being 'sectioned' and taken to a psychiatric facility.

Being 'sectioned' is the term that is often used when someone is detained under the Mental Health Act. The Mental Health Act 2007 is the law in the United Kingdom that can allow someone to be admitted, detained and treated in hospital against their wishes. It can be a very distressing experience for the person, their family and friends, and is only used when all other options have been considered. These usually include researching available support in the community or exploring whether the person would agree to go into hospital on a voluntary basis.

The decision to detain someone under the Mental Health Act is only considered when someone is very unwell, and is not taken lightly. The criteria for detention are that someone has to be suffering from a mental disorder of a 'nature or degree which warrants detention in a hospital for assessment or treatment' and that the person needs to be admitted to hospital in the interests of their own health or safety or with a view to the protection of others.

The decision to section someone is taken after a Mental Health Act assessment. There are several different ways that it can get to this stage. It may be that someone is already in contact with their local mental health team who become so concerned about their current mental health that they decide to arrange an assessment. Sometimes family and friends become concerned and they contact the local mental health team or crisis team themselves. It could also be the case that a situation becomes so urgent that emergency services, such as the police, have to be called. The police can also remove someone from a public place if they are behaving in a way that puts themselves or others at risk, under Section 136 of the Mental Health Act, and take them to a 'place of safety' (this is often a dedicated suite at a local hospital but can, unfortunately, sometimes be a police cell). These emergency sections can last up to 72 hours during which time arrangements must be made to assess if the individual requires further intensive support.

For a person to be sectioned three people involved in a Mental Health Act assessment taking place in the United Kingdom have to agree that the person needs to be detained in hospital and meets the criteria mentioned above. Usually, these three people are an approved mental health professional (who is a professional, such as a social worker, who has had extra training to carry out these assessments) and two doctors. Wherever possible, one of these doctors should know the person. The initial section is often a Section 2, which is for a period of 28 days to allow for 'assessment and treatment'.

The approved mental health professional will speak with the person's nearest relative or carer when considering admitting someone to hospital under a section.

Under the Mental Health Act, a key person in the family is designated as the nearest relative. This is someone who is defined under a hierarchy of relatives in the Mental Health Act, and it is not necessarily going to be the same person as someone's next of kin. The nearest relative has certain rights under the Mental Health Act. They have the right to request that a Mental Health Act assessment is considered and they can contact their local social services department or local mental health team to use this right. The nearest relative should receive written reasons if the approved mental health professional does not apply to detain their relative in hospital under the Mental Health Act.

When a person has been detained under Section 2 of the Mental Health Act for an initial period of 28 days, if they are still deemed to meet the criteria for detention, they can be further detained under Section 3 of the Act, which allows a longer period of time for assessment and treatment. The treatment section lasts up to six months and can be renewed (for a further six months, then annually).

The process is the same for adolescents as it is for adults.

Whilst someone is detained under the Mental Health Act, they are not free to leave the hospital and may be prevented in a variety of ways, including locked doors and secure fencing. They may be allowed out on what is called Section 17 leave, but this is at the discretion of the treating team and is carefully monitored.

After admission, the hospital team will decide upon the level of risk that the patient is deemed to present. This can be risk to self or others. This evaluation of risk should take the form of a dynamic risk assessment and should be reviewed regularly. There are different levels of monitoring which range from 15-minute checks to one-to-one (or sometimes two- or three-to-one) continuous arms-length observation for very high risk patients.

There are some significant differences in the way mentally ill patients are treated in the United Kingdom compared to other parts of the world. In the United Kingdom a person can be detained in order to 'prevent deterioration' in their condition. In the United States and Canada, it is somewhat more difficult to justify detaining patients involuntarily. Involuntary commitment in these countries is justifiable only when the patient is at significant risk of harm to self or others. In Canada, the United States and Australia, individuals can be sectioned by one single psychiatrist, but in the United States, there appears to be considerably more interest, particularly from the legal profession, in ensuring that people are not detained unnecessarily.

The law in the United States stipulates that people should be detained in the 'least restrictive environment'. In addition, the need for involuntary treatment has to be based upon a significant history of unsuccessful community treatment.

In Australia, mental health law tends to focus more upon 'treatability' than is the case in other parts of the world. The Australian Mental Health Act refers to 'illness' rather than 'disorder' and, in most cases, no patient or patient's representative has the right to refuse treatment.

The law in New Zealand is somewhat different. The Mental Health Act (Compulsory Assessment and Treatment Act) is now over 20 years old and was based upon the former United Kingdom

Mental Health Act of 1983. New Zealand's ratification of the 2006 United Nations Convention on the Rights of Persons with Disabilities has resulted in the concept of 'compulsory treatment' as being contrary to best practice. However, it is reported that more people than ever are being detained in New Zealand (Gordon and O'Brien 2014). One of the main areas of difference relates to the initial assessment period, the first being up to five days and the second for up to 14 days. During this time, individuals have the right to have their compulsory assessment status reviewed by a family court or a district court judge. The main problem for many people in New Zealand was reported to be the high number of individuals who do not have access to legal aid and the difficulty in challenging what is, essentially, a clinical decision. In addition, unlike the United Kingdom, Australia and Canada, New Zealand does not have commissions that exercise some form of independent monitoring of, or initiative to reduce, the use of involuntary detention. The threshold for compulsory care under New Zealand legislation is that the person must be clinically assessed as having an 'abnormal state of mind, of such a degree that it poses a serious danger to the health or safety of the person or of others, or seriously diminishes the capacity of the person for self-care' (Ministry of Health 2012, p.9). Either of the above criteria could have significant implications for individuals with autism as it would be open to debate as to what constitutes an 'abnormal state of mind' and 'capacity for self-care' given the difficulties that some individuals face with regard to maintaining hygiene and self-care, especially at times of heightened anxiety.

There are also issues around medication which are particularly pertinent for individuals with autism. In the United Kingdom, the NICE (2011) guidelines for the assessment and treatment of both children and adults with autism specifically outline that it is not appropriate to treat the *core features* of autism with medication, as this has been proved to be ineffective. There is also a recognised risk of significant side-effects in any medication. In the United Kingdom, if someone is detained under the Mental Health Act, their 'responsible clinician' (who will usually be a psychiatrist) can insist upon medication being given, even if the person does not wish it. This is clearly a very contentious area because, although medication is not effective in managing the core deficits present in autism, it can be extremely effective in managing co-morbid mood disorders, anxiety and depression.

However, what was reported to me when writing this book was that a number of young women were prescribed high doses of benzodiazepines (a group of drugs used for their sedative and muscle-relaxant properties) such as lorazepam (Ativan) or diazepam (Valium) when their behaviour became challenging. These types of medication are highly addictive, and resulted in making them feel sedated or 'spaced out' for much of the time. However, this did not really address the core reasons behind their behaviour. Many felt that they were offered very little in the way of therapeutic support, other than groups, which many of them found difficult to attend.

In the United States, because of a stated commitment to the autonomy and dignity of persons with mental health conditions, Mental Health America strongly agrees with the judgement of the United States Supreme Court in that all persons have a right to refuse medication and that medication may not be imposed involuntarily unless rigorous standards and procedures are met. These procedures should include an impartial decision maker who is focused upon the best medical interests of the individual and not of the treating establishment.

Once a person has been an inpatient for a period of time, in the United Kingdom they can apply for a Mental Health Tribunal. If someone is detained under Section 2 of the Mental Health Act, they can apply after 14 days. If they are on a Section 3, they have to wait six months. The patient can make this application themselves or it can be made by the patient's legal representative or nearest relative. At a tribunal, all the information about the person's case and treatment is presented in front of a panel which consists of a judge, a tribunal doctor and an independent expert. After hearing all of the evidence, the panel will make a decision about the person's detention. This may include deciding that the person no longer needs to be detained.

In the United States, persons facing involuntary confinement have a right to a number of procedures including: a judicial hearing at which at least one mental health professional is required to testify; the right to be legally represented; an independent mental health evaluation; and the right to appeal.

In the United Kingdom, when a person is released from hospital following detention for mental health difficulties, they will often be placed on a community treatment order (CTO). CTOs were introduced in 2008 and represent a supervised discharge programme. Patients can be recalled to hospital whilst on a CTO if their mental health deteriorates or they do not comply with the conditions of the CTO, which may include mandatory regular contact with their mental health team. A person can be recalled temporarily for reassessment and, in some cases, the CTO will be revoked and they will be detained under section again. It is possible to be discharged from a CTO if the responsible clinician feels that significant improvement has been made and maintained.

Similar arrangements, with local variations, exist in the United States, Canada, Australia and New Zealand.

The rise of mental health difficulties amongst adolescents is of significant concern in the United Kingdom. In 2011 there were 3626 admissions to inpatient units. This represented a steep rise.

In the United Kingdom, CAMHS Tier 4 services provide specialised inpatient treatment for young people with emotional, behavioural or mental health difficulties. NHS England (who are responsible for all inpatient adolescent beds in the United Kingdom) commissioned a review into these services in April 2013 (CAMHS Tier 4 Steering Group 2014).

Results from this review revealed several key areas in need of urgent improvement:

> *Lack of beds:* It was reported that some children were being sent hundreds of miles away from their homes in order to access inpatient care. Many had to be admitted onto adult mental health wards because there were no available beds in adolescent units.

> » *Staff shortages:* The report also found that there was a lack of adequately skilled staff trained specifically to work with young people.

> » *Lack of community services:* Concerns were raised over reductions in specialist community services which often led to delayed discharges whilst hospital staff endeavoured to ensure that appropriate post-discharge follow-up services were in place. The report cites unclear recovery pathways, lack of case managers, and ineffective discharge planning to be at the root of the issue.

It appears likely that young people on the autism spectrum are disproportionately represented in CAMHS inpatient services.

Data from one adolescent inpatient unit, from an informal audit my colleagues and I carried out, was as follows:

> » 52 young people admitted, 16 boys and 36 girls

> » Of the girls who were admitted:

>> - 19 per cent had a diagnosis of ADHD

>> - 30 per cent had a diagnosis of autism spectrum disorder[1]

>> - 6 per cent had a dual diagnosis of autism spectrum disorder/ADHD.

This information represents only one unit's admission data and may not be representative of all services. However, it certainly warrants further discussion and exploration, particularly with regard to the specific difficulties experienced by individuals with autism. Most of the young women interviewed for this book who had spent time as inpatients reported it as a very stressful time, first because they were placed on a ward with other young people with mental health difficulties (but not autism) and found that the bullying and rejection they had experienced in their day-to-day life continued whilst they were in hospital. Some found the noise, the bright

---

1   Compared with a population prevalence rate of 0.2 per cent for females with autism.

lights and the constant proximity of others exacerbated their stress. Their sensory issues were very often not understood or taken into account and none could effectively articulate these difficulties. At times when their behaviour became difficult to manage or they were presenting a risk to themselves, many reported finding being restrained or held unbearable. For some being held triggered memories of previous sexual abuse or exploitation. L, the young woman referred to earlier in this chapter, found the imposition of 'someone else's routine' particularly hard to deal with. In addition, as cited in the NHS review (CAMHS Tier 4 Steering Group 2014), staff shortages are a common theme in inpatient units. This means that shifts are often covered by locum or agency staff. Frequent staff changes and unfamiliar faces were another concern that emerged from the reported experiences of inpatient care. This can be particularly difficult for young women on the autism spectrum. Conversely, however, a few of the young women interviewed actually enjoyed the experience of being an inpatient. They described feeling less 'weird' when in an environment where everyone had difficulties, and some reported feeling safer away from the stresses of their normal life.

This appears to support the argument for accommodating individuals with autism in dedicated inpatient wards, with staff trained to meet their specific needs. In learning disability services, this is already the case. In the United Kingdom, children and adults with a learning disability (an IQ lower than 70 is usually the cut-off for learning disability services) are usually accommodated in specialised autism services. Specific autism services tend also to employ speech and language therapists and sensory-integration trained occupational therapists, alongside psychologists, nurses and medical staff. This allows them to provide both positive behaviour support and behavioural analysis, and also to advise on communication difficulties and sensory integration interventions. In the United Kingdom, there are a number of inpatient units specifically for people with high-functioning autism for both adolescents and adults.

However, not all young people with autism have a diagnosis before their first inpatient admission. All general adolescent hospital inpatient units tend to be staffed with a multi-disciplinary team. These teams will usually include a psychologist or psychotherapist. However, speech and language therapists tend to be relatively rare and occupational therapists are usually employed in adolescent inpatient teams to provide therapeutic activities such as arts and crafts, and are not always sensory-integration trained.

Siegel *et al.* (2012) reported on a significant growth in the United States of inpatient units specifically for young people with autism and other developmental disorders. They reported that between 67.5 per cent and 87.5 per cent of admitted children had autism and discussed findings from a case study of one such unit. This unit adopted a bio-behavioural approach and the team included psychiatrists, psychologists, speech and language therapists and occupational therapists. The average length of stay was 42.3 days. This was much longer than the average admission time of ten days for adolescents. This longer admission time was accounted for by the severity of behaviour reported upon admission, the time needed for a bio-behavioural approach and the lack of appropriate follow-up care. However, they did report positive outcomes for patients where this approach was taken. A further study (Siegel *et al.* 2015) supported these findings. Interestingly, they reported that since the study began in 2014, 26.5 per cent of those young people diagnosed with autism and included in the study were female, although the sample did include young people with intellectual disability and this may have skewed the results due to the higher number of females with severe autism compared to those without intellectual disability. However, 58 per cent of the young people in this specialist unit were not reported to have any intellectual disability. Siegel *et al.* (2014) outline the approach that was taken. This included the development of an individual behaviour plan based upon the principles of applied behaviour analysis (ABA) and positive behaviour support (PBS). The therapeutic interventions offered included functional communication training, occupational therapy, milieu training and family therapy. In all cases, and perhaps most importantly, in addition to addressing the acute presenting symptomology, the teams in these units also explored and addressed the underlying chronic factors that had led to the development of the presenting behaviour.

Using a positive behaviour support approach in an inpatient setting

A positive behaviour support approach is becoming an increasingly popular way of managing the challenges of extreme or potentially damaging behaviour in inpatient settings, particularly for those individuals who have not responded to other evidence-based treatments. Such behaviours can include verbal or physical aggression, self-harm and matters related to self-care and hygiene, all of which can be pertinent for both young people and adults on the autism spectrum.

Functional assessment (or functional analysis) provides the cornerstone of any such approach. Careful analysis of the particular 'problem' behaviour (including the frequency, severity and definition of the behaviour), any antecedents (i.e. what was happening immediately before), what the consequences were (intended or otherwise) and whether there were any relevant environmental conditions or motivating factors are all taken into account (see Kanfer and Saslow 1969). Carrying out a strong functional assessment also allows for discussion of what might already have been tried with the individual. The idea is to try to establish the 'meaning' of a particular behaviour, with a view to finding a solution that best fits the individual.

The main difference between adopting a PBS approach and some other approaches is the focus upon the cause of the negative or challenging behaviour and bringing about a paradigm shift in terms of the attitude of, and approach taken by, the treating team. In the past, there has often been a focus upon 'consequences' for behaviour that is deemed unacceptable. This approach is explicitly discouraged in a PBS programme.

The main barrier to the success of this type of programme in an inpatient unit can be lack of consistency in the staff team. The environment can be stressful in the extreme, and burnout and stress are very common. In addition, this type of approach is often counterintuitive to many people. Culturally many people have grown up being used to more traditional approaches to discipline and punishment and it can be difficult to eradicate this type of attitude. As a consequence, any attempt to implement a PBS approach needs to include training that supports staff to challenge any preconceived ideas about discipline and morality.

It is important to acknowledge that the day-to-day environment in most inpatient units can be tense at times and difficult situations can quickly escalate. However, what is clear is that for individuals with autism, the traditional inpatient management techniques, which can include both restraint and seclusion, are unlikely to help manage a difficult situation, particularly if the person has significant sensory processing difficulties.

The biggest challenge for those working in inpatient settings is overcoming the reliance upon medication to manage behaviour, and for the whole clinical team to effectively buy in to the concept of a PBS approach, rather than seeing it as something the psychologist 'does' with a particular patient. The success of any PBS support initiative depends to a large extent upon the degree of cooperation between the various members of the multi-disciplinary treatment team.

It is important to point out at this juncture that the majority of day-to-day support in both adult and adolescent inpatient units, both in the United Kingdom and elsewhere, is carried out by support workers or healthcare assistants. These team members face a number of issues. Generally they receive relatively low pay, run the daily risk of injury, and often have limited access to supervision and/or training opportunities. They can also be prone to burnout and low morale. Staff retention is a challenge and very often units face high levels of staff turnover, which makes it difficult to ensure consistency of approach. There is a strong argument, therefore, for an increase in the level of training in autism and ongoing support which could be offered to those individuals in these very necessary, and challenging, roles.

References

Austen, B. (2009) The Development of Guidance for Commissioning and Delivery of Services for People Aged 16+ With Asperger Syndrome. A literature search for the South West Development Centre Regional Oversight Group.

CAMHS Tier 4 Steering Group (2014) *Child and Adolescent Mental Health Services (CAMHS) Tier 4 Report.* NHS England. Accessed on 3 May 2017 at www.england.nhs.uk/wp-content/uploads/2014/07/camhs-tier-4-rep.pdf.

Gordon, S.E. and O'Brien, A. (2014) New Zealand's mental health legislation needs reform to avoid discrimination. *New Zealand Medical Journal 127*, 1403, 55–65.

Kanfer, F.H. and Saslow, G. (1969) Behavioral Diagnosis. In C.M. Franks (ed.) *Behavior Therapy: Appraisal and Status.* New York, NY: McGraw-Hill.

Mental Health Act 2007. Accessed on 3 May 2017 at www.legislation.gov.uk/ukpga/2007/12/notes/division/6.

Ministry of Health (2012) *Guidelines to the Mental Health (Compulsory Assessment and Treatment) Act 1992.* Wellington: Ministry of Health. Accessed on 1 June 2017 at www.health.govt.nz/system/files/documents/publications/guide-to-mental-health-act.pdf.

Siegel, M., Doyle, K., Chemelski, B. *et al.* (2012) Specialized inpatient psychiatry units for children with autism and developmental disorders: A United States survey. *Journal of Autism and Developmental Disorders 42*, 9, 1863–1869.

Siegel, M., Milligan, B., Chemelski, B. *et al.* (2014) Specialized inpatient psychiatry for serious behavioural disturbance in autism and intellectual disability. *Journal of Autism and Developmental Disorders 44*, 12, 3026–3032.

Siegel, M., Smith, K.A., Mazefsky, C. *et al.* (2015) The autism inpatient collection: Methods and preliminary sample collection. *Molecular Autism 6*, 61, 1–10.

Chapter 4

Social Relationships and Bullying

This chapter explores the incidence of bullying of girls on the autism spectrum, their vulnerability (particularly sexually) and the potential impact of this upon their mental health.

The chapter also provides tips for parents, carers and professionals working with this group around keeping them safe.

As stated in earlier chapters, girls on the autism spectrum tend to have relatively strong social skills, compared to boys on the spectrum. They may often not receive a diagnosis until they reach adolescence. However, many, if not all, report difficulties with making and maintaining peer relationships.

There is some evidence to suggest that girls on the autism spectrum effectively get by by imitating the interaction style of their peers during early childhood. When relationships become more complex, during early adolescence, this strategy becomes less effective (Bauminger *et al.* 2008; Carrington, Templeton and Papinczak 2003). Adolescent female relationships rely upon reciprocal sharing, emotional support and social problem solving, whereas boys' relationships tend to be more about 'doing' than 'talking'.

Nichols, Moravcik and Tetenbaum (2009) report that girls with autism tend to need longer to process and respond to information than neuro-typical girls and thus find it increasingly difficult to respond to the fast-paced conversations conducted by their peers. The researchers also found that in typical adolescent relationships, when boys experienced conflict and disagreement, they were much more likely to deal with it in an overt way, often by engaging in acts of aggression and fighting but, generally, this tended to be resolved quite quickly. In contrast, girls tend to behave very differently. Their way of handling conflict will often be to spread rumours, talk about people when they are not present, and gossip about or ignore those they disagree with or dislike.

Card *et al.* (2008) and Nichols *et al.* (2009) also noted the variety of subtle non-verbal ways in which girls express displeasure, such as eye rolling and pulling faces. These behaviours were referred to as 'relational aggression'. Understanding this type of conflict is particularly challenging for girls on the autism spectrum, who may struggle to read and interpret these non-verbal signals. These differences were speculated to account for much of the social isolation reported by girls on the spectrum.

One mother, in a study by Cridland *et al.* (2014), reported that she had found it difficult to pinpoint any specific difficulties with friendship until her daughter reached the age of around eight or nine, but that after this age it became increasingly apparent. She also stated that she wished she had been aware of the difficulties earlier, as she could then have supported her by teaching her about facial expression and how to read people.

Some girls on the autism spectrum report that they get on better with boys than with other girls, as their friendships tended to be based predominantly upon shared interests.

Cridland *et al.* (2014) also reported that some girls in their study appeared to have particular difficulty with the two-way reciprocal nature of adolescent friendship and that, at times, there appeared to be a reduced need for social interaction in girls on the spectrum, or possibly a different perception of the function of social interaction.

L, the young woman referred to in the previous chapter, did describe feeling lonely at times but reported only wanting to have a friend in order that she could participate in activities with her (such as going to the cinema or out for a meal). She appeared puzzled, and slightly perturbed, when questioned about how she might support a friend who was having difficulties, or what she would do if a friend arrived unexpectedly at her home (her answer was that she would pretend she was not in).

Another mother in the Cridland *et al.* study reported that her daughter struggled socially when out with a group of friends – particularly when they all hugged and kissed each other as a form of greeting. This mother reported that her daughter simply would not have known when it was appropriate to do this. There are also reported differences with regard to having an interest in fashion and make-up, which are often 'social facilitators' for girls. Many girls in the Cridland *et al.* study reported choosing clothing solely for comfort and not understanding the unwritten social rules about 'dressing up' for an evening out. However, interestingly, some of the young women interviewed for this book were the opposite of this and were very interested in fashion and make-up, some to the point of obsession. Others were interested, but somehow got it wrong and their clothing and make-up appeared garish or over the top, which again could make them vulnerable.

In their early years, many mothers of girls on the autism spectrum reported to some extent actively fostering and supporting friendships for their daughters, by arranging play-dates and other joint social activities, usually with the children of mothers they had become friendly with at the school gates. They also reported that this became increasingly difficult as their children grew up, as peers often became more vocal about who they wished (and did not wish) to play with. Roberts and Smith (1999) found that typically developing children tend to develop their attitudes about difference and disability based upon their parents' attitudes. There was no difference if these attitudes were expressed verbally or inadvertently passed on (Cummings *et al.* 2006).

Jamison and Oeth Schuttler (2015) carried out a study examining social competence, self-perception and quality of life in adolescent females with and without autism. They concluded that adolescent females on the autism spectrum may experience the 'most significant impact of social impairment on their functioning' (p.2). They also reported that little has been studied with regard to the social and emotional health of young women on the spectrum, or how they cope with the shifting emphasis of relationships away from parents to peers. They found significant evidence of girls on the spectrum reporting feelings of low self-worth, anxiety and depression. These girls also reported particularly poor perception of their own appearance, their friendships and general quality of life.

Having problems with friendships is clearly upsetting for some girls on the spectrum. However, what is potentially much more serious is the likelihood of not just social exclusion but actual victimisation and bullying. Any young person with a history of problems with interpersonal relationships and difficulties with verbal and non-verbal communication is likely to be at risk of this, more so in today's society. With the rise in the use of social media such as Facebook, there is often no escape: bullying and comments may continue both in and out of school. Even with the use of 'emojis' (the smiley and cross faces used on these sites to represent different emotions), it can still be difficult for girls on the spectrum to work out exactly what is meant by a comment when it appears on their screen.

Bullying, as described in Schroeder *et al.* (2014), usually occurs when there is a perceived power imbalance. This power imbalance, particularly in adolescence, can be due to a variety of factors including age, size, perceived status and 'differences' (due to disability, sexual orientation, etc.).

Bullying is common amongst the neuro-typical population. According to Schroeder *et al.*, one third of all children between the ages of 11 and 13 report some degree of bullying. In a paper by Wang *et al.* (2010), 10 per cent of children reported 'chronic bullying'. Bullying and victimisation by peers contributes towards school avoidance, poor academic achievement and mental health difficulties, including anxiety, depression and even suicidal ideation. As stated earlier in this chapter, bullying for girls rarely takes the form of direct comments or physical acts. For girls it can be subtle eye rolling or laughing behind someone's back. Girls on the autism spectrum are also more likely to misinterpret even friendly teasing and banter as bullying.

There is a growing research literature that suggests that children with disabilities of any kind are at significantly increased risk of bullying and rejection. A literature review by Rose, Monda-Amaya and Espelage (2011) reported an overall figure of 50 per cent of children with additional needs having been bullied or victimised by their peers.

Having a group of supportive friends who will stand by you is one of the major reported protective factors against bullying. This is one key area where young people on the autism spectrum may struggle. In addition, being marginalised and shut out of peer activities is also going to reduce the young person's opportunity to practise social skills and learn the rules of peer interaction. Difficulties with theory of mind make it harder for the young person on the spectrum to internalise feedback from others about how their behaviour is being perceived. In addition, Biovin, Hymel and Bukowski (1995) and Gray (2004) noted that some young people with autism were more likely to have a strong and highly visible reaction to bullying which made them even more vulnerable.

Van Roekel, Scholte and Didden (2010) carried out a study specifically looking at bullying amongst adolescents with autism. The study examined:

» the prevalence of bullying amongst this population

» the extent to which they correctly perceived bullying behaviour and

» theory of mind involvement in these perceptions.

Their results showed that adolescents with autism who had been bullied tended to interpret the majority of situations as potentially bullying. Van Roekel *et al.* speculated that this may have been due to frequent negative feedback from others over a period of time.

Cappadocia, Weiss and Pepler (2012) and Shtayermman (2007) both found a clear link between peer victimisation and bullying and high levels of anxiety in young people on the autism spectrum.

Shtayermman (2007) found when researching a sample of young people with autism that 20 per cent of their participants who reported high levels of bullying and victimisation would also meet diagnostic criteria for a major depressive disorder, 30 per cent for a generalised anxiety disorder and 50 per cent exhibited significant levels of suicidal ideation.

Storch *et al.* (2012) also studied peer victimisation and bullying in youth with autism, with a specific focus on the relationship with co-occurring anxiety and loneliness. Their study investigated the experiences of 60 young people and found, surprisingly, that this group reported fairly low levels of peer bullying. The authors of this study speculated whether this was due to the young people either not being aware of being bullied or simply under-reporting. Nearly half of their sample did, however, report feelings of loneliness, although it has been suggested that when young people with autism report feeling lonely, they may place greater emphasis on the physical state of being lonely rather than the emotional state.

One particular area that parents interviewed for this book felt particularly concerned about was the possibility that their daughters may become involved in sending intimate pictures of themselves to others via the internet. Some felt that their daughter's desire to be popular, and their lack of appreciation of appropriate boundaries, or their own vulnerability, might make them easy targets for both their peers and those seeking to groom young women.

Sexting – defined as 'the production and dissemination of sexually explicit images by children and young adults via mobile telephones or personal computer consoles' (Merriam-Webster 2017) – is a growing trend. The growth of internet access for young people has led to a dramatic increase in the potential for sharing intimate images with a wide audience. Rollins (2015) highlighted the cases of two American teenagers who committed suicide after explicit pictures of them were circulated. Young people can also face the possibility of criminal charges if the recipient of these 'sexts' is a minor. In the course of researching this book, one incident was reported of a young adult with autism who, because of social naivety and a degree of immaturity, had sent explicit pictures to another young person who was only 15 years of age and found themselves potentially being placed upon the sex offender register.

Allyson, *et al.* (2013) in their paper exploring differences in 'sexting' behaviour across the genders reported that girls generally reported more negative experiences than boys, and identified the potential risks of cyberbullying, social humiliation and psychological distress as possible outcomes.

The study by Storch *et al.* (2012) suggested that intervention to help young women on the autism spectrum to improve their social skills should begin as early as possible. They felt that the focus should be upon attempting to modify inappropriate styles of interaction and reducing anxiety. However, although social skills training is advocated as an evidence-based intervention for school-age children with autism, the effectiveness of such programmes is reported to be variable, with the greatest challenge cited as helping the young person to generalise any teaching to outside of the therapeutic setting. Mackay, Knott and Dunlop (2007) also examined the effectiveness of a group intervention with young people with autism and reported similar findings.

Group work is often considered a cost-effective and efficient way of providing a service in both educational and clinical service provision. Howlin and Yates (1999) described a year-long intervention programme for ten adults with autism, which focused upon improving conversational skills. Group members and families reported improvement. However, other studies have demonstrated fewer positive results and raised questions about (1) whether these improvements were maintained or (2) whether they were generalised.

A variety of intervention approaches are available in the United Kingdom, ranging from books specifically targeting prosody and tone of voice to enhance communication, through to advice regarding navigating leaving home, parties, first sexual encounters, and guides for making and keeping friends. The National Autistic Society also produces help sheets for people with autism, specifically around developing social skills. However, in order to truly understand and support young women on the autism spectrum, it is necessary to consider carefully the key skills (or lack of them) that are likely to impact upon their ability to make and maintain friendships, to avoid bullying and victimisation and to keep themselves safe.

When observing the way that girls on the spectrum play and interact with other children from a very early age, it is easy to see how making and maintaining friendships can be difficult. They will often be very keen to play with dolls and miniature figures and will, superficially, appear to have very good imaginative skills. However, when this play is observed for any length of time, it can quickly become formulaic or repetitive. In addition, what quickly becomes apparent is the difficulty that these girls have in taking on board someone else's ideas. Quite often, any attempt to move a game in a different direction, or introduce an alternative theme is met with either anger or, more commonly, complete confusion. Poor theory of mind skills mean that they simply cannot contemplate a different way of playing. If the girl on the spectrum is either playing with children younger than herself or has a fairly dominant personality, this is usually tolerated for a while. Problems begin to emerge in mid-childhood, when negotiation and compromise become a more important skill.

Another key area to consider is the young person's understanding of what friendship is and what she actually wants from a relationship. Questions about friendships and relationships are included in the ADOS, which is used in many diagnostic assessments. These questions ask, 'What does being a friend mean to you?', 'How do you know someone is your friend?' and 'How is a friend different from someone who you just work or go to school with?' Many girls on the autism spectrum can provide a superficial answer to this and will say, 'A friend is someone who is there for you' or 'A friend is kind to you.' However, what is often missing is a true understanding of the reciprocal two-way nature of friendship, more specifically, that in a friendship there is some degree of expectation that you will also be there for the other person!

Cridland *et al.* (2014) highlighted the differences in the way some of the girls on the spectrum they interviewed for their study viewed social relationships. They seemed to take a much more pragmatic, activity-based approach which appeared more to do with attending a chosen social event together. This may, to some extent, explain the confusion and upset experienced by girls on the spectrum when their friendships fail. When working therapeutically with L, the young woman referred to earlier in the chapter, she reported feeling upset when her friends drifted away from her. However, her upset was more about the break in her routine rather than missing the individual friend per se. It had also not occurred to her that her friend may want more from the relationship, beyond just attending a social event with her. L also talked about her desire for an intimate relationship at some point but acknowledged that she would struggle having someone 'in her space' and 'interfering with her routine'.

Current knowledge regarding the social and romantic functioning in individuals with autism is limited. Henault and Attwood (2002) and Stokes and Kaur (2005) reported that although many individuals with autism may seek out and desire intimate relationships, many will lack the social skills to initiate or maintain such relationships appropriately. When these relationships break down, a lack of social skills combined with inflexible thinking and difficulty moving on from situations could lead to accusations of stalking (Stokes and Newton 2004).

In society generally (at least in Western cultures) there tend to be unspoken, but fairly predictable routines associated with courtship behaviour, for example, contacting by telephone, text or via social media. There is a fairly subtle dividing line between this type of behaviour and persistent or unwanted attention.

Stokes, Newton and Kaur (2007) found that individuals on the autism spectrum were more likely to engage in intrusive or socially unacceptable behaviour when attempting to initiate a romantic relationship. In addition, they were more likely to persist longer in pursuit of a romantic interest in the face of negative or no response from the person they were interested in. They also reported that individuals on the autism spectrum were also more likely to touch inappropriately in the belief that the target person must reciprocate their interest, demonstrate obsessional interest and make inappropriate comments. They also found an increased likelihood that those on the autism spectrum may be more inclined to monitor what their romantic interest was doing, follow or pursue them or even make threats against them. Some also threatened to self-harm when the person withdrew from them. They were also less likely to engage in some of the more typical courtship behaviours such as talking on the telephone or asking for a date. In addition, there were more reported difficulties with regard to 'reading' when someone was interested romantically and in appreciating the distress that persistence in pursuing them might cause.

This perhaps encapsulates the difficulties faced by young women on the autism spectrum. They are faced with a dichotomy – on the one hand they seek intimacy and closeness with other people but, on the other, they do not have the social imagination to work out what another person may be looking for in a relationship. Interventions, therefore, may need to start by going right back to basics and teaching about the nature of friendship. Women on the autism spectrum can, and do, have successful relationships but there needs to be a degree of openness and understanding about the difficulties that this might bring.

With regard to sexual relationships and sexual knowledge specifically, Brown-Lavoie, Viecili and Weiss (2014) report on a gap in the research literature regarding the risk of sexual victimisation and abuse for girls on the autism spectrum and the variables that contribute to this risk. Understanding the nature of age-appropriate sexual interest, limited sexual knowledge and experience and social deficits are some of the factors cited. They reported that individuals with autism gained most of their sexual knowledge from non-social sources and less from talking to their peers, leading to poorer perceived and actual knowledge about sex and sexual relationships.

Stokes and Kaur (2005) and Stokes et al. (2007) noted that, according to parental reports, children with autism had a poor understanding of privacy issues relating to sexual behaviour and learned less from interacting with their peers compared to typically developing children. Brown-Lavoie *et al.* (2014) conclude that individuals with autism are likely to have fewer opportunities to internalise accurate information due to misunderstanding intentions and missing social subtleties. Brown-Lavoie *et al.* also report that young people with autism also gained a significant amount of their sexual knowledge by 'making mistakes', and that they were likely to have poorer knowledge than their typically developing peers, both of how to protect themselves from sexually transmitted diseases and of safe sexual practices.

Although there has been some conjecture about the links between social and behavioural deficits in young people with autism and poorer sexual well-being (Henault 2005; Sevlever, Roth and Gillis 2013), there is little in the available literature that explores the increased risk of sexual victimisation in individuals with autism. Brown- Lavoie *et al.* (2014) reported that 78 per cent of their group of young people with autism felt they had been victimised sexually, compared to 47.7 per cent of the control group without autism. They also found that individuals with autism were two to three times more likely to experience sexual victimisation or rape.

Parents of children with autism also report concern about how to raise such topics with their children in an appropriate way. Holmes and Himle (2014) found that young people with autism are just as likely to engage in sexual activity as their typically developing peers (see also Byers *et al.* 2013; Hellemans *et al.* 2007). However, the parents they interviewed reported only having covered basic topics such as privacy, puberty and hygiene, pregnancy and some fairly basic information about relationships. They did not report having attempted to explain more complex issues such as sexuality or sexual health.

Tullis and Zarigrillo (2013) reported that 'reactive education' for young people on the spectrum appears to be the norm, in other words only implementing sexual education programmes for this group in response to a problem or behaviour that is deemed to be 'deviant'. They suggest that a more proactive approach to sex education would be beneficial.

Speirs (2006) produced a specific sex education curriculum for pupils with autism who have a reasonable level of language and communication ability, which is still available, and Stanfield (2000) developed the 'circles of intimacy' model to explain the rules around touch for people on the autism spectrum.

A study by Hatton and Tector (2010) revealed some of the vulnerability in this population. One young person in the group of young people they interviewed stated, 'I thought to get a boyfriend you had to agree to have sex with them and so I told the first boyfriend I had that I knew about this and would have sex.' This young woman also stated, 'I wish I had learned to keep myself safe and when someone asks you to "go for a walk", it sometimes means they want to touch you. I did not understand' (p.71).

Hatton and Tector also report the upset and confusion created for one girl they interviewed who had gained a bad reputation for herself because she thought she was obliged to have sex with every boy who approached her. She also discussed the distress and anxiety that this caused her parents. Sensory issues and the understanding and interpretation of touch were also highlighted in the Hatton and Tector study. For two of their participants, this had resulted in them deciding that touching was too unpredictable and 'scary'. Another reported that experiencing sexual feelings made her body feel 'out of balance'. This particular interviewee talked a great deal about her need to keep her senses regulated and in control.

One young woman who was engaged in a sexual relationship talked about her need to ensure that it was on her terms and under her control. She was aware that this could be perceived as selfish but talked about it being a 'coping strategy'.

There is of course another issue, rarely investigated or indeed discussed outside of the learning disability or forensic literature – that of hypersexuality and autism. In individuals, particularly boys, on the autism spectrum who have intellectual impairment, inappropriate masturbation is common. However, as a clinician, I have come across numerous reports by parents of young girls on the spectrum 'self-stimulating' or engaging in precocious sexual activity. This has, at times, led to raised concerns about possible sexual abuse, which can be upsetting and troubling for parents. However, it appears that very little has been written in the literature about the early sexual experiences of females. It is entirely possible that due to hypersensitivity, some females, like the young woman referred to in the Hatton and Tector study, may find sexual arousal uncomfortable. However, it is equally possible that others may find it intensely pleasurable.

One study by Muller (2011) found that with regard to the neurobiology of sexual behaviour, the frontal and temporal cortices are believed to be involved in modulating sexual drive, whereas sub-cortical structures including the amygdala and hippocampus are believed to be implicated in the modulation of sexual desire and genital response. In forensic studies differences in the amygdala-hippocampal brain structures have been linked to hypersexuality, and Muller (2011) speculated that brain changes associated with autism could potentially lead to hypersexuality in some individuals on the spectrum.

In summary, it appears that young (and older) women on the autism spectrum face a number of challenges with regard to both intimate relationships and friendship generally. The key to helping these women seems to be around specific teaching (of social norms and of the expectations of a relationship) and clear, unambiguous and, more importantly, proactive advice about sex and sexual health.

References

Allyson, L., Coskunpinar, A., Steiner, J. et al. (2013) Understanding differences in sexting behaviours across gender, relationship status and sexual identity and the role of expectancies in sexting. Cyberpsychology, Behaviour and Social Networking 16, 8, 568–574.

Bauminger, N, Solomon, M., Aviezer, A. et al. (2008) Friendship in high-functioning children with autism spectrum disorder: Mixed and non-mixed dyads. Journal of Autism and Developmental Disorders 38, 7, 1211–1229.

Biovin, M., Hymel, S. and Bukowski, W.M. (1995) The roles of social withdrawal, peer rejection, and victimization by peers in predicting loneliness and depressed mood in childhood. Development and Psychopathology 7, 4,765–785.

Brown-Lavoie, S.M., Viecili, M.A. and Weiss, J.A. (2014) Sexual knowledge and victimization in adults with autism spectrum disorders. *Journal of Autism and Developmental Disorder 44*, 9, 2185–2196.

Byers, E.S., Nichols, S., Voyer, S.D. *et al.* (2013) Sexual well-being of a community sample of high-functioning adults on the autism spectrum who have been in a romantic relationship. *Autism 17*, 4, 418–433.

Cappadocia, M., Weiss, J. and Pepler, D. (2012) Bullying experiences among children and youth with autism spectrum disorders. *Journal of Autism and Developmental Disorders 42*, 2, 266–277.

Card, N.A., Stucky, B.D., Sawalani, G.M. *et al.* (2008) Direct and indirect aggression during childhood and adolescence: A meta-analytic review of gender differences, intercorrelations, and relations to maladjustment. *Child Development 79*, 5, 1185–1229.

Carrington, S., Templeton, E. and Papinczak, T. (2003) Adolescents with Asperger syndrome and perceptions of friendships. *Focus on Autism and Other Developmental Disabilities 18*, 4, 211–218.

Cridland, E.K., Jones, S.C., Caputi, P. *et al.* (2014) Being a girl in a boys' world: Investigating the experiences of girls with ASD during adolescence. *Journal of Autism and Developmental Disorders 44*, 6, 1261–1274.

Cummings, J.G., Pepler, P., Mishna, F. *et al.* (2006) Bullying and victimization among students with exceptionalities. *Exceptionality Education 16*, 193–222.

Gray, C. (2004) Gray's guide to bullying parts I–III. *Jenison Autism Journal 16*, 1, 2–19.

Hatton, S. and Tector, A. (2010) Sexuality and relationship education for young people with autism spectrum disorders. *British Journal of Special Education 37*, 2, 69–76.

Hellemans, H., Colson, K., Verbraeken, C. *et al.* (2007) Sexual behavior in high-functioning male adolescents and young adults with autism spectrum disorder. *Journal of Autism and Developmental Disorders 37*, 2, 260–269.

Henault, I. (2005) *Asperger's Syndrome and Sexuality: From Adolescence through Adulthood.* London: Jessica Kingsley Publishers.

Henault, I. and Attwood, T. (2002) The Sexual Profile of Adults with Asperger's Syndrome: The Need for Understanding, Support and Sex Education. Paper presented at the Inaugural World Autism Congress, Melbourne, Australia, November.

Holmes, L.G. and Himle, M.B. (2014) Brief report: Parent–child sexuality communication and autism spectrum disorders. *Journal of Autism and Developmental Disorders 44*, 11, 2964–2970.

Howlin, P.A. and Yates, P. (1999) The potential effectiveness of a social skills group for adults with autism. *Autism: The International Journal of Research and Practice 3*, 3, 299.

Jamison, T.R. and Oeth Schuttler, J. (2015) Examining social competence, self-perception, quality of life and internalizing and externalizing symptoms in adolescent females with and without autism spectrum disorder: A quantitative design including between-groups and correlational analyses. *Molecular Autism 6*, 53.

Mackay, T., Knott, F. and Dunlop, A.W. (2007) Developing social interaction and understanding in individual with autism spectrum disorder: A group work intervention. *Journal of Intellectual and Developmental Disability 32*, 4, 279–290.

Merriam-Webster (2017) *Sexting.* Springfield, MA: Merriam-Webster Inc. Accessed on 1 June 2017 at www.merriam-webster.com/dictionary/sexting.

Muller, J.L. (2011) Are sadomasochism and hypersexuality in autism linked to amygdalahippocampal lesion? *Journal of Sexual Medicine 8*, 11, 3241–3249.

Nichols, S., Moravcik, G.M. and Tetenbaum, S.P. (2009) *Girls Growing Up on the Autism Spectrum: What Parents and Professionals Should Know About the Pre-Teen and Teenage Years.* London: Jessica Kingsley Publishers.

Roberts, C.M. and Smith, P.R. (1999) Attitudes and behaviour of children towards peers with disabilities. *International Journal of Disability, Development and Education 46*, 1, 35–50.

Rollins, J. (2015) Sexting cyberchildren: Gender, sexuality and childhood in media and law. *Sexuality and Culture 19*, 1, 57–71.

Rose, C.A., Monda-Amaya, L.E. and Espelage, D.L. (2011) Bullying perpetration and victimization in special education: A review of the literature. *Remedial and Special Education 32*, 2, 114–130.

Schroeder, J.H., Cappadocia, C., Bebko, J.M. *et al.* (2014) Shedding light on a pervasive problem: A review of research on bullying experiences among children with autism spectrum disorders. *Journal of Autism and Developmental Disorders 44*, 7, 1520–1534.

Sevlever, M., Roth, M.E. and Gillis, J.M. (2013) Sexual abuse and offending in autism spectrum disorders. *Sexuality and Disability 31*, 2, 189–200.

Shtayermman, O. (2007) Peer victimization in adolescents and young adults diagnosed with Asperger's syndrome: A link to depressive symptomatology, anxiety symptomatology, and suicidal ideation. *Issues in Comprehensive Pediatric Nursing 30*, 3, 87–107.

Speirs, F. (2006) *Sex and Relationship Education: A Programme for Learners..* Nottingham: The Shepherd School. Accessed on 1 June 2017 at www.fionaspeirs.co.uk/resources/sex-and-relationship-education.

Stanfield, J. (2000) *Circles of Intimacy.* Santa Barbara, CA: James Stanfield Publishing Company.

Storch, E., Larson, M., Ehrenreich-May, J. *et al.* (2012) Peer victimisation in youth with ASD and co-occurring anxiety: Relation with psychopathology and loneliness. *Journal of Developmental and Physical Disabilities 24*, 6, 575–590.

Stokes, M. and Kaur, A. (2005) High functioning autism and sexuality: A parental perspective. *Autism 9*, 3, 263–286.

Stokes, M. and Newton, N. (2004) Autistic spectrum disorders and stalking. *Autism 8*, 3, 337–338.

Stokes, M., Newton, N. and Kaur, A. (2007) Stalking and social and romantic functioning among adolescents and adults with autism spectrum disorder. *Journal of Autism and Developmental Disorders 37*, 10, 1969–1986.

Tullis, C.A. and Zarigrillo, A.N. (2013) Sexuality education for adolescents and adults with autism spectrum disorders. *Psychology in the Schools 50*, 9, 866–875.

Van Roekel, E., Scholte, R.H.J. and Didden, R. (2010) Bullying amongst adolescents with autism spectrum disorders. *Journal of Autism and Developmental Disorders 40*, 1, 63–73.

Wang, J., Iannotti, R.J., Luk, J.W. *et al.* (2010) Co-occurrence of victimization from five subtypes of bullying: Physical, verbal, social exclusion, spreading rumors, and cyber. *Journal of Pediatric Psychology 35*, 10, 1103–1112.

Chapter 5

Self-Harm

This chapter examines self-harming behaviour in girls on the autism spectrum. Links are made with sensory processing issues. Tips for supporting girls who exhibit this type of behaviour are included within this chapter.

There is an extensive literature around self-harming behaviour in individuals on the autism spectrum. However, this tends to focus predominantly upon people who are generally non-verbal, and who have a significant learning difficulty. Little research appears to have taken place that explores the function of self-harm in higher-functioning people, particularly females, on the autism spectrum.

Devine (2014) studied self-injurious behaviour in children on the autism spectrum and found that between 35 per cent and 50 per cent of children with autism will engage in behaviours such as hitting or biting themselves or banging their heads.

Head banging, in particular, can be especially detrimental. Newell *et al.* (1999) analysed the head-banging behaviour of an eight-year-old with autism and found that the peak impact force was near to that experienced by professional boxers. In addition, the frequency of the blows recorded was much greater than the frequency that would typically be expected to occur during a boxing match, thus making the potential for tissue damage extremely high.

Duerden *et al.* (2012b) explored the function of self-harming behaviour in both children and adolescents on the autism spectrum. Self-injurious behaviour represents serious acts of self-harm that can lead to hospitalisation in children with an ASD, as described in Mandell (2008). Duerden *et al.* (2012b) explored seven factors which they found to be risk factors, which included atypical sensory processing, impaired cognitive ability, abnormal social and language functioning, age and the need for routines and rituals. They also explored severity of self-harm and the impact of-gender.

Duerden *et al.* used items from the Repetitive Behaviour Scale – Revised (RBS-R) (Bodfish *et al.* 1999) in order to classify different types of self-harming behaviour. These behaviours include:

» hitting or slapping one's own head, face or body

» banging the head, or other part of the body, against an object such as the floor, wall or piece of furniture

» hitting the head, or other part of the body, with an object

» biting one's hand, or other body part

» pulling at either hair or skin

» picking or scratching the arms, legs or body

» inserting foreign objects

» picking at skin.

They found that one of the key factors associated with self-injurious behaviour in children with autism is their need for sensory stimulation. Individuals with autism display a wide range of abnormal, or different, sensory responses including visual, auditory, oral, olfactory and touch.

Various theories have been proposed to explain these sensory processing differences. Gillberg (1995) and Oswald *et al.* (1994) both speculated that they might be due to an overactive opoidergic system, whereby raised levels of endorphins are released due to high levels of stress and anxiety, resulting in an analgesic or numbing sensation and a reduced perception of sensory stimuli. In other words, high stress levels, which are often reported in individuals with autism, may lead to them feeling less pain when they self-harm.

The latest edition of the DSM, DSM-5 (APA 2013), now includes a specific category that evaluates sensory differences experienced by individuals on the autism spectrum. Both hyper- and hypo-sensitivity to pain have been reported in some individuals with autism. Individuals can experience either, depending upon the situation (Baranek *et al.* 2006). Individuals with hyper-sensitivity may attempt to avoid situations where overstimulation may occur and those with hypo-sensitivity may be more inclined to engage in sensory-seeking behaviours to increase the amount of sensation they experience (Dunn 2001).

One feature I have noted with regard to self-harming behaviour, particularly amongst girls on the autism spectrum who are detained in inpatient units, is the severity of the self-harm. It is not unusual to see evidence of pens, pencils and other objects being inserted deep inside self-inflicted wounds with almost unbelievable tolerance of the pain that these wounds undoubtedly must cause. An extensive search of the literature found few studies that have explicitly examined the pain threshold of individuals on the autism spectrum.

Pain is defined as an unpleasant experience both from a sensory and an emotional perspective, and sensitivity to pain comprises two elements – the way an individual perceives that pain and their subjective emotional response to this pain. The experience of pain is a very effective way of alerting someone to a potentially dangerous or damaging action. In the course of my work in a specialist CAMHS autism team, many parents reported that their children had, or appeared to have, an exceptionally high threshold for pain. One mother in particular reported particular distress because she had not noticed that her child had been burned by an iron which had been left switched on. There was no indication that she had been hurt, as she neither cried nor drew any attention to the burn. The mother only realised how badly her child was burned when she undressed her ready for bed in the evening. In contrast, other parents reported that their children appeared to have a very low threshold for pain, often crying or fussing unduly about relatively minor injuries such as a paper cut.

In a systematic review of studies of pain sensitivity in individuals with autism by Yasuda *et al.* (2016), 15 studies were identified, five of which were case studies and ten experimental studies. All of the case studies reported hypo-sensitivity to pain. However, the experimental studies revealed mixed results, with both hyper- and hypo-sensitivity to pain being reported. Yasuda *et al.* went on to compare both pain detection and pain tolerance thresholds in individuals with autism compared to neuro-typical controls. Their results suggested that the sensory perception thresholds for the group with autism were not significantly impaired (in other words, they appeared to experience the sensation of pain in a similar way). However, the researchers found that what appeared to be different in the group with autism were the pain processing pathways, which seemed to lead to a poorer ability to describe, or provide an emotional evaluation of, their pain.

An interesting study by Jennett, Hagopian and Beaulieu (2011) discussed a case of a 17-year-old girl with autism and intellectual impairment, who was hospitalised because of significant self-harming. They found that when she was restrained (by which they meant held firmly by the arms), her heart rate reduced to a normal resting rate. As soon as the restraint was discontinued, her heart rate increased again. It would appear that she was calmed by being held gently but firmly. There is research (Isley *et al.* 1991; Smith *et al.* 1992) that shows that a number of individuals on the spectrum seek to wrap themselves tightly in either clothing or a blanket when they feel anxious or agitated. The authors also reported cases of individuals requesting to be restrained or held whilst self-harming.

In children and adults with more significant cognitive impairment, self-injurious behaviour is often seen as a feature of frustration and poor communicative ability. Kurtz *et al.* (2003) and Reeve and Carr (2000) both report that encouraging the development of communicative ability can have a positive impact upon the levels of self-injurious behaviour.

Duerden *et al.* (2012b) also reported on gender differences in self-injurious behaviour in autism and it would appear that girls are more likely to self-harm than boys. However, these were reports of studies carried out with individuals with significant cognitive impairment.

Bjarehed and Lundh (2008) observed that deliberate self-harm is also common in typically developing adolescents and Lundh, Walgby-Lundh and Bjarehed (2011) looked more specifically at the type of psychological problems that are likely to serve as risk factors for self-harm. Deliberate self-harm is not established as a formal psychiatric diagnosis. However, self-harm is often the most common reason for an inpatient admission. Linehan (1993) hypothesised that problems with emotional vulnerability is a major risk factor. She also speculated that because engaging in self-harm tends to elicit a negative response from parents, teachers and peers, this may lead to anxiety, shame and guilt and this may, in turn, lead to further emotional problems.

Lundh *et al.* (2011) found evidence to suggest that there is a strong relationship between psychological problems and self-harm in girls but not boys. They also found that self-harm in boys tended to be a more transient and temporary behaviour compared to girls.

Adolescent girls today are growing up in a complex world where the media portrays endless images of females with perfect bodies and perfect lives, which are generally not achievable for the majority. Combined with this is often early access to pornographic material and sexual material online and the growth of a competitive and often discontented culture. One of the ways in which this anxiety and discontent appears to manifest itself is in self-harm. Social media also appears to have added to the apparent growth in self-harm, with many sites sharing pictures of self-harming behaviour and describing ways in which this can be carried out.

Cerdorian (2005) reported that in the United States, a conservative estimate suggested that three million Americans harmed themselves by cutting or burning. It is likely that this figure is much higher today. Most self-harming behaviour is carried out in private and those who engage in self-harming are often secretive

(Froeschle and Moyer 2004). The most likely group to engage in self-harming behaviour is reported to be intelligent, middle- to upper-class girls, often with the first incidence occurring between the ages of 12 and 14. Self-harm, particularly amongst adolescents, can be 'contagious', with many copying the behaviour of their peers (Galley 2003).

Giletta et al. (2012) looked at types of self-injury in typically developing adolescents. They studied young people between the ages of 12 and 15 who had been admitted to psychiatric units (none had a prior history of either learning difficulties or psychosis). They found the most common forms of self-harming behaviour were cutting or carving of skin, burning of skin, biting/hitting self, drawing blood by scratching, and inserting objects under skin or nails.

Farber (2008) speculated that inflicting pain and injury on oneself is a behaviour that emerges when individuals feel alone and helpless and can also be a mechanism for dealing with psychological pain. It was further speculated that if an individual's feelings are numbed due to depression, or because they are dissociating, experiencing physical pain can make them feel alive. For some, self-harming also brings a means of having control when they perceive that everything else in their life is out of control.

In terms of how girls in particular self-harm, the most common area to cut is the arms, usually the forearms, although many also cut their legs and other parts of their body. They may use fingernails, razor blades, knives or anything else they find that is sharp (broken shards of CDs or other small pieces of plastic are particularly popular). The young person may also attempt to burn herself with a cigarette or cigarette lighter. Girls may also attempt to self-ligate by using their hair, bedding or clothing or wire from binders or notebooks. This type of behaviour can be addictive and can become a habitual way of dealing with stress (Bywaters and Rolfe 2002).

James et al. (2012) analysed over 500 reports of self-harm that took place in inpatient settings. Most of these reports involved females. Interestingly, although self-harming behaviour is often perceived as a 'cry for help' or as 'attention seeking', James et al.

found that the majority of the incidents reported took place in private (bedrooms, bathrooms or toilets) and most occurred in the evening. The most common interventions to support individuals in inpatient units who were self-harming were reported as verbal de-escalation and/or physical restraint, and the most common antecedents were reported to be either psychological distress or conflict with staff.

Swinton, Hopkins and Swinton (1998) reported that 70 per cent of service users admitted to psychiatric units self-harmed during the course of their admission.

Managing self-harm in inpatient settings can be very challenging. The primary aim of such services is to keep the service user safe. However, this very often involves measures such as continuous observation or replacement of normal clothing with anti-tear items. If verbal de-escalation fails, it can be necessary to employ physical restraint techniques and/or administer medication. This is often viewed by both service users and staff as infringing the human rights and dignity of those involved. This type of management is likely to result in additional challenges for young women on the autism spectrum, particularly with regard to sensory issues. Earlier in the chapter, the case study of a 17-year-old girl with autism was discussed. This particular girl clearly found being held a calming experience. However, the sensory profiles of individuals on the spectrum can vary widely, with some being hypo-sensitive (and thus more likely to need a firm pressure) whilst others will be hyper-sensitive to touch and will find being held in restraint extremely distressing. A full evaluation of an individual's sensory profile would be helpful and would undoubtedly reduce the distress experienced by many females with autism who experience an inpatient admission. However, the presence of a therapist trained in sensory integration is not a feature of many inpatient teams. In addition, it has been reported (McHale 2010) that self-harm is often perceived negatively by clinical and support staff working with young people as, at times, this can wrongly be seen as 'attention-seeking' behaviour.

Around a quarter of the incidents reported in James *et al.* (2012) (21%) cited conflict between staff and service user as being the antecedent for self-harming behaviour. It was further reported that the cause of the conflict was usually either a request by the service user being denied or the service user being asked to do something. This is, of course, a study of inpatient services. However, it does raise speculation about the function of self-harm in other environments. More particularly, it raises the question of the role of self-harm as a means of demand avoidance. This could have implications for the study of girls with the pathological demand avoidance profile.

Poor emotion recognition or emotional literacy may also play a part in the underlying reasons for self-harm amongst girls on the autism spectrum. Linehan's (1993) biosocial theory suggested that the defining feature of someone with a borderline (or emotionally unstable) personality disorder is a very poor ability to regulate emotional reactions. Linehan linked this to the impact of the young person having experienced an 'emotionally invalidating' environment as a child, suggesting that this lack of emotional 'containment' leads to less opportunity to learn how to regulate intense emotions. They may then turn to self-harm as a means of avoiding unwanted (or difficult to deal with) emotions, thoughts or feelings. Individuals who self-harm report that it quickly relieves emotion pain, anxiety or tension (Kemperman *et al.* 1997). Some also report that self-harm temporarily reduces feelings of anger, anxiety and shame. In terms of young women on the autism spectrum, the reason for using self-harm may be linked, not to an emotionally invalidating environment, but rather to poor emotional literacy. There has been a great deal of research into the emotional recognition skills of males on the autism spectrum, but little has been studied specifically about the abilities of women on the spectrum. Ketelaars *et al.* (2016) have attempted to address this with their study of high-functioning females with autism.

It has been speculated that individuals with autism have specific difficulties with emotion processing, particularly those which impact upon social interaction (Humphreys *et al.* 2007).

However, the majority of the studies have been based upon male samples. In a meta-analysis of 48 studies Uljarevic and Hamilton (2013) found evidence for a deficit in visual emotion recognition (however, effect sizes were small and there was a high degree of inter-group variation). It would also appear that this deficit was greater for negative emotions such as fear and sadness (Humphreys *et al.* 2007; Wallace, Coleman and Bailey 2008).

One possible hypothesis which could explain this is that some individuals with autism may have alexithymia. Alexithymia is a specific impairment in the ability to identify and describe one's own feelings and emotions. A number of studies, including Berthoz and Hill (2005) and Hill, Berthoz and Frith (2004), used the Bermond-Vorst Alexithymia Questionnaire (BVAQ, Bermond 1998) and found that up to 50 per cent of individuals may have alexithymia. This questionnaire includes items such as, 'When I am distressed, I know whether I am afraid, sad or angry.' This study found that their sample of females with high-functioning autism were able to accurately identify vocally expressed emotions. However, they were slower than their neuro-typical counterparts. One of the reasons suggested by the authors was that it reflects the additional amount of mental energy needed by women on the spectrum, or that it simply takes them longer to work out the emotion. Either of these hypotheses could lead to a negative outcome in a social situation when a quick response or change in behaviour is required. Interestingly, the researchers also found that when even quite subtle emotions were presented visually, women on the spectrum had no problem in recognising them.

Of perhaps greater interest with regard to self-harm was the finding that women on the autism spectrum, whilst having few problems acknowledging their feelings (i.e. they could recognise that they were feeling a particular way and could recognise the signs of physiological arousal such as increased heart rate or breathing), were very poor at labelling or describing them. Many individuals with autism describe how it can be difficult to speak, particularly when anxious, so combining an already poor ability to describe how one is feeling with the impact of stress upon the ability to verbally express anything, it is perhaps not surprising that some turn to self-harm.

This is of particular relevance to both parents and clinicians providing therapeutic support to girls on the spectrum, especially those in inpatient settings. Personal clinical experience has demonstrated both the very poor ability to accurately describe how they feel (very often becoming confused between anxiety and sadness or anxiety and anger) and the need for specific, almost step-by-step tuition to help them to link bodily sensations and physiological arousal to specific emotions.

Another interesting feature to emerge from the literature may be of specific relevance to those young women with pathological demand avoidance. When researching self-harm and the behaviour of those diagnosed initially with borderline personality disorder, it was reported that borderline personality disorder is associated with high levels of demand avoidance/escape behaviours when faced with stressful (or perceived stressful) situations, one of which is self-harm (Bijttebier and Vertommen 1999).

In terms of helping young women on the spectrum who do self-harm it may be necessary to return to the issue of borderline personality disorder. As described in earlier chapters, borderline personality disorder is a formal psychiatric diagnosis and does appear in the DSM-5. However, it is essentially a description of observed behaviour, which includes poor emotion regulation and maladaptive ways of coping with difficult feelings. Many young women with autism develop these types of behaviour because they too are unable to manage difficult feelings. The therapeutic approach with the strongest evidence base for supporting young women with features of borderline personality disorder is dialectical behavioural therapy (DBT, Mooney 2010). Dialectical behavioural therapy is described as a 'multi-modal' comprehensive and flexible treatment programme for young people and adults with emotion regulation difficulties. It includes weekly individual therapy and between-sessions coaching and what is referred to as 'skills training'. The skills training aspect of a DBT programme may be of particular help to young women on the autism spectrum as part of this programme aims to improve emotional literacy. Individuals work on 're-structuring' negative or unhelpful thoughts. However, as with other forms of cognitive behavioural therapy, the therapist needs to be aware that, even if the person they are working with appears cognitively able, it may still be necessary to start at a relatively simple level in terms of emotional recognition and the ability to link thoughts and feelings to body sensations of anger, anxiety or sadness.

For parents faced with a child who is self-harming, knowing quite what to do and how to handle the situation is extremely challenging. Girls who are self-harming become very adept at finding, and secreting, items that are sharp and can be used to cut themselves. As stated above, these can include sharp edges off plastic cups, broken pens, pieces of CDs, tiny pieces of plaster off the wall. The list goes on. Making sure that obvious items such as glass or razor blades are kept well out of reach is one way of limiting opportunity, but this will not stop a determined self-harmer. Encouraging the young person to put an elastic band around their wrist and flick it when they feel the urge to self-harm can help, as can placing an ice cube on the skin. However, ice can cause burns if left on the skin for too long.

Parents can also help their daughters to talk about their feelings and there are many good resources available that aim to improve emotional literacy. However, if a young person is continuing to self-harm it could be argued that aside from discouragement and support in other ways, the most important factor to consider is to minimise the risk of secondary infection, so ensuring that there is always a good supply of antiseptic wipes and plasters readily available is vital.

References

American Psychiatric Association (2013) *Diagnostic and Statistical Manual of Mental Disorders* (5th edition). Washington, DC: American Psychiatric Association.

Baranek, G.T., David, F.J., Poe, M.D. *et al.* (2006) Sensory experiences questionnaire: Discriminating sensory features in young children with autism, developmental delays, and typical development. *Journal of Child Psychology and Psychiatry 47*, 6, 591–601.

Bermond, B. (1998) *Bermond-Vorst Alexithymia Questionnaire.* Amsterdam: University of Amsterdam.

Berthoz, S. and Hill, E.L. (2005) The validity of using self-reports to assess emotion regulation abilities in adults with autism spectrum disorder. *European Psychiatry 20,* 3, 291–298.

Bijttebier, P. and Vertommen, H. (1999) Coping strategies in relation to personality disorders. *Personality and Individual Differences 26,* 5, 847–856.

Bjarehed, J. and Lundh, L.G. (2008) Deliberate self-harm in 14-year-old adolescents: How frequent is it, and how is it associated with psychopathology, relationship variables and styles of emotional regulation? *Cognitive Behaviour Therapy 37,* 1, 26–37.

Bodfish, J.W., Symonds, F.W., Parker, D.E. *et al.* (1999) *The Repetitive Behaviour Scale.* Western Carolina Centre Research Reports, Morganton.

Bywaters, P. and Rolfe, A. (2002) *Look Beyond the Scars: Understanding and Responding to Self-Injury and Self-Harm.* London: NCH. Accessed on 3 May 2017 at www.selfinjurysupport.org.uk/docfiles/selfharm-nch.pdf.

Cerdorian, K. (2005) The needs of adolescent girls who self-harm. *Journal of Psychosocial Nursing 43,* 8, 40–46.

Devine, D.P. (2014) Self-injurious behaviour in autistic children: A neurodevelopmental theory of social and environmental isolation. *Psychopharmacology 231,* 6, 979–997.

Duerden, E.G., Oatley, H.K., Mak-Fan, K.M. *et al.* (2012a) Risk factors associated with self-injurious behaviors in children and adolescents with autism spectrum disorders. *Journal of Autism and Developmental Disorders 42,* 11, 2420–2470.

Duerden, E.G., Szatman, P. and Roberts, S.W. (2012b) Towards a better understanding of self-injurious behaviour in children and adolescents with autism spectrum disorders. *Journal of Autism and Developmental Disorders 42,* 11, 2515–2518.

Dunn, W. (2001) The sensations of everyday life: Empirical, theoretical, and pragmatic considerations. *American Journal of Occupational Therapy 55,* 6, 608–620.

Farber, S.K. (2008) Autistic and dissociative features in eating disorders and self-harm. *Modern Psychoanalysis 33,* 1, 23–49.

Froeschle, J. and Moyer, M. (2004) Just cut it out: Legal and ethical challenges in counseling students who self-mutilate. *Professional School Counseling 7,* 4, 231–235.

Galley, M. (2003) Student self-harm: Silent school crisis. *Education Week 23,* 14, 1–3.

Giletta, M., Scholte, R.H., Engels, R.C. *et al.* (2012) Adolescent non-suicidal injury: A cross-national study of community samples from Italy, the Netherlands and the United States. *Psychiatry Research 197,* 1–2, 66–72.

Gillberg, C. (1995) Endogenous opioids and opiate antagonists in autism: Brief review of empirical findings and implications for clinicians. *Developmental Medicine and Child Neurology 37,* 3, 239–245.

Hill, E., Berthoz, S. and Frith, U. (2004) Brief report: Cognitive processing of own emotions in individuals with autistic spectrum disorder and in their relatives. *Journal of Autism and Developmental Disorders 34,* 2, 229–235.

Humphreys, K., Minshew, N., Leonard, G.L. *et al.* (2007) A fine-grained analysis of facial expression processing in high-functioning adults with autism. *Neuropsychologia 45,* 4, 685–695.

Isley, E.M., Kartsonis, C., McCurley, C.M. *et al.* (1991) Self-restraint: A review of etiology and applications in mentally retarded adults with self-injury. *Research in Developmental Disabilities 12,* 1, 87–95.

James, K., Stewart, D., Wright, S. *et al.* (2012) Self-harm in adult inpatient psychiatric care: A national study of incident reports in the UK. *International Journal of Nursing Studies 49,* 10, 1212–1219.

Jennett, H., Hagopian, L.P. and Beaulieu, L. (2011) Analysis of heart rate and self-injury with and without restraint in an individual with autism. *Research into Autism Spectrum Disorders 5*, 3, 1110–1118.

Kemperman, I., Russ, M.J., Clark, W.C. *et al.* (1997) Pain assessment in self-injurious patients with borderline personality disorder using signal detection theory. *Psychiatry Research 70*, 3, 175–183.

Ketelaars, M.P., In't Velt, A., Mol, A. *et al.* (2016) Emotion recognition and alexithymia in high functioning females with autism spectrum disorder. *Research in Autism Spectrum Disorders 21*, 51–60.

Kurtz, P.F., Chin, M.D., Huete, J.M. *et al.* (2003) Functional analysis and treatment of self-injurious behavior in young children: A summary of 30 cases. *Journal of Applied Behavior Analysis 36*, 2, 205–219.

Linehan, M.M. (1993) *Cognitive Behavioral Treatment of Borderline Personality Disorder.* New York: Guilford Press.

Lundh, L.G., Walgby-Lundh, M. and Bjarehed, J. (2011) Deliberate self-harm and psychological problems in young adolescents: Evidence of a bidirectional relationship in girls. *Scandinavian Journal of Psychology 52*, 5, 476–483.

Mandell, D.S. (2008) Psychiatric hospitalisation among children with autism spectrum disorders. *Journal of Autism and Developmental Disorders 38*, 6, 1059–1065.

McHale, J. (2010) Self-harm: What's the problem? A literature review of the factors affecting attitudes towards self-harm. *Journal of Psychiatric and Mental Health Nursing 17*, 8, 732–740.

Mooney, S. (2010) Managing the unmanageable: Cognitive behaviour therapy for deliberate self-harm. *Psychoanalytic Psychotherapy 24*, 2, 135–149.

Oswald, D.P., Ellis, C.R., Singh, N.N. *et al.* (1994) Self-Injury. In J.L. Matson (ed.) *Autism in Children and Adults: Etiology, Assessment, and Intervention.* Pacific Grove, CA: Brooks/Cole Publishing.

Newell, K.M., Sprague, R.L., Pain, M.T. *et al.* (1999) Dynamics of self-injurious behaviours. *American Journal of Mental Retardation 104*, 1, 11–21.

Reeve, C.E. and Carr, E.G. (2000) Prevention of severe behavior problems in children with developmental disorders. *Journal of Positive Behavior Interventions 2*, 3, 144–160.

Smith, R.G., Iwata, B.A., Vollmer, T.R. *et al.* (1992) On the relationship between self-injurious behavior and self-restraint. *Journal of Applied Behavior Analysis 25*, 2, 433–445.

Swinton, M., Hopkins, R. and Swinton, J. (1998) Reports of self-injury in a maximum security hospital. *Criminal Behaviour and Mental Health 8*, 1, 7–16.

Uljarevic, M. and Hamilton, A. (2013) Recognition of emotions in autism: A formal meta-analysis. *Journal of Autism and Developmental Disorders 43*, 7, 1517–1526.

Wallace, S., Coleman, M. and Bailey, A. (2008) An investigation of basic facial expression recognition in autism spectrum disorders. *Cognition and Emotion 22*, 7, 1353–1380.

Yasuda, Y., Hashimoto, R., Nakae, A. *et al.* (2016) Sensory cognitive abnormalities of pain in autism spectrum disorder: A case control study. *Annals of General Psychiatry 15*, 8, 1–8.

Chapter 6

Anxiety and Depression

This chapter explores anxiety disorders (including obsessive compulsive disorder) and depression in girls on the autism spectrum. Strategies for adapting both cognitive behavioural therapy and dialectical behavioural therapy approaches to help them manage their anxiety are included.

Anxiety

Evidence suggests that an estimated 40 per cent of individuals on the autism spectrum will suffer from high levels of anxiety (Van Steensel, Bögels and Perrin 2011). Clinical experience would suggest that this figure is likely to be higher, particularly amongst those with the pathological (or extreme) demand avoidance profile. In an earlier version of the DSM, the DSM-III (APA 1980), 'sudden excessive anxiety' and 'unexplained panic attacks' were included amongst the core criteria for a diagnosis of autism. However, subsequent versions of the DSM (IV and 5) do not include this. The reason for this is not entirely clear. Hallett *et al.* (2013) cite the meta-analysis by White *et al.* (2009) which found that between 11 per cent and 84 per cent of children with a diagnosis of autism display anxiety. Of the 31 studies analysed 30 per cent were diagnosed with specific phobias, 17 per cent had obsessive compulsive disorder, 17 per cent had social anxiety and 15 per cent reported features of 'generalised' anxiety. Their results suggested that children with autism were twice as likely to develop anxiety disorders compared with their neuro-typical peers. High levels of anxiety have a negative impact upon education, social relationships and social participation and on other members of the immediate family group (Reaven 2011). There is also an increased likelihood that these anxiety disorders will persist into adulthood.

The presence of anxiety in those with autism is well documented. However, less has been researched and reported regarding what specifically, in terms of traits or particular triggers, affects anxiety levels. Liew *et al.* (2015) looked at social problem solving, social competence, the experience of being teased or bullied and being deterred from engaging in repetitive or sensory behaviours. Whatever the cause, anxiety levels amongst those on the autism spectrum are much higher than those experienced or reported in either the general population or in other neurodevelopmental conditions (Gadow, DeVincent and Schneider 2009; Green *et al.* 2000). It has also been reported (Micali, Chakrabarti and Fombonne 2004; Piven *et al.* 1991) that anxiety-related disorders are more common in the relatives of individuals with autism. Settipani *et al.* (2012) and Puleo and Kendall (2011) also reported that the higher the level of autistic traits (even without a formal diagnosis) in adolescents with anxiety disorders, the greater the resistance to traditional cognitive behavioural interventions was compared to adolescents with fewer autistic traits. These studies also found that the causes of social anxiety and the causes of obsessive compulsive behaviours in individuals with autism were different, and they responded to different interventions. Social anxiety is likely to be reduced or at least supported through social skills training, more specifically through interventions that aim to improve social problem solving. The authors also found some support for their hypothesis that linked either punishment for, or prevention of, repetitive behaviours and/or sensory processing difficulties to higher levels of anxiety-related compulsive behaviours. They suggested that interventions for managing this type of anxiety might be more effective if the focus was upon developing an understanding of the individual's need for repetitive behaviours and their sensory needs.

This is of particular relevance to parents living with girls on the autism spectrum who display high levels of anxiety and who tend to be focused upon playing computer games or viewing YouTube videos whilst they are at home. Parents are often concerned about the extent to which this type of activity is useful and whether or not it should be encouraged. In view of the research results, it may be that acknowledging the need for a certain amount of repetitive behaviour, certainly in the immediate time after the young person has been at school or engaging in socially draining interaction, could be helpful in reducing anxiety levels.

With regard to sensory processing difficulties, a study by Wigham *et al.* (2015) further explored the link between anxiety, sensory processing difficulties and repetitive behaviours in individuals with autism. Wigham *et al.* (2015) aimed to examine these links with specific reference to the 'intolerance of uncertainty' (IU). Dunn (1997) reported that sensory input can be experienced as heightened and unpleasant or alternatively as a reduced or 'dulled' sensation. Both types of response can occur in the same individual and can fluctuate over time. Green *et al.* (2012) studied toddlers with an autism diagnosis and found that sensory over-responsiveness predicted higher levels of anxiety. In a later study, Green *et al.* (2013) further examined young people with a diagnosis of autism using fMRI scanning of their brains. They found higher levels of activation in the sensory areas of the brain in those young people who reported sensory over-responsiveness. They also found increased levels of activation in the areas of the brain associated with emotional responsiveness, namely the amygdala, the hippocampus and the orbito-frontal cortex which they felt suggested a strong link between sensory processing difficulties and emotion regulation, including anxiety. In addition, 'insistence upon sameness' was suggested by Lidstone *et al.* (2014) as a strategy used by individuals with autism to control their environment and thus manage their anxiety levels.

Wigham *et al.* (2015) also explored the concept of 'intolerance of uncertainty'. This is a theoretical model that was initially developed for a non-autistic population (Dugas *et al.* 1998).

The main principle of this model was that uncertainty is stressful and can be anxiety-provoking. In addition, unexpected events can be negative. This construct has been widely tested across a variety of anxiety disorders with the general population and may have a neurological basis (Grupe and Nitschke 2013), presumably as a way of maintaining survival and safety at a very basic level. This may in part link with the resistance to change and insistence upon sameness observed in individuals with autism.

Wigham *et al.* (2015) suggested that psychological interventions for young people with autism should incorporate specifically targeting cognitions around IU and encouraging them to develop more flexible thinking in the face of uncertainty, and that this may help to reduce anxiety.

Obsessive compulsive disorder

Given the findings that the majority of individuals with autism will seek out repetitive activities in order to calm and reduce anxiety, and that studies show that some 17 per cent of those diagnosed with autism would also meet diagnostic criteria for obsessive compulsive disorder, it is interesting to consider the research that has been undertaken to further examine the links between the two conditions.

Restricted and repetitive interests and behaviour were amongst the original key features of autism identified by Kanner in the 1940s and have remained in the diagnostic criteria ever since. Ruzzano and Borsboom (2016) attempted to further examine the relationship between autism and obsessive compulsive disorder. They were specifically investigating whether autism and obsessive compulsive disorder represent two distinct but often co-morbid disorders or whether there is a more significant overlap. Similarities in symptoms between the two disorders (such as insistence upon sameness, doing things at a particular time or saying things a certain way) are often cited in such discussions. South, Ozonoff, and McMahon (2005) examined certain neural abnormalities found in the brains of those with both autism and obsessive compulsive disorder and suggested there may be similarities in both conditions. Others argue that there are fundamental differences between the two. In particular, there appeared to be a less frequent occurrence of behaviours such as excessive handwashing or checking and counting in individuals with autism (Lewin *et al.* 2011).

Markarian *et al.* (2010) and Storch, Abramowitz and Goodman (2008) felt that obsessive compulsive behaviours were strategies, albeit not particularly helpful ones, developed to deal with the distress caused by obsessive and intrusive thoughts, whereas repetitive behaviour in autism, as mentioned earlier in this chapter, may be used either to manage sensory difficulties or to reduce anxiety.

Hazen *et al.* (2008), when reporting on a series of case studies of children with obsessive compulsive behaviour (but without autism), concluded that these children also demonstrated a degree of intolerance of some sensory stimuli. Dar, Kahn and Carmeli (2012) also found that unusual sensory processing has been linked to symptoms of obsessive compulsive disorder in later life. These studies suggest that there are some overlaps between the two conditions, which are still not fully understood.

However, when developing intervention strategies that may support those experiencing the need to engage in compulsive behaviours, it may be necessary to examine the function of such behaviours. In individuals with autism, repetitive actions are often calming, whereas in individuals who have obsessive compulsive disorder (without autism), the need to engage in repetitive actions often causes extreme distress. This is often linked to deep-rooted fears about what may happen (to self or family members) if the repetitive actions are not completed.

Autism and depression

Solomon, Miller and Taylor (2012) carried out a study to investigate depression and what they referred to as 'internalising psychopathology' in individuals with autism; more specifically they wished to examine whether there were significant gender differences in the likelihood of experiencing depressive symptoms. They reported that typically developing boys and girls have a similar risk of developing depression during childhood, but the risk for girls goes up dramatically during adolescence (Nolen-Hoeksema and Girgus 1994). This is evidenced by the high level of reported depression amongst teenaged girls.

It has also been found that young people with autism are at significantly increased risk of internalising their difficulties compared to typically developing peers. It was, therefore, hypothesised in Solomon *et al.* (2012) that girls with autism would be doubly at risk of developing depression. This hypothesis was found to be accurate and is clearly worrying for those living with or supporting someone with the condition.

A study by Wallace *et al.* (2016) noted that 70 per cent of individuals currently diagnosed with autism do not have any significant intellectual disability, so it is interesting to note that over 25 per cent of adults with autism (without a learning difficulty) were not able to engage in paid work or any other meaningful daytime activities (Taylor and Selzer 2011). Whether this was because they chose not to engage or whether due to low mood, anxiety or depression, engaging in meaningful day-to-day activities became impossible.

A number of models have been developed to help understand the cognitive processes involved in both anxiety and depression (Beck 1963; Ellis 1962). Ellis cited 'irrational beliefs' as the source of emotional difficulties, whereas Beck proposed a model of 'distorted thinking'. These underlying beliefs and assumptions often lead to automatic negative thoughts and an inability to consider more positive cognitions. The fundamental principle of cognitive behavioural therapy (CBT) focuses upon modifying or challenging these automatic negative thoughts. This type of programme can prove difficult for individuals with autism who may struggle with cognitive flexibility. Unfortunately for many, they will, in addition to a degree of rigidity, have experienced a high level of social rejection and relationship difficulties, alongside academic and work problems. Undoubtedly, this would, to some extent, serve to reinforce their negative beliefs. In addition, as many individuals with autism have poor emotional literacy and a reduced ability to verbalise thoughts and feelings, standard CBT programmes can prove problematic. McGillivray and Evert (2014) also highlight the amount of time it can take people on the autism spectrum to establish a meaningful therapeutic relationship. This study recruited young people (male and female) with a diagnosis of high-functioning autism aged between 15 and 25. The specific aim of the study was to reduce negative and anxious thinking patterns and reported symptoms of stress, anxiety and depression. Their study took place over nine two-hour sessions and included topics such as recognising emotions in self and others and the relationship between thoughts and feelings. It also included support in managing the 'critical voice', that is, automatic negative thoughts, and an introduction to a variety of coping styles. The programme also introduced them to the physiological impact of stress. Their post-course results suggested there had been a significant improvement in the young people's reported feelings of depression but not in their anxiety. It was felt that in terms of depression, the intervention helped to reduce the number of negative thoughts they had about themselves. However, the authors speculated (as has been suggested elsewhere in this chapter) that for people with autism, anxiety may well be mediated by different physiological processes.

A study by Sharpley *et al.* (2016) reported on differences that have been found in the plasma and salivary concentration of cortisol in young people with autism. Cortisol is a hormone that regulates a wide range of processes throughout the body including metabolism and the immune response. It also has a very important role in helping the body respond to stress. The young people examined in their study were found to have unusual levels of cortisol compared to neuro-typical peers. High levels of cortisol are a strong indicator of chronic stress and anxiety and are also associated with depression. High levels of cortisol can also contribute to a range of illnesses including coronary heart disease. In contrast, abnormally low levels of cortisol can contribute towards chronic pain, irritable bowel syndrome, post-traumatic stress disorder and fibromyalgia. Low levels of cortisol (hypocortinolaemia) can also be associated with chronic anxiety and stress. Bitsika *et al.* (2014) found that boys with autism had low levels of cortisol.

Sharpley *et al.* (2016) studied 39 girls with autism spectrum disorder between the ages of 6 and 17 and established that there were some recorded differences in overall cortisol levels compared with their neuro-typical peers, which suggests that further investigation of this area is important. In addition to measuring cortisol levels, the researchers also looked at a subjective assessment of the girls' mood. Their findings were somewhat concerning in that over a third of the girls studied (where the mean age was 10 years and 1 month) reported that they had thoughts of dying or killing themselves 'sometimes' or 'often'. The authors concluded that this added further support to the hypothesis that girls on the autism spectrum are more likely than typically developing girls to be at risk of suffering depression.

Wallace *et al.* (2016) investigated the role of poor executive function ability in adults with autism and its impact upon co-morbid depression and anxiety. 'Executive function' is the term used to describe higher-order cognitive abilities such as working memory, planning, flexibility and organisational ability, in terms of both problem solving and emotional regulation. In a study of 400 children with autism, Granader *et al.* (2014) found that the most significant difficulty identified was that of 'behavioural flexibility' and a further study by Lawson *et al.* (2015) found that poor behavioural flexibility was associated with an increased reporting of symptoms of anxiety and depression. This finding was replicated in the Wallace *et al.* study when assessing adults, and leads to speculation about how cognitive rigidity and depression in autism are linked. This particular study did not, interestingly, include any females with autism. They did, however, point to the possible effectiveness of developing programmes that aim to develop more flexible thinking skills, hypothesising that if inflexible thinking leads to an insistence upon sameness, this could also lead to further anxiety when things do not go according to plan. Kenworthy *et al.* (2014) reported promising results from a randomised controlled trial, but acknowledged that further research is required.

In terms of therapeutic approaches, cognitive remediation therapy may be a potentially useful intervention for individuals with autism. The primary aim of cognitive remediation therapy is to reduce 'cognitive deficits' which can include areas such as attention, memory and executive function. Cognitive remediation therapy endeavours to improve these abilities through a variety of exercises. It is not meant to replace other forms of therapy, but rather to complement them. Tchanturia, Lounes and Holttum (2014) report that it has been used with some success in treating major depressive disorders, obsessive compulsive disorder and eating disorders. There is, however, only one published study (Eack *et al.* 2013) that examines the use of cognitive remediation therapy with an autistic population. Eack *et al.* reported promising improvements following a group intervention that included both a computer-based neurocognitive training programme and a social cognitive programme.

My own experience of attempting a cognitive remediation programme with individuals on the autism spectrum is that, whilst individuals are perfectly capable of carrying out tasks that aim to improve cognitive flexibility in a classroom or clinic-based setting, actually applying these principles to real-life situations in a dynamic way often proves difficult. Given the difficulties faced by many individuals with autism with regard to social imagination or 'mentalising', it may be that programmes of this type would need to be carried out in-vivo, with the therapist or parent providing real-time, real-life examples for the young person to work on.

Of particular interest from a clinical perspective are those young women who present with features of pathological (or extreme) demand avoidance. The extreme and distressing behaviour displayed by those with this form of autism is widely believed to be driven by high levels of anxiety leading to an overwhelming need for control. This need can be all-consuming with some girls obsessively resisting all demands, sometimes to their own detriment and including things they really enjoy doing. Some become so controlling that every aspect of their life (and often those of their parents and caregivers) becomes minutely 'scripted'. Any deviation from this 'script' can result in severe behavioural meltdowns, which resemble full-blown panic attacks. Others will camouflage or mask their anxiety in public and find themselves unable to manage their anxiety and distress once in the safety of their own home. Many of the young women who were kind enough to share their experiences for this book reported the level of stress caused by the need to mask and hide their anxiety in public; their embarrassment about (sometimes) public meltdown was palpable. Also, many reported the need to withdraw and effectively recharge their social batteries after any kind of social encounter or situation where the social and/or physical demands were high.

Many of the parents of younger girls with autism, and pathological demand avoidance particularly, reported the attraction of computer games such as Minecraft or The Sims. Some would choose to play all day on these games and, intuitively, it is possible to see the attraction for a girl with a strong need to control her environment, as what could be better than a whole world that is yours to do with what you will? Parents do, however, worry about the extent to which these games can become all-consuming, to the point that the young person becomes reluctant to leave their room or attend school. It is a fine balance between allowing the use of these games as a form of relaxation and escape from social and educational pressures, and running the risk of them becoming an intractable obsession.

Anxiety, depression and well-being

A recent study by Bargiela, Seward and Mandy (2016) interviewed 14 women on the autism spectrum about their experiences of diagnosis, support and managing their mental health issues. Of the 14 interviewed, seven reported being able to support themselves through paid employment. One was signed off work due to mental health problems. Their mean age at the time of diagnosis was 21 years; all but one reported currently experiencing significant anxiety. A theme emerged from this study which suggested that many of the women had experienced being dismissed, or ignored, when they tried to seek help. Some reported feeling misunderstood and having been told, 'You are not autistic.'

Almost all of the women reported having experienced mental health difficulties at some time, with the most common being anxiety, depression and eating disorders. Passive behaviour or adopting the role of a 'model child' appeared to contribute to their diagnosis being overlooked. Most reported masking or camouflaging their difficulties at school and whilst in public, and nearly all reported meltdowns at home. The strain of pretending to be 'normal' was cited as a common reason for this. Many attempted to adopt a vivacious and bubbly persona in public and some had used alcohol and other substances to boost social confidence. Most reported that their greatest source of social support were fellow 'Aspies', usually contacted through social media fora.

Clearly there remains a great deal of work to be done in terms of developing appropriate support mechanisms to manage the unique challenges faced by girls and young women on the autism spectrum, particularly in regard to helping them manage their anxiety levels.

References

American Psychiatric Association (1980) *Diagnostic and Statistical Manual of Mental Disorders* (3rd edition). Washington, DC: American Psychiatric Association.

Bargiela, S., Seward, R. and Mandy, W.J. (2016) The experiences of late-diagnosed women with autism spectrum conditions: An investigation of the female autism phenotype. *Journal of Autism and Developmental Disorders 46*, 10, 3281-3294.

Beck, A.T. (1963) Thinking and depression: Theory and therapy. *Archives of General Psychiatry 10*, 561-571.

Bitsika, V., Sharpley, C., Sweeney, J. *et al.* (2014) HPA and SAM axis responses as correlates of self- vs parental ratings of anxiety in boys with an autistic disorder. *Journal of Physiological Behaviour 127*, 1-7.

Dar, R., Kahn, D.T. and Carmeli, R. (2012) The relationship between sensory processing, childhood rituals and obsessive-compulsive symptoms. *Journal of Behaviour Therapy and Experimental Psychiatry 43*, 1, 679-684.

Dugas, M.J, Gagnon, F., Ladouceur, R. *et al.* (1998) Generalized anxiety disorder: A preliminary test of a conceptual model. *Behaviour Research and Therapy 36*, 2, 215-226.

Dunn, W. (1997) The impact of sensory processing abilities on the daily lives of young children and their families: A conceptual model. *Infants and Young Children 9*, 4, 23–35.

Eack, S.M., Greenwald, D.P., Hogarty, S.S. *et al.* (2013) Cognitive enhancement therapy for adults with autism spectrum disorder: Results of an 18-month feasibility study. *Journal of Autism and Developmental Disorders 43*, 2866–2877.

Ellis, C.J. and Schneider, J. (2009) Comparative study of children with ADHD only, autism spectrum disorder + ADHD, and chronic multiple tic disorder + ADHD. *Journal of Attention Disorders 12*, 5, 474–485.

Granader, Y., Wallace, G.L., Hardy, K.K. *et al.* (2014) Characterizing the factor structure of parent reported executive function in autism spectrum disorders: The role of cognitive inflexibility. *Journal of Autism and Developmental Disorders 44*, 12, 3056–3062.

Green, J., Gilchrist, A., Burton, D. *et al.* (2000) Social and psychiatric functioning in adolescents with Asperger syndrome compared with conduct disorder. *Journal of Autism and Developmental Disorders 30*, 4, 279–293.

Green, S.A., Ben-Sasson, A., Soto, T.W. *et al.* (2012) Anxiety and sensory over-responsivity in toddlers with autism spectrum disorders: Bidirectional effects across time. *Journal of Autism and Developmental Disorders 42*, 6, 1112–1119.

Green, S.A., Rudie, J.D., Colich, N.L. *et al.* (2013) Over-reactive brain responses to sensory stimuli in youth with autism spectrum disorders. *Journal of the American Academy of Child and Adolescent Psychiatry 52*, 11, 1158–1172.

Grupe, D.W. and Nitschke, J.B. (2013) Uncertainty and anticipation in anxiety: An integrated neurobiological and psychological perspective. *Nature Reviews Neuroscience 14*, 7, 488–501.

Hallett, V., Lecavalier, L., Sukhodolsky, D.G. *et al.* (2013) Exploring the manifestations of anxiety in children with autism spectrum disorders. *Journal of Autism and Developmental Disorders 43*, 10, 2341–2352.

Hazen, E., Reichert, E., Piacentini, J. *et al.* (2008) Case series: Sensory intolerance as a primary symptom of paediatric obsessive compulsive disorder. *Annals of Clinical Psychiatry 20*, 4, 199–203.

Kenworthy, L., Anthony, L.G., Naiman, D.Q. *et al.* (2014) Randomised controlled effectiveness trial of executive function intervention for children on the autism spectrum. *Journal of Child Psychology and Psychiatry 55*, 4, 374–383.

Kenworthy, L., Yerys, B.E., Anthony, L.G. *et al.* (2008) Understanding executive control in autism spectrum disorders in the laboratory and in the real world. *Neuropsychology Review 18*, 4, 320–338.

Lawson, R.A., Papadakis, A.A., Higginson, C.I. *et al.* (2015) Everyday executive function impairments predict comorbid psychopathology in autism spectrum and attention-deficit/hyperactivity disorders. *Neuropsychology 29*, 3, 445–453.

Liew, S., Thevaraga, N., Hong, R.Y. *et al.* (2015) The relationship between autistic traits and social anxiety, worry, obsessive-compulsive and depressive symptoms: Specific and non-specific mediators in a student sample. *Journal of Autism and Developmental Disorders 45*, 3, 858–872.

Lewin, A.B., Wood, J.J., Gunderson, S. *et al.* (2011) Phenomenology of comorbid autism spectrum and obsessive-compulsive disorders among children. *Journal of Developmental and Physical Disabilities 23*, 6, 543–553.

Lidstone, J., Uljarevic, M., Sullivan, J. *et al.* (2014) Relations among restricted and repetitive behaviours, anxiety and sensory features in children with autism spectrum disorders. *Research in Autism Spectrum Disorders 8*, 2, 82–92.

Markarian, Y., Larson, M.J., Aldea, M.A. *et al.* (2010) Multiple pathways to functional impairment in obsessive-compulsive disorder. *Clinical Psychology Review 30*, 1, 78–88.

McGillivray, J.A. and Evert, H.T. (2014) Group cognitive behavioural therapy programme shows potential in reducing symptoms of depression and stress among young people with ASD. *Journal of Autism and Developmental Disorders 44*, 8, 2041–2051.

Micali, N., Chakrabarti, S. and Fombonne, E. (2004) The broad autism phenotype: Findings from an epidemiological survey. *Autism International Journal of Research and Practice 8*, 1, 21–37.

Nolen-Hoeksema, S. and Girgus, J.S. (1994) The emergence of gender differences in depression during adolescence. *Psychological Bulletin 115*, 3, 424–443.

Piven, J., Landa, R., Gayle, J. *et al.* (1991) Psychiatric disorders in the parents of autistic individuals. *Journal of the American Academy of Child and Adolescent Psychiatry 30*, 3, 471–478.

Puleo, C.M. and Kendall, P.C. (2011) Anxiety disorders in typically developing youth: Autism spectrum symptoms as a predictor of cognitive-behavioural treatment. *Journal of Autism and Developmental Disorders 41*, 3, 275–286.

Reaven, J. (2011) The treatment of anxiety symptoms in youth with high functioning autism spectrum disorder: Developmental considerations for parents. *Brain Research 1380*, 255–263.

Ruzzano, L. and Borsboom, D. (2016) Repetitive behaviours in autism and OCD: New perspectives from a network analysis. *Journal of Autism and Developmental Disorders 45*, 1, 192–202.

Settipani, C.A., Puleo, C.M., Conner, B.T. *et al.* (2012) Characteristics and anxiety symptom presentation associated with autism spectrum traits in youth with anxiety disorders. *Journal of Anxiety Disorders 26*, 3, 459–467.

Sharpley, C.F., Bitsika, V., Andronicos, N.M. *et al.* (2016) Further evidence of HPA-axis dysregulation and its correlation with depression in ASD: Data from girls. *Physiology and Behaviour 167*, 110–117.

Solomon, M., Miller, M. and Taylor, S. (2012) Autism symptoms and internalising pathology in girls and boys with autism spectrum disorders. *Journal of Autism and Developmental Disorders 42*, 1, 48–59.

South, M., Ozonoff, S. and McMahon, W.M. (2005) Repetitive behaviour profiles in Asperger syndrome and high-functioning autism. *Journal of Autism and Developmental Disorders 35*, 2, 145–158.

Storch, E., Abramowitz, J. and Goodman, W. (2008) Where does obsessive-compulsive disorder belong in DSM-V? *Depression and Anxiety 25*, 4, 336–347.

Taylor, J.L. and Seltzer, M.M. (2011) Employment and post-secondary educational activities for young adults with autism spectrum disorders during the transition to adulthood. *Journal of Autism and Developmental Disorders 41*, 5, 566–574.

Tchanturia, K., Lounes, N. and Holttum, S. (2014) Cognitive remediation in anorexia nervosa and related conditions: A systematic review. *European Eating Disorders Review 22*, 6, 254–262.

Van Steensel, F., Bögels, S. and Perrin, S. (2011) Anxiety disorders in children and adolescents with autistic spectrum disorders: A meta-analysis. *Clinical Child and Family Psychology Review 14*, 3, 302–317.

Wallace, G.L., Kenworthy, L., Pugliese, C.E. *et al.* (2016) Real-world executive functions in adults with autism spectrum disorder: Profiles of impairment and associations with adaptive functioning and co-morbid anxiety and depression. *Journal of Autism and Developmental Disorders 46*, 3, 1071–1083.

White, S.W., Oswald, D., Ollendick, T. *et al.* (2009) Anxiety in children and adolescents with autism spectrum disorders. *Clinical Psychology Review 29*, 3, 216–229.

Wigham, S., Rodgers, J., South, M. *et al.* (2015) The interplay between sensory processing abnormalities, intolerance of uncertainty, anxiety and restricted and repetitive behaviours in autism spectrum disorder. *Journal of Autism and Developmental Disorders 45*, 4, 943–952.

Chapter 7

Dissociative Disorders and Psychosis

Although rare, both dissociative episodes following trauma and psychotic episodes (usually after periods of extreme stress) are experienced by girls on the autism spectrum. This chapter provides advice for parents, carers and professionals on how to support young people through periods of crisis.

Autism and psychosis

Autism frequently co-exists with other psychiatric disorders and, in the early years of research into the disorder, the common features of autism and schizophrenia were assumed to be the same (Eisenberg and Kanner 1958).

In the late 1970s autism spectrum disorders and schizophrenia were split into two distinct diagnostic categories in the DSM-III (APA 1980). The debates about the boundaries between the two disorders continue to this day. Both autism and schizophrenia share common neurobiological features and common genetic risk factors. In addition, the presence of autistic traits in early childhood is said to increase the risk of psychosis in later life (Bevan Jones *et al.* 2012), and a number of individuals who later present with schizophrenia in adulthood would also fulfil diagnostic criteria for childhood autism (Unenge Hallerback, Lugnegard and Gillberg 2007).

A number of studies have examined the extent to which autism may be a risk factor for the development of later psychosis (Clarke *et al.* 1989). A large-scale study by Volkmar and Cohen (1991) found that rates of schizophrenia in an autistic population were no higher than in a neuro-typical population and Tsanikos *et al.* (2006), in a study of adults with autism (and intellectual disability), found they had no greater risk of developing psychosis. However, they did speculate that, as a high number of this group were routinely prescribed anti-psychotic medication, it was entirely possible that any features of psychosis were merely well controlled. Although the NICE guidelines in the United Kingdom do not recommend the use of anti-psychotic medication to treat the 'core features of autism' (NICE 2017), it is frequently prescribed to manage aggressive or violent behaviour.

A study carried out by Stahlberg *et al.* in 2004 found that 15 per cent of a group of individuals with a diagnosis of high-functioning autism had features of either bipolar affective disorder or psychotic disorders. In a follow-up study, they aimed to explore this further and recruited 155 individuals (94 males and 61 females) with a diagnosis of high-functioning autism. Using the SCID-IV (Structured Clinical Interview for DSM-IV Axis 1 Disorders, First *et al.* 2002), they found that only two individuals met full criteria for a diagnosis of psychosis. However, 13 per cent reported experiencing recurrent auditory hallucinations. They did not report any gender differences. In contrast, a study by Maric *et al.* (2003) reported that sub-clinical psychotic features were more likely to be observed in girls.

It was speculated by Kyriakopoulos *et al.* (2015) that a group of children they studied who presented with what appeared to be psychotic symptoms may, in fact, represent a distinct sub-group of autism. Buitelaar and Van der Gaag (1998), Van der Gaag *et al.* (1995) and Sprong *et al.* (2008) all referred to a group of children who were described as having multiple complex developmental disorder (MCDD). These children all had similar presentations which included idiosyncratic fears, panic episodes and explosive emotional outbursts. Kyriakopoulos *et al.* (2015) speculated that using the criteria developed for multiple complex developmental disorder, those children most at risk of developing psychotic episodes might be identified.

Although these criteria are outlined clearly in the Buitelaar paper, the concept of multiple complex developmental disorder as a separate diagnostic category did not receive widespread support and it is not included in the new DSM-5 (APA) or the proposed ICD-11 revision of the currently used ICD-10. However, when looking at the behavioural features described (see below) the similarities between multiple complex developmental disorder and the presentation of those children who have the pathological demand avoidance profile of autism are striking, and do raise important questions about sub-types or different presentations of autism spectrum disorders.

The criterion for multiple complex developmental disorder (Buitelaar *et al.* 1998) is an impaired ability to regulate one's emotional state characterised by:

» unusual fears or extreme anxiety reactions

» frequent anxiety or panic attack

» behavioural meltdowns which can involve immature or violent outbursts

» difficulties in social interaction: lack of interest or avoidance of or disturbed/ambivalent relationships

» evidence of thought disorder

» irrational thinking, intrusive thoughts or unusual ideas, repeating nonsense words

» easily confused

» paranoid thoughts or over-engagement with fantasy figures or ideas.

It was suggested that a diagnosis could be made on the basis of the presence of five of the above features (which had to include at least one from each category).

The multiple complex developmental disorder criterion highlights formal thought disorder as a key feature of early psychoticism. In children and young people with autism, this can be difficult to distinguish from language and communication difficulties. Many comments and observations made by individuals on the spectrum could be perceived as 'odd' or 'unusual'. However, a study by Weisbrot *et al.* (2005) found that certain children with autism, who were highly anxious, did experience odd thoughts, strange beliefs and illogical thinking. In addition, some also reported visual hallucinations when extremely stressed and anxious.

Kyriakopoulos *et al.* (2015) studied a group of children admitted to a specialist inpatient unit in London between 2003 and 2012. This unit receives referrals on a national basis for children with the most severe and complex developmental and neuropsychiatric conditions. The clinicians who worked in this unit were faced with the difficult task of identifying children with autism who had psychotic features and those with early-onset schizophrenia.

Eighty-four patients with autism (of which 25% were female), with an average age of 11 years and 1 month, were included in their study. Their results identified two distinct groups of patients with autism – those with psychotic features and those without. When the researchers compared their findings with the multiple complex developmental disorder profile, they found that it matched their autism spectrum disorder group almost perfectly. This led them to conclude that, although having multiple complex developmental disorder as a separate diagnostic profile was not necessarily appropriate, the presence of thought disorder, irrational fears and phobias and frequent idiosyncratic and bizarre anxiety reactions in children with autism could be an indicator of a small sub-group.

Another key finding of this study was that these children, when admitted, had extremely low scores on the CGAS (Children's Global Assessment Scale). The CGAS is frequently used in adolescent inpatient units upon admission and discharge as an outcome measure. Low CGAS scores indicate a high level of impairment in both mental health and everyday functioning. In addition, this group of children were likely to need to spend significantly longer in hospital compared to the group with autism who did not display psychotic features.

Bevan-Jones *et al.* (2012) followed a group of children who were identified with traits of autism at the age of seven. From this original sample 78 per cent (8232) were followed up at the age of 12. Of these, 11.55 per cent reported experiencing psychotic features.

All of the above studies appear to suggest that some sort of psychotic episode can take place in young people with autism and that this is usually associated with high levels of anxiety or stress. Nylander, Lugnegard and Hallerback (2008) and Tebartz van Elst *et al.* (2013) support this.

It cannot be under-estimated how worrying and, indeed, terrifying this type of behaviour can be for parents of children on the autism spectrum. My own clinical experience has provided numerous examples of this type of reaction to stress and many parents have reported that their child appears 'unreachable' or completely out of control, sometimes with a strange or glassy gaze. Some report them resorting to behaviours such as rocking and muttering to themselves. This type of reaction has also been reported in adults, particularly females, who describe great shame following an incident where they feel they have lost control.

Care does need to be taken when interpreting this behaviour as psychotic. Many individuals with autism resort to self-talk as a calming strategy when falling asleep or when feeling anxious. Van Schalkwyk *et al.* (2011) noted that this behaviour often lessens once anxiety levels fall. They also noted that structure, routine and predictability also help.

Starling and Dosseter (2009) also highlight the difficulties in distinguishing between an internal voice and an external (psychotic) voice in people with high-functioning autism.

Delusions and unusual beliefs are also not uncommon and may to others appear idiosyncratic or odd. However, these are not necessarily psychotic. In addition, many behaviours such as stereotypical speech, echolalia, unusual mannerisms or facial grimaces are also seen in individuals on the spectrum, but are not necessarily evidence of psychosis.

Supporting someone through a psychotic episode

Hallucinations, voices and delusions can be frightening, feel threatening and increase anxiety. Families of those who are affected in this way are likely to feel equally scared. Witnessing someone you care about experiencing a psychotic episode can be upsetting. There is growing evidence that the experience of extreme stress can trigger this type of reaction in some individuals on the autism spectrum. The first step in supporting someone in this situation would be to help them manage the stressor. For many this may require reducing demands entirely for a short time and allowing the person to calm. Talking through how they feel may help if they are able to verbalise their feelings. Ensuring consistency and clarity in daily routines may also help.

Psychotic episodes are frequently preceded by a 'prodromal' stage which includes subtle changes in the person's thoughts, emotions and perceptions. They may become more paranoid or feel that they are being judged or talked about. There may also be a decline in functional skills such as self-care; washing, eating or keeping their environment tidy; or a decline in academic or work achievement.

Dissociation

Dissociative disorders fall into three major categories: dissociative amnesia, dissociative identity disorders and depersonalisation/ derealisation disorders. These tend to be associated with traumatic events and involve 'splitting' of the conscious mind in order to protect the individual from the painful emotions and psychological distress that result from this trauma. For some individuals, when they reach the point of no longer feeling able to regulate themselves or when they become emotionally overwhelmed, they may begin to 'dissociate'. Someone in this state may experience loss of memory or appear paralysed or stuck in one place. They may report intrusive flashbacks or voices. Some individuals even develop conflicting images of themselves or form actual co-existing personalities ('alters'). The most common feature of a dissociative disorder is amnesia, where the person is unable to recall specific information or an event.

Dissociative identity disorder (DID) is often referred to as multiple personality disorder and individuals can develop a number of different 'personalities' (usually between 5 and 10) that can emerge at any time. The switch from one personality to another can often be sudden and dramatic. The individual may or may not be aware of the other personalities. Dissociative identity disorder remains a controversial diagnosis amongst professionals and there is conflicting evidence about the efficacy and potential harm of psychotherapeutic approaches.

Both dissociative amnesia and dissociative identity disorder tend to be more prevalent in females, with most being diagnosed in adolescence or early adulthood.

There is limited research evidence with regard to the prevalence of these types of difficulty in girls with autism. However, in the course of clinical work and research for this book, a number of young people have reported features of this type of difficulty. These have tended to be girls with the pathological demand avoidance profile who report this type of experience starting in their early teens. This is a potentially interesting area for future research, given the 'Jekyll and Hyde' switches in mood reported by many parents of children with this profile. In addition, pathological demand avoidance is driven by highly elevated levels of anxiety, permeating across all aspects of daily life. The development of dissociative identity disorder tends to be associated with childhood trauma and, again, this could be an interesting area for future research with girls on the autism spectrum, particularly those with pathological demand avoidance, where their behaviour is often extreme and may have led to them experiencing certain situations (such as overly punitive management of their behaviour, for example, being restrained or physically removed from an area) or the reaction of others when they have experienced a behavioural meltdown as sufficiently traumatic to trigger a dissociative disorder.

Neuroscientific research has begun to identify the types of dissociative process which may be a factor in this area in a number of individuals with autism. Links have been made to a separation of the psyche (thought processes) from the soma (the body). Dissociation is described as a psychic survival tool which arises when an individual separates out and, in some way, compartmentalises aspects of traumatic experiences in order to allow them to continue to function (Howell 2005). In addition, it would appear that when in a dissociative state, self-harm and other potentially harmful acts appear to become easier to carry out. The person is reported to become almost 'de-humanised'.

Autism and trauma responses

Morrow Kerns, Newschaffer and Berkowitz (2015) speculated whether young people with autism may be at increased risk of encountering traumatic events and experiencing the negative effects of these in later life. Traumatic events in childhood are strongly associated with future mental illness. Morrow Kerns *et al.* used the term 'trauma' to describe an event or events that are experienced as threatening or frightening and which can have a long-term impact upon the individual. Trauma experiences can range from relatively minor (such as mild teasing), which should be relatively easy to forget, to severe trauma which can result in depression, anxiety, self-harm and even suicidal ideation. Trauma can be a single event or a chronic, repeated set of circumstances or behaviour which continues over a long period of time. The experience of trauma is, of course, subjective and individuals react differently depending upon their personality and previous life history. The most commonly recognised effects of trauma are 'traumatic stress', where the individual experiences a persistent disturbance in their mood or anxiety levels, and PTSD, which usually involves a specific set of trauma-related symptoms such as flashbacks, nightmares and a feeling of emotional numbness that persists for longer than a month after the event or events (DSM-5, American Psychiatric Association 2013).

A high proportion of young people will be exposed to potentially traumatic events. Finkelhor *et al.* (2005) cited figures of up to 60 per cent of youth in the United States. The effects of these traumatic experiences are wide-ranging and can include difficulties with affect regulation, behaviour difficulties, somatic illnesses and a greater incidence of immunological and gastrointestinal illnesses in later life (Anda *et al.* 2006).

A number of studies have highlighted the increased risk of experiencing potentially traumatising incidents in young people with learning or other developmental difficulties (Hibbard and Desch 2007). Additional risk factors include poor communication skills, social isolation and family stress, all of which are likely to be prevalent in an autistic population.

There is also some evidence to suggest a possible neurological involvement with regard to the experience of trauma in the brains of young people with autism. Neuro-imaging of the brains of children with autism demonstrated alterations, or differences in the functional connectivity of the amygdala and pre-frontal cortex (Mazefsky *et al.* 2013). Similar abnormalities were observed in a group of individuals with a history of chronic childhood trauma and PTSD (Grant *et al.* 2011). This may suggest that for children and young people with autism, the potential impact of trauma could be enhanced.

As has already been mentioned in previous chapters, it appears likely that young people with autism also have differences in the levels of cortisol in their blood in response to novel or threatening situations which could lead to an increased vulnerability to the effects of trauma because of their inherently weak stress response system. White *et al.* (2014) also identified further physiological differences in individuals with autism, including an enhanced startle reflex, which could also contribute to the experience of traumatic stress.

Catatonia

Catatonia is described as a neuropsychiatric syndrome characterised by motor, cognitive, affective and sometimes autonomic disturbances. Someone in a catatonic state can appear mute and as if in a stupor. They can be unresponsive and seemingly impossible to connect with. Following recovery, the most commonly experienced feeling is anxiety. Catatonia has been strongly linked with schizophrenia.

There is a considerable body of evidence to suggest that autism, catatonia and childhood psychosis may represent three distinct manifestations of the same brain disorder. Shorter and Wachtel (2013) refer to this as an 'iron triangle'.

The revised version of the DSM (DSM-5, APA 2013) now includes a new category of 'catatonia, not otherwise specified'. It also includes catatonic symptoms as indicative of a variety of disorders including psychosis and mood disorders. The DSM-5 defines catatonia as being characterised by at least three of the following symptoms:

» catalepsy (muscular rigidity and lack of mobility)

» waxy flexibility (holding a posture if a limb is moved)

» stupor

» agitation

» mutism

» negativism

» posturing

» mannerisms

» stereotypies

» grimacing

» echolalia

» echopraxia (mirroring of motor movements).

Research now suggests that catatonia can occur as a co-morbid syndrome in individuals with autism. The studies by Wing and Shah (2000a), Billstedt, Gillberg and Gillberg (2005) and Ghaziuddin, Dhossche and Marcotte (2012) report that between 12 per cent and

18 per cent of young people with autism spectrum disorders will display some catatonic features. Wing and Shah (2000a) found that the typical age of onset was between 10 and 19 years and often emerged gradually.

Diagnosis of catatonia as a separate condition to autism is often problematic as many of the features of autism (mutism, echolalia, stereotyped movements and repetitive behaviours) are also signs of catatonia. Hare and Malone (2004) felt that catatonic symptoms in individuals with autism were simply an 'autistic expression'. However, it has been observed that in some individuals with autism, there does appear to be what both Hare and Malone and Wing and Shah refer to as 'catatonia-like deterioration' or 'autistic catatonia'. Specific features of this deterioration were reported as a slowing of movement, slower speech, difficulty in completing actions (appearing to become 'stuck') and increased reliance on others to prompt activity combined with a lessening of motivation.

A variety of explanations for this have been suggested, ranging from possible genetic susceptibility to changes in neural circuitry. Wing and Shah (2000b) suggest that there may also be psychological factors involved, as they found that there were reports of traumatic incidents and extreme levels of anxiety prior to the onset of catatonic symptoms. This may also be associated with the 'freeze' response in the fight/flight/freeze response to stress.

The severity of the catatonic features reported in Wing and Shah (2000b) varied from minor to significant with some individuals becoming completely immobile and needing support with all aspects of daily living.

It is acknowledged that autistic catatonia is very difficult to treat and in severe cases can be life threatening (particularly if the individual is unwilling or unable to eat or drink). Treatment for catatonia ranges from high doses of lorazepam (one of the benzodiazepine group of drugs) through to ECT (electroconvulsive therapy). However, Wing and Shah (2000b) felt that a more psychological approach that focused upon reducing stress and anxiety along with prompting to maintain a daily routine and participate in meaningful and pleasurable activities could be helpful. They also advocated for psychoeducation programmes for parents and carers.

A case study on an 11-year-old boy with autism and catatonia was reported by Bozkurt and Mukaddes (2010). Their conclusions pointed to anxiety and depression as being the most likely triggers for an episode of catatonia. Prior to the symptoms of catatonia emerging, the boy's mother reported an increase in periods of crying and irritability. The young man also began to display more aggressive behaviour. This mirrors the findings of Wing and Shah (2000b) who also found that life events, including stress at school, could trigger these type of symptoms.

In summary, those working with individuals on the autism spectrum, whether children or adults, need to be aware of the possibility of catatonia developing. Any individual who experiences a gradual decline in verbal interaction, self-care and willingness to engage socially (compared to how they used to present) could be at risk. In these cases it would appear prudent to attempt (where possible) to minimise stress whilst at the same time continuing to encourage the individual to participate in meaningful and pleasurable activities.

References

American Psychiatric Association (1980) *Diagnostic and Statistical Manual of Mental Disorders* (3rd edition). Washington, DC: American Psychiatric Association.

American Psychiatric Association (2013) *Diagnostic and Statistical Manual of Mental Disorders* (5th edition). Washington, DC: American Psychiatric Association.

Anda, R.F., Felitti, V.J., Bremner, J.D. *et al.* (2006) The enduring effects of abuse and related adverse experiences in childhood. *European Archives of Psychiatry and Clinical Neuroscience 256*, 3, 174–186.

Bevan Jones, R., Thapar, A., Lewis, G. *et al.* (2012) The association between early autistic traits and psychotic experiences in adolescence. *Psychiatry Research 135*, 1–3, 164–169.

Billstedt, E., Gillberg, C. and Gillberg, C. (2005) Autism after adolescence: Population-based 13- to 22-year follow-up study of 120 individuals with autism diagnosed in childhood. *Journal of Autism and Developmental Disorders 35*, 3, 351–360.

Bozkurt, H. and Mukaddes, M. (2010) Catatonia in a child with autistic disorder. *Turkish Journal of Paediatrics 52*, 4, 435–438.

Buitelaar, J.K. and Van der Gaag, R.J. (1998) Diagnostic rules for children with PDD-NOS and multiple complex developmental disorder. *Journal of Child Psychology and Psychiatry 39*, 6, 911–919.

Clarke, D.J., Littlejohns, C.S., Corbett, J.A. *et al.* (1989) Pervasive developmental disorders and psychoses in adult life. *British Journal of Psychiatry 155*, 5, 692–699.

Eisenberg, L. and Kanner, L. (1958) Early Infantile Autism, 1943–1955. In C.F. Reed, I.E. Alexander and S.S. Tomkins (eds) *Psychopathology: A Source Book.* Cambridge, MA: Harvard University Press.

Finkelhor, D., Ormrod, R., Turner, H. *et al.* (2005) The victimization of children and youth: A comprehensive, national survey. *Child Maltreatment 10*, 1, 5–25.

First, M.B., Spitzer, R.L., Gibbon, M. *et al.* (2002) *Structured Clinical Interview for DSM-IV-TR Axis 1 Disorders, Research Version, Patient Edition. (SCID-I/P).* New York: Biometrics Research, New York State Psychiatric Institute.

Ghaziuddin, N., Dhossche, D. and Marcotte, K. (2012) Retrospective chart review of catatonia in child and adolescent psychiatric patients. *Acta Psychiatrica Scandinavica 125*, 1, 33–38.

Grant, M.M., Cannistraci, C., Hollon, S.D. *et al.* (2011) Childhood trauma history differentiates amygdala response to sad faces within MDD. *Journal of Psychiatric Research 45*, 7, 886–895.

Hare, D.J. and Malone, C. (2004) Catatonia and autistic spectrum disorders. *Autism 8*, 2, 183–195.

Hibbard, R.A. and Desch, L.W. (2007) Maltreatment of children with disabilities. *Pediatrics 119*, 5, 1018–1025.

Howell, E. (2005) *The Dissociative Mind.* Hillsdale, NJ: The Analytic Press.

Kyriakopoulos, M., Stangaris, A., Manolesou, S. *et al.* (2015) Determination of psychosis-related clinical profiles in children with autism spectrum disorders using latent class analysis. *European Journal of Child and Adolescent Psychiatry 24*, 3, 301–307.

Maric, N., Krabbendam, L., Vollebergh, W. *et al.* (2003) Sex differences in symptoms of psychosis in a non-selected, general population sample. *Schizophrenia Research 63*, 1–2, 89–95.

Mazefsky, C.A., Herrington, J., Siegel, M. *et al.* (2013) The role of emotion regulation in autism spectrum disorder. *Journal of the American Academy of Child and Adolescent Psychiatry 52*, 7, 679–688.

Morrow Kerns, C., Newschaffer, C.J. and Berkowitz, S.J. (2015) Traumatic childhood events and autism spectrum disorder. *Journal of Autism and Developmental Disorders 45*, 11, 3475–3486.

NICE (2017) *Quality Statement 6: Treating the Core Features of Autism: Medication.* London: NICE. Accessed on 1 June 2017 at www.nice.org.uk/guidance/qs51/chapter/quality-statement-6-treating-the-core-features-of-autism-medication

Nylander, L., Lugnegard, T. and Hallerback, M. (2008) Autism spectrum disorders and schizophrenia spectrum disorders in adults – is there a connection? A literature review and some suggestions for future clinical research. *Clinical Neuropsychiatry 5*, 1, 43–54.

Shorter, E. and Wachtel, L.E. (2013) Childhood catatonia, autism and psychosis past and present: Is there an iron triangle? *Acta Psychiatrica Scandinavica 128*, 1, 21–33.

Sprong, M., Becker, H.E., Schothorst, P.F. *et al.* (2008) Pathways to psychosis: A comparison of the pervasive developmental disorder subtype Multiple Complex Developmental Disorder and the 'At Risk Mental State'. *Schizophrenia Research 99*, 1–3, 38–47.

Stahlberg, O., Soderstrom, H., Rastam, M. *et al.* (2004) Bipolar disorder, schizophrenia and other psychotic disorders in adults with childhood onset ADHD and/or autism spectrum disorders. *Journal of Neurotransmission 111*, 7, 891–902.

Starling, J. and Dosseter, D. (2009) Pervasive developmental disorders and psychosis. *Current Psychiatry 11*, 3, 190–196.

Tebartz van Elst, L., Pick, M., Biscaldi, M, *et al.* (2013) High functioning autism spectrum disorder as a basic disorder in adult psychiatry and psychotherapy: Psychopathological presentation, clinical relevance and therapeutic concepts. *European Archives of Psychiatry and Clinical Neuroscience 263* (suppl. 2), 189–196.

Tsanikos, E., Costello, H., Holt, G. *et al.* (2006) Psychopathology in adults with autism and intellectual disability. *Journal of Autism and Developmental Disorders 36*, 8, 1123–1129.

Unenge Hallerback, M., Lugnegard, T, and Gillberg, C. (2007) Is autism spectrum disorder common in schizophrenia? *Psychiatry Research 198*, 1, 12–17.

Van der Gaag, R.J., Buitelaar, J., Van den Ban, E. *et al.* (1995) A controlled multivariate chart review of multiple complex developmental disorder. *Journal of the American Academy of Child and Adolescent Psychiatry 34*, 8, 1096–1106.

Van Schalkwyk, G., Peluso, F., Qayyum, Z. *et al.* (2015) Varieties of misdiagnosis in autism spectrum disorder: An illustrative case series. *Journal of Autism and Developmental Disorders 45*, 4, 911–918.

Volkmar, F.R. and Cohen, D.J. (1991) Comorbid association of autism and schizophrenia. *American Journal of Psychiatry 148*, 12, 1705–1707.

Weisbrot, D.M., Gadow, K.D., DeVincent, C.J. *et al.* (2005) The presentation of anxiety in children with pervasive developmental disorders. *Journal of Child and Adolescent Psychopharmacology 15*, 3, 477–496.

White, S.W., Mazefsky, C.A., Dichter, G.S. *et al.* (2014) Social-cognitive, physiological and neural mechanisms underlying emotion regulation impairments: Understanding anxiety in autism spectrum disorder. *International Journal of Developmental Neuroscience 39*, 22–36.

Wing, L. and Shah, A. (2000a) Catatonia in autistic spectrum disorders. *British Journal of Psychiatry 176*, 357–362.

Wing, L. and Shah, A. (2000b) Possible causes of catatonia in autistic spectrum disorders: Reply. *British Journal of Psychiatry 177*, 180–181.

Chapter 8

Eating Disorders

This chapter examines the development of eating disorders in young women on the autism spectrum. Sensory and food texture issues are explored along with psychological motivation behind the development of restricted or abnormal eating patterns in girls on the autism spectrum. Case studies are used to illustrate the issues, and intervention and support strategies are discussed.

Eating difficulties experienced by children on the autism spectrum

Selective eating, defined as accepting only a limited variety or type of food and refusal of many types of food, is a common problem experienced by many children with autism (Bandini *et al.* 2010). Compared to other groups, children with autism are five times more likely to develop selective eating patterns (Sharp *et al.* 2013). Selective eating can cause stress to parents who may worry that their child may not be getting adequate nutrition. Bicer and Alsaffer (2013), amongst others, reported that a high percentage (over 60%) of children they studied who were on the autism spectrum displayed either selective or picky eating patterns (selective eating refers to eating only a very limited range of foods, for example, all white foods such as pasta or bread, whereas picky eating tends to refer to being particular about specific brands or appearing to have limited appetite). Ledford and Gast (2006) conducted a literature review of all studies published between 1994 and 2004 that looked at the feeding difficulties of children on the autism spectrum, and found that between 46 per cent and 89 per cent of all children with autism had atypical eating patterns.

The clinical picture of children with autism who have this type of behaviour is quite complex, and links have been made with repetitive behaviours, anxiety and sensory issues (Johnson *et al.* 2014; Matson, Fodstad and Dempsey 2009; Nadan *et al.* 2011; Paterson and Peck 2011).

The complexity of the presentation of this type of difficulty makes it difficult to plan interventions without a multi-disciplinary team, and in extreme cases, some children have refused to eat at all and have needed feeding via a gastrostomy tube.

Parents and carers of children with autism often report facing unique challenges with regard to feeding and daily eating routines. Difficulties reported range from being fussy about brands or particular types of food to general disruption at mealtimes. Even simple changes by manufacturers to a recipe, or the packaging they use, can result in a refusal to eat certain foods.

A small number of studies, including Ahearn *et al.* (2001), have examined the specific preferences and dislikes of children on the autism spectrum. These difficulties were found to emerge at an early age and are often reported in a developmental history as 'problems with weaning'. This can be introducing solid food, gagging on lumps or refusal to chew lumpy food. Parents also frequently report having concerns about whether their child is getting adequate nutrition and about the general quality of their diet.

In studies of typically developing children, those with high taste and smell sensitivity were significantly less willing to try new foods (Coulthard and Blissett 2009) and those with tactile defensiveness were also very selective about what they would eat (Smith *et al.* 2005). It is hardly surprising, therefore, that children with autism, who are very likely to have sensory difficulties, will often struggle with eating. Kral *et al.* (2015) found that children with autism, particularly those with oral sensitivity, were more likely to under- or over-eat than typically developing children.

A study by Coury *et al.* 2012 also highlighted the gastrointestinal difficulties experienced by many children on the autism spectrum, which include constipation, diarrhoea, bloating and reflux, all of which will impact upon feeding and willingness to eat. A surprisingly high number of parents giving developmental histories in the course of clinical assessments I have undertaken have reported problems with reflux and colic when their children have been babies. In addition, there is some research, and much anecdotal evidence, that points to children with autism presenting with unusual eating patterns, having fixed rituals/routines around eating and mealtimes and displaying strong reactions to new or unusual foods (e.g. Ahearn *et al.* 2001). Many children with autism display a strong preference for carbohydrates, snack and processed foods, and reject fruit and vegetables. It is unclear the extent to which these difficulties persist into adolescence and adulthood.

The link between autism and eating disorders

There has been much speculation over the years regarding the connection between eating disorders and autism. Both genetic and behavioural links have been found (see Huke *et al.* 2013 for a full review). Research has largely focused upon the presence of similar cognitive processing styles observed in both individuals with autism and those with a diagnosis of an eating disorder. As is the case for autism, it has been speculated that eating disorders also lie upon a continuum which ranges from no symptoms through to those who exhibit certain features (or traits) through to those who fulfil diagnostic criteria.

Aside from similarities in cognitive performance, there are other reported biological and behavioural similarities between the two disorders (Carton and Smith 2014), including a higher incidence of social anxiety and a tendency towards engaging in rituals and compulsions. There also appears to be an above-chance co-occurrence of eating disorders and autism within families. One sample (Wentz-Nilsson, Gillberg and Rastam 1998) found that 31 per cent of first-degree relatives in a group diagnosed with anorexia nervosa exhibited a high level of autistic traits. Gillberg, Rastam and Gillberg (1994) also noted that having an autism spectrum disorder diagnosis made recovery from an eating disorder significantly less likely.

The DSM-5 (APA 2013) categorises eating disorders as follows:

» *anorexia nervosa (restricting):* severely restricted food intake by maintaining a very low calorie diet, only eating one meal a day or limiting the type of food eaten

» *bulimia nervosa:* cycles of binge eating followed by purging by either vomiting or using diuretics or laxatives

» *binge eating disorder:* as above but minus the purging

» *pica:* eating of non-food items which lasts for longer than a month

» *rumination disorder:* regurgitation of food which is subsequently re-chewed, swallowed or spat out

» *avoidant/restrictive food intake disorder:* a disturbance of normal eating patterns which can result in insufficient nutritional input.

Several young people with whom I have worked clinically have received a diagnosis of avoidant/restrictive food intake disorder. However, in terms of the link between eating disorders and autism, the majority of the research has focused upon anorexia nervosa.

Anorexia nervosa is described as a 'disabling mental disorder' which results in poor quality of life and high levels of co-morbidity with other disorders. It predominantly affects females (Westwood *et al.* (2016) cite a gender ratio of 10:1). It is characterised by abnormally low body weight and a morbid fear of gaining weight.

A number of studies have highlighted traits associated with autism that are also observed in individuals with anorexia nervosa. These include difficulties with flexible thinking, difficulties seeing the bigger picture and theory of mind difficulties, including difficulty in appreciating the impact of one's actions upon other people (Baron-Cohen, Leslie and Smith 1985; Tchanturia *et al.* 2004). Issues have also been reported for individuals with anorexia nervosa in terms of emotional literacy and emotional processing (Davies *et al.* 2011; Russell *et al.* 2009).

Westwood *et al.* (2016) speculate that girls in particular on the autism spectrum (whether diagnosed or undiagnosed) may be more likely to develop an eating disorder in adolescence due to a combination of their underlying autistic traits and the social and cultural pressure to conform to an 'ideal' body shape as determined by the popular media. Consistently at the current time, this is portrayed as an extremely thin (and often unrealistic) image.

In their study, Westwood *et al.* used the autism-spectrum quotient (AQ) as a screen for autistic traits. The AQ was originally developed by Simon Baron-Cohen *et al.* in 2001. It is a self-report that measures functioning in five domains including social skills, attention shifting, attention to detail, communication and imagination. It has good reliability and has been used extensively in both research and clinical populations.

Westwood *et al.* (2016) clearly outline the difficulties faced by researchers examining the links between these two disorders. First, as cited earlier in this chapter, eating/feeding difficulties in individuals with autism are very common and are often linked to sensory processing difficulties. This is often combined with a high need for control which is found in many children and adults on the autism spectrum (more particularly those with the pathological demand avoidance profile). Second, the types of 'autistic' difficulties seen in individuals with an eating disorder may well be equally or predominantly due to the adverse effects of low nutritional intake and low body weight.

A number of researchers have focused upon the neurobiological underpinnings of the disorder. However, what was interesting was that these difficulties have been found to persist both in the acute phase of the illness and following recovery. This has sparked a great deal of research examining the impact of extreme weight loss upon cognitive processes.

Fuglset *et al.* (2013) examined structural brain changes in four females with anorexia nervosa. The most frequently reported brain findings in adults with anorexia nervosa involve an overall reduction of white matter and grey matter and an increased volume in the ventricles and in cerebrospinal fluid (Frank *et al.* 2004). Some studies (Wagner *et al.* 2006) report that the brain returns to normal after weight has been normalised, whereas others (such as Friederich *et al.* 2012) suggest that these structural brain changes may be irreversible.

Very few studies have been carried out on adolescents (when eating difficulties very often first emerge). One study that did look at this age group reported on a group of 12–18-year-olds in the early stages of anorexia nervosa and found a reduction in global grey matter (Gaudio *et al.* 2011). The authors concluded that an overall reduction in brain mass could be seen as an inevitable result of extreme weight loss, as it follows that starving the body of nutrition is also going to starve the brain.

The Fuglset *et al.* (2015) study also found that global grey matter was reduced. However, they also found that there were cerebral tissue alterations in a variety of brain areas including those associated with emotional processing, sensory information processing and language comprehension.

Returning to the Westwood *et al.* (2016) meta-analysis which used the AQ to examine autistic traits in females with anorexia nervosa, their results suggested that patients with a diagnosis of anorexia scored significantly higher on the AQ than did a healthy control group, specifically with regard to difficulties with social skills, communication and flexibility of thought. Their findings were in line with previous research carried out by Huke *et al.* (2013) which reported an autism prevalence rate of 22.9 per cent in an eating disordered population. However, Westwood *et al.* did suggest that these findings should be treated with caution as all of the participants in the anorexia nervosa group were acutely unwell at the time of the study with very low average BMI (body mass index) of between 14.6 and 16.4. As discussed earlier, acute starvation can exacerbate what are perceived as autistic traits.

What would be necessary to further clarify this would be to take a detailed developmental history (using a standardised tool such as the ADI-R or the DISCO) to establish whether these traits had been present since early childhood. A study by Mandy and Tchanturia (2015) did assess ten women with an eating disorder using the ADOS-2 (the second edition of the ADOS, which as described in previous chapters is one of the tools frequently used in diagnostic assessments). They found that of the ten women assessed, three met the cut-off score for a diagnosis of autism. A further two met other criteria for an autism diagnosis. Pellicano and Hiller (2013) cited Odent (2010) who speculated that anorexia nervosa may be a specific manifestation of autism in girls and women. Pellicano and Hiller refer to how anorexia has been colloquially referred to as the 'female Asperger's' but discuss the need for caution in speculating whether this is in fact the case or whether the effects of starvation on the brain produce a 'phenotype' of autism.

Courty *et al.* (2013) also studied the profiles of females diagnosed with anorexia nervosa and those diagnosed with autism. They used the EQ (empathy quotient) and the SQ (systemising quotient) which were developed by Baron-Cohen *et al.* (2003) and Baron-Cohen and Wheelwright (2004) for research purposes to measure levels of empathy and the tendency to systemise (organise things). They also included the IRI (Interpersonal Reactivity Index) which is a multi-dimensional questionnaire about empathy which includes four sub-scales: perspective taking (PT), which examines the ability to take into account the views of others; fantasy (FS), which measures how much the individual relates to fantasy figures; personal distress (PD), which assesses 'self-orientated' feelings and the degree to which the participant feels anxiety when confronted with negative situations; and empathetic concerns (EC), which assesses feelings of sympathy and concern for others. This study indicated that the anorexia group and the autistic group were very similar in terms of their tendency to feel anxious when faced with negative situations and, interestingly, in their ability to identify with fantasy figures.

Once again, this may be pertinent when considering the profile of those individuals who present with pathological demand avoidance, as relating to fantasy figures and taking on other personas is a particular feature of this profile. Pathological demand avoidance is now recognised by the National Autistic Society in the United Kingdom as being part of the wider autism spectrum and is generally characterised by anxiety that drives an overwhelming need to control the environment, often resulting in the complete refusal to comply with any demands. When pushed to follow another person's direction, the individual will often go into meltdown and become extremely emotionally dysregulated and out of control. It could be hypothesised that these individuals could be categorised as 'externalisers' in terms of their demand avoidance.

However, what is interesting when considering the findings of Courty *et al.* (2013) regarding the tendency to identify with fantasy figures observed in the women with autism and some of the anorexic group they studied is the similarity to the behavioural presentation of many (girls in particular) with the pathological demand avoidance profile, where retreating into different roles and obsessively playing out a variety of scenarios is quite common. When working clinically with children with extreme demand avoidance, it has frequently emerged that their mothers have also identified similar behaviour patterns in themselves when younger, in terms of needing to control their environment. They reported having moved from overt control of their environment (through fairly public meltdowns) to alternative methods such as controlling their eating, thus internalising their need for control. This raises the question, does this represent a different temperamental presentation of pathological demand avoidance? Temperament has been defined as 'constitutionally based individual differences in emotional, motor and attentional reactivity and self-regulation' which are generally consistent across situation and time (Robarth 1989, p.109).

In the literature, over-control has been linked to social isolation, difficulties with relationships, cognitive rigidity, detail versus bigger-picture processing and inhibited emotional expression. This has been linked to a variety of mental health difficulties including depression, anorexia nervosa and obsessive compulsive disorder.

Konstantellou (2014), in a research thesis, wrote about the link between the need for control and eating disorders, particularly in relation to psychological distress. Lack of control over one's environment and feelings was cited by Bruch (1978) as fuelling the need for internal control. Surgenor et al. (2002) also discuss the strong desire for control with regard to eating disorders. However, little is known about what underlies this need for control. Sassaroli and Ruggiero (2011) refer to this as a 'coping belief' which is driven by the need to control the outside world.

Lynch, Hempel and Dunkley (2015) report that those who present with features of over-control are likely to have been punished or reprimanded for making mistakes or for overt displays of emotion when they were younger and, as a consequence, learn to internalise their anger and frustration. It is an interesting hypothesis, therefore, that some adult women who have the pathological demand avoidance profile may have learned to do this as a way of managing their need for control. As women with autism tend to be more socially motivated than men with autism, they may realise that extreme behaviour and loss of control would tend to isolate them socially even further. Thus controlling their behaviour, and more specifically their eating, may prove to be an effective way of managing their anxiety and tolerating uncertainty in other areas of their lives. Very little research in this area has been carried out and this hypothesis would need further empirical study. However, one mother of a daughter diagnosed with pathological demand avoidance (whose story is recounted in full in Chapter 10) observed that she had been struggling with an eating disorder for most of her own adult life. It was only when she went through the process of providing a developmental history for her daughter that she recognised both autistic and demand avoidance features in herself. She reported that as she entered adolescence it became much more important to her to 'fit in' and she stated that she attempted to become 'the life and soul of the party', always being the one who organised social events whilst at university. In hindsight, she now looks back and recognises this as being a way of controlling how social events took place. By being the person who organised everything, she minimised the anxiety and uncertainty about attending an event where she did not know what would happen. She now also recognises that her need to control also fuels her eating disorder – the more anxious she becomes, or the more unpredictable her life is, the more she needs to control her food intake.

Interventions for anorexia nervosa and the implications for their use with individuals on the autism spectrum

Dr Elizabeth Shea, a clinical psychologist working in the Birmingham Food Refusal Service in the United Kingdom, wrote an article entitled 'Eating disorder or disordered eating' (Shea 2015a). In this article she provides examples to illustrate the difference between the two. She also provides advice on managing avoidant and restrictive food intake disorder (ARFID) and describes how this differs from anorexia nervosa. ARFID is described as deliberate restriction of food based upon sensory properties and concerns about the adverse consequences of eating certain foods. This can include a fear of vomiting, choking or contamination. This can lead to weight loss and vitamin and mineral deficiency. Dr Shea reports that this type of difficulty is very common in individuals with autism. She also describes the exaggerated 'disgust and contamination response' that is often seen in individuals with autism:

> Imagine I squash a sheep's eye between two slices of bread and offer it to you as a 'nice, tasty sandwich'. Your disgust response is likely to be triggered and it is doubtful you will be able to place it in your mouth, never mind eat it. Again, this is an adaptive response to foods (or indeed to non-foods) that could be dangerous if eaten. Young people with ASC [autism spectrum conditions] tend to display this response when faced with unfamiliar or disliked foods, even if they are socially and culturally appropriate. (Shea 2015b)

In terms of intervention, Dr Shea (2015b) commented that, although some of the young people involved did not appear troubled by their restrictive diet and appeared to stay surprisingly well, it was parents who were reporting significant restrictions to family life and anxiety about what would happen if their child's chosen food or brand of food was not available. Some of the young people Dr Shea worked with did report that at times they felt anxious about being different and 'fitting in' with other children.

The advice provided, which may at first appear counterintuitive, is for parents to attempt to reduce their own anxiety around food and nutrition. Dr Shea advises initially allowing the young person to select her preferred and 'safe' foods, before any attempt is made to increase the range of foods she will tolerate. This will at least maintain the young person's weight and growth. Following this new foods can be slowly introduced. At this point, she advises those working with these young people to think again about the sheep's eye scenario and the degree of disgust that most people would have to overcome in order to even be in close proximity to it. This is designed to provide some insight into the challenge that increasing the range of food tolerated presents to some young people with autism. Prior to attempting this, the use of relaxation strategies is recommended in an attempt to reduce anxiety levels. The suggested approach is then to try a graded exposure to the new food.

My own clinical experience of developing an intervention programme for a young person on the autism spectrum who would only drink milk (no solid food was tolerated) would support this. With this young person, the process of introducing food of any kind was painfully slow (because you are not only dealing with an enhanced 'disgust' response, but also with extremely rigid thinking). Initially the young person was persuaded to sit outside the room where food was being consumed, gradually working up to sitting in the room, before progressing to sitting at the table, tolerating the sight of food on the plate in front of them and ultimately putting a tiny piece into their mouth (but not chewing or swallowing). This approach has been demonstrated to be clinically effective, particularly with older, more cognitively able children. This is usually most effective when paired with specific anxiety management work and sensory integration and/or desensitisation techniques to minimise the impact of hyper or hypo-sensitivities.

Using this approach, one of the young women Dr Shea worked with was able to slowly expand the range of food she could tolerate and at the age of 15 was able, for the first time, to go to a restaurant and choose food from the menu, an activity that had previously seemed unachievable. This young woman is now at university and is able to tolerate a range of foods that she can enjoy with peers and, most importantly for her, she no longer feels 'odd' or stands out in any way.

Cognitive remediation therapy

Tchanturia, Larsson and Adamson (2016) examined how patients with anorexia nervosa with high and low levels of autistic traits responded to group cognitive remediation therapy (CRT). They studied 35 patients in an eating disorders unit with a diagnosis of anorexia nervosa.

Cognitive remediation therapy is a set of exercises or interventions that are designed to improve cognitive functioning in certain areas. It has been demonstrated as effective in a number of randomised controlled trials for both those with traumatic brain injury and those with schizophrenia. It has also been used extensively with individuals with anorexia nervosa (e.g. Davies and Tchanturia 2005).

In the Tchanturia *et al.* (2016) study, participants in group therapy were split into those without high ASD traits and those with. Their results showed that the anorexia nervosa group without ASD traits demonstrated significantly higher scores when subsequently questioned about their ability to change following the intervention compared with those with high ASD traits. The researchers speculated that this may have been because much of the group discussion was carried out using 'Socratic' questioning. Socratic questioning uses a series of open questions to allow the participant to reach their own conclusions. An example of this type of question might be, 'What is another way of looking at this?' Tchanturia *et al.* felt that this may have proved difficult for those women with high levels of autistic traits and speculated that they would need to be provided with more concrete and less ambiguous examples and questions. My own experience of using CRT exercises with a young person on the autism spectrum is that whilst they were perfectly able to rationalise at a cognitive level, it was not possible to subsequently generalise this knowledge in everyday activities and tasks.

Family therapy as a treatment for anorexia nervosa

Traditional treatments for anorexia nervosa include both group work and family therapy – both of which could prove problematic for girls on the autism spectrum. If deficits are present in theory of mind, understanding their own feelings is going to be difficult. Discussing and comprehending the impact of their eating disorder on family members (as often takes place in family therapy sessions) is likely to be even more difficult.

Cognitive analytic therapy

Cognitive analytic therapy (CAT) involves a three-stage process that aims to consider and address why unhealthy eating patterns may have developed and recognise how these patterns contribute to the maintenance of eating difficulties. It then works on identifying and implementing change.

Cognitive behavioural therapy

Cognitive behavioural therapy (CBT) has a strong evidence base for effectiveness in a variety of disorders and aims to modify, or reformulate, unhealthy cognitions and thinking patterns.

All of the above approaches can present difficulty for the individual on the autism spectrum. One of the key impairments in autism is the lack of social imagination, or the ability to foresee (or even think about) consequences or possible different outcomes. Rigid thinking makes it difficult to move on from cognitions. In addition, clinical experience has shown that girls on the autism spectrum with anorexia nervosa appear to be very proficient at not eating, and whether this is due to rigidity or differences in the perception of the feeling of hunger is difficult to establish. Many children on the autism spectrum either fail to notice that they are hungry or thirsty or eat until they are over-full. As mentioned earlier in the chapter, there is also the issue of the kudos and social acceptance craved by many girls on the autism spectrum. Being 'good' at not eating and consequently becoming thin may lead to an increase in popularity. All of these factors make treating this disorder in girls on the spectrum more challenging.

Dudova, Kocourkova and Koutec (2015) looked at the therapeutic prognosis for girls with Asperger's syndrome and early-onset anorexia nervosa. They found that cognitive rigidity was, indeed, the greatest barrier to improvement. They cited the approach taken by Kerbeshian and Burd (2009) with a 12-year-old girl with high-functioning autism and a partial anorexia diagnosis which highlighted the importance of focusing upon improving the ability to mentalise (the ability to infer the thoughts, feelings and emotions of others).

What is very clear in the literature are the not inconsiderable challenges faced by clinicians working with this group of young people and the need for modification of standard therapeutic approaches including family therapy. Dudova *et al.* (2015) also felt it was important that clinicians working in this area should be familiar with working with young people on the spectrum, as their autism was the greatest barrier to recovery. They cite a treatment regime described by Fisman *et al.* (1996) whereby a structured behavioural approach was implemented along with treatment with risperidone (an atypical anti-psychotic medication), reportedly to good effect. It may be that the strategies that have proved effective in working with children on the autism spectrum who have feeding difficulties (such as graded exposure to different food types) could be adapted for use with young women on the autism spectrum with anorexia nervosa.

References

American Psychiatric Association (2013) *Diagnostic and Statistical Manual of Mental Disorders, 5th Edition: DSM-5. Arlington, VA:* American Psychiatric Association.

Ahearn, W. H., Castine, T., Nault, K. *et al.* (2001) An assessment of food acceptance in children with autism or pervasive developmental disorder–not otherwise specified. *Journal of Autism and Developmental Disorders 31,* 5, 505–511.

Bandini, L.G., Anderson, S.E., Curtin, C. *et al.* (2010) Food selectivity in children with autism spectrum disorders and typically developing children. *Journal of Pediatrics 157,* 2, 259–264.

Baron-Cohen, S. (2003) *The Essential Difference.* New York: Basic Books.

Baron-Cohen, S., Leslie, A.M. and Frith, U. (1985) Does the autistic child have a 'theory of mind'? *Cognition 21,* 1, 37–46.

Baron-Cohen, S. and Wheelwright, S. (2004) The Empathy Quotient (EQ): An investigation of adults with Asperger syndrome and high-functioning autism, and normal sex differences. *Journal of Autism and Developmental Disorders 34,* 2, 163–175.

Baron-Cohen, S., Wheelwright, S., Skinner, R. *et al.* (2001) The Autism-spectrum quotient (AQ): Evidence from Asperger syndrome/high-functioning autism, males and females, scientists and mathematicians. *Journal of Autism and Developmental Disorders 31,* 1, 5–17.

Bicer, A.H. and Alsaffar, A.A. (2013) Body mass index, dietary intake and feeding problems of Turkish children with autism spectrum disorder (ASD). *Research in Developmental Disabilities 34,* 11, 3978–3987.

Bruch, H. (1978) *The Golden Cage: The Enigma of Anorexia Nervosa.* Cambridge, MA: Harvard University Press.

Carton, A.M. and Smith, A.D. (2014) Assessing the relationship between eating disorder pathology and autistic traits in a non-clinical adult population. *Eating and Weight Disorders – Studies in Anorexia, Bulimia and Obesity 19,* 3, 285–293.

Coulthard, H. and Blissett, J. (2009) Fruit and vegetable consumption in children and their mothers: Moderating effects of child sensory sensitivity. *Appetite 52,* 2, 410–415.

Coury, D.L., Ashwood, P., Fasano, A. *et al.* (2012) Gastrointestinal conditions in children with autism spectrum disorder: Developing a research agenda. *Pediatrics 130* (suppl. 2), 160–168.

Courty, A., Maxia, A.S., Lalanne, C. *et al.* (2013) Levels of autistic traits in anorexia nervosa: A comparative psychometric study. *BMC Psychiatry 13,* 222.

Davies, H., Schmidt, U., Stahl, D. *et al.* (2011) Evoked facial emotional expression and emotional experience in people with anorexia nervosa. *International Journal of Eating Disorders 44,* 6, 531–539.

Davies, H. and Tchanturia, K. (2005) Cognitive remediation therapy as an intervention for acute anorexia nervosa: A case report. *European Eating Disorders Review 13,* 5, 311–316.

Dudova, I., Kocourkova, J. and Koutec, J. (2015) Early-onset anorexia nervosa in girls with Asperger syndrome. *Neuropsychiatric Disease and Treatment 11,* 1639–1643.

Fisman S., Steele, M., Short, J. *et al.* (1996) Case study: Anorexia nervosa and autistic disorder in an adolescent girl. *Journal of the American Academy of Child and Adolescent Psychiatry 35,* 7, 937–940.

Frank, G.K., Bailer, U.F., Henry, S. *et al.* (2004) Neuroimaging studies in eating disorders. *CNS Spectrums 9,* 7, 539–548.

Friederich, H.C., Walther, S., Bendszus, M. *et al.* (2012) Grey matter abnormalities within cortico-limbic-striatal circuits in acute and weight-restored anorexia nervosa patients. *Neuro Image 59,* 2, 1106–1113.

Fuglset, T.S., Endestad, T., Landro, N.I. *et al.* (2015) Brain structure alterations associated with weight change in young females with anorexia nervosa: A case series. *Neurocase 21*, 2, 169–177.

Gaudio, S., Nocchi, F., Franchin, T. *et al.* (2011). Gray matter decrease distribution in the early stages of anorexia nervosa, restrictive style in adolescents. *Psychiatry Research Neuroimaging 191*, 1, 24–30.

Gillberg, C., Rastam, M. and Gillberg, L.C. (1994) Anorexia nervosa: Who sees the patients and who do the patients see? *Acta Paediatrica 83*, 9, 967–971.

Huke, V., Turk, J., Saeidi, S. *et al.* (2013) Autism spectrum disorders in eating disorder populations: A systematic review. *European Eating Disorders Review 21*, 5, 345–351.

Johnson, C.R., Turner, K., Stewart, P.A. *et al.* (2014) Relationships between feeding problems, behavioral characteristics and nutritional quality in children with autism spectrum disorders. *Journal of Autism and Developmental Disorders 44*, 9, 2175–2184.

Kerbeshian, J. and Burd, L. (2009) Is anorexia nervosa a neuropsychiatric developmental disorder? *World Journal of Biological Psychiatry 9*, 10, 648–657.

Konstantellou, A. (2014) An Investigation of Intolerance of Uncertainty and Associated Factors in Anorexia Nervosa. Doctoral thesis, Kings College, London. Accessed on 3 May 2017 at https://kclpure.kcl.ac.uk/portal/en/theses/an-investigation-of-uncertainty-and-intolerance-of-uncertainty-and-associated-factors-in-anorexia-nervosa(a3885975-5855-42b5-aaf4-c920f7a1f786).html.

Kral, T.V.E., Souders, M.C., Tompkins, V.H. *et al.* (2015) Child eating behaviours and caregiver feeding practices in children with autism spectrum disorders. *Public Health Nursing 32*, 5, 488–497.

Ledford, J.R. and Gast, D.L. (2006) Feeding problems in children with autism spectrum disorders: A review. *Focus on Autism and Other Developmental Disabilities 21*, 3, 153–166.

Lynch, T.R., Hempel, R.J. and Dunkley, C. (2015) Radically open dialectical behavioural therapy for disorders of over-control: Signalling matters. *American Journal of Psychotherapy 69*, 2, 141–164.

Mandy, W. and Tchanturia, K. (2015) Do women with eating disorders who have social and flexibility difficulties really have autism? A case series. *Molecular Autism 6*, 1, 1–10.

Matson, J.L., Fodstad, J.C. and Dempsey, T. (2009) The relationship of children's feeding problems to core symptoms of autism and pervasive developmental disorders – not otherwise specified. *Research in Autism Spectrum Disorders 3*, 3, 759–766.

Odent, M. (2010) Autism and anorexia nervosa. *Medical Hypothesis 75*, 1, 79–81.

Paterson, H. and Peck, K. (2011) Sensory processing ability and eating behaviour in children with autism. *Journal of Human Nutrition and Dietetics 24*, 301.

Pellicano, L. and Hiller, R. (2013) Anorexia and autism: A cautionary note. *Psychologist 26*, 780.

Rothbart, M.K. (1989) Biological Processs in Temperament. In G.A. Komstramm, J. Bates and M.K. Rothbart (eds) *Temperament in Childhood*. Sussex: Wiley.

Russell, T.A., Schmidt, U., Doherty, L. *et al.* (2009) Aspects of social cognition in anorexia nervosa: Affective and cognitive theory of mind. *Psychiatry Research 168*, 3, 181–185.

Sassaroli, S. and Ruggiero, M. (2011) The Need of and the Compulsion to Control and the Tendency to Worry in Eating Disorders. In S. Sassaroli and M. Ruggiero (eds) *Cognitive Therapy of Eating Disorders on Control and Worry*. Eating Disorders in the 21st Century. New York: Nova Science Publishers Inc.

Sharp, W.G., Berry, R.C., McCracken, C. *et al.* (2013) Feeding problems and nutrient intake in children with autism spectrum disorders: A meta-analysis and comprehensive review of the literature. *Journal of Autism and Developmental Disorders 43*, 9, 2159–2173.

Shea (2015a) Eating disorder or disordered eating? Eating patterns in autism. Network Autism. Accessed on 3 May 2017 at http://network.autism.org.uk/good-practice/case-studies/eating-disorder-or-disordered-eating-eating-patterns-autism.

Shea (2015b) Understanding and managing eating issues on the autism spectrum. Network Autism. Accessed on 3 May 2017 at http://network.autism.org.uk/knowledge/insight-opinion/understanding-and-managing-eating-issues-autism-spectrum.

Smith, A.M., Roux, S., Naidoo, N.T. *et al.* (2005) Food choice of tactile defensive children. *Nutrition 21*, 1, 14–19.

Surgenor, L.J., Horn, J., Plumridge, E.W. *et al.* (2002) Anorexia nervosa and psychological control: A re-examination of selected theoretical accounts. *European Eating Disorders Review 10*, 2, 85–101.

Tchanturia, K., Happe, F., Godley, J. *et al.* (2004) 'Theory of mind' in anorexia nervosa. *European Eating Disorders Review 12*, 6, 361–366.

Tchanturia, K., Larsson, E. and Adamson, J. (2016) How anorexia nervosa patients with high and low autistic traits respond to group cognitive remediation therapy. *BMC Psychiatry 16*, 334.

Wagner, A., Greer, P., Bailer, U.F. *et al.* (2006) Normal brain tissue volumes after long-term recovery in anorexia and bulimia nervosa. *Biological Psychiatry 59*, 3, 291–293.

Wentz-Nilsson, E., Gillberg, C. and Rastam, M. (1998) Familial factors in anorexia nervosa: A community-based study. *Comparative Psychiatry 39*, 6, 392–399.

Westwood, H., Eisler, I., Mandy, W. *et al.* (2016) Using the Autism Spectrum Quotient to measure autistic traits in anorexia nervosa: A systematic review and meta-analysis. *Journal of Autism and Developmental Disorders 46*, 3, 964–977.

Chapter 9

The Impact of Mental Health Issues on Parents and Siblings

This chapter explores the emotional impact of caring for a girl on the autism spectrum with mental health issues. The chapter also examines the difficulties of managing self-harming and challenging behaviour and discusses the difficulties faced by families in finding an appropriate school and dealing with school refusal or exclusion.

The impact of having a child on the autism spectrum upon parents

A number of studies point to the potentially detrimental impact of having a child on the autism spectrum upon parents and other family members. Ekas and Whitman (2011) and Estes *et al.* (2009) both reported increased symptoms of depression in parents of children with autism. Autistic symptom severity has been cited as a major source of parenting stress. Davis and Carter (2008), Ingersoll and Hambrick (2011) and Morgan (1988) discussed the impact of having a child with autism on the family as a whole.

Pruitt *et al.* (2016) specifically examined the well-being and parenting experiences of mothers with children on the autism spectrum and found that this group experience consistently higher levels of stress and depression compared to mothers of children with other developmental disorders. Benson and Karlof (2009) also reported higher levels of reported anger in mothers with children on the spectrum.

Pruitt *et al.* (2016) also explore overall family functioning when the household includes a child with autism. They cited Olson's (2000) study which identified three factors that impact upon families – cohesion, flexibility and communication. Cohesion refers to the emotional bond the family has; flexibility refers to the ability of the whole family to adapt and change aspects of family life to accommodate the needs of the young person with autism. The study also pointed out the importance of maintaining good lines of communication between family members.

The Pruitt study also found that only family cohesion was associated with a more positive parenting experience. They explained this further by clarifying that those families who were emotionally close and felt supported by their wider family reported the highest level of positive experiences. This is likely to be a relevant issue in today's society where availability of extended families able to offer support, certainly in Western cultures, tends to be less common.

Karst and Vaughan von Hecke (2012) highlighted that in addition to increased parenting stress and the potential for mental health issues, parents of a child with an autism spectrum disorder are also likely to experience significant financial strain (particularly if the child is not attending school and one parent has to provide full-time care). In addition, they also reported higher marital break-up and divorce rates amongst these families.

These studies resonated with my own experience of 15 years working clinically with these families. Those reporting the greatest levels of stress tended to be either single-parent families (usually the mother) bringing up children alone and those where the wider family were either not available or failed to accept the level of difficulty the immediate family of the child with autism were experiencing.

Seltzer *et al.*, in a longitudinal study of parents *Autism* published in 2001, found that 50 per cent of parents over 50 who had a child with developmental difficulties still had the young person living with them compared to 17 per cent of those with typically developing children, which the author of the study took to reflect the potentially lifelong impact on families of having a family member with autism. Even if the individual did not have a learning difficulty, problems with daily living, holding down a job, managing money and mental health issues all added to the challenge of living independently.

It has been found that mothers of children on the autism spectrum tend to be more affected by stress and anxiety around their children's behaviour and emotional dysregulation (Davis and Carter 2008) and poor social skills (Allen, Bowles and Weber 2013) than the fathers of children on the autism spectrum; whereas, in contrast, fathers of children with autism tended to be more affected by the severity of their child's autism (Rivard *et al.* 2014). Mothers generally tend to access more in the way of social support (via social media support groups, for example) than fathers (Pozo, Saria and Brioso 2013). Fathers tend to engage more in self-blame, distraction and denial and generally are less involved with social support groups or social media networks. Pozo *et al.* concluded that on the whole, mothers and fathers develop very different coping strategies.

Vohra *et al.* (2014) discuss the multiple and varied challenges faced by parents with a child on the autism spectrum who also has co-morbid mental health difficulties. Often young people on the spectrum will need services from a variety of healthcare professionals throughout their lives which can be an additional burden, both in terms of finances and time. Studies by Cidav, Marcus and Mandell (2012), Kogan *et al.* (2008) and Wang and Leslie (2010) all report further on this.

Vohra *et al.* (2014) focuses upon the experiences of families in the United States and cites dissatisfaction with the quality of care provided post-diagnosis and access to services as key stressors. The same is also true in the United Kingdom where access to post-diagnostic support is patchy at best and where support often has to be accessed via third-sector (voluntary) providers. For parents in the United States, finding they had inadequate insurance coverage to meet their child's complex needs was also cited as an additional stressor.

In the United Kingdom, where care is theoretically provided under the umbrella of the National Health Service, free at the point of access, parents are increasingly reporting chronically over-stretched services which are unable to provide anything in the way of routine support. Services are tending to be able to provide care only for those families in absolute crisis.

The impact of having a sibling with autism

The impact upon parents of caring for a child with autism has been well researched. However, there is also an impact upon the siblings of these children. Lovell and Weatherall (2016) report on the emotional, social and physical challenges that are associated with having a brother or sister on the spectrum. Dyke, Mulroy and Leonard (2009) note that to alleviate the burden on their parents, siblings often take on additional chores and household responsibilities, and Macks and Reeve (2007) noted that parents who had a child with additional needs tended to be less emotionally available to their other children as a result of the burden of caring for the child with difficulties.

Relative to typically developing children, siblings of young people with autism have been found to have higher levels of emotional problems (Petalas *et al.* 2009) and 'internalising' behaviours (Fisman *et al.* 2000).

In addition, Meyer, Ingersoll and Hambrick (2011) and Neece, Blacher and Baker (2010) both found that the greater the levels of hyperactivity and conduct problems the sibling with autism had, the more likely the siblings were to report symptoms of depression. The Lovell and Weatherall (2016) study replicated these findings and also reported that these symptoms were, to some extent, mediated by the availability of social support.

Social support groups for siblings of children with developmental difficulties have been shown to improve depressive symptoms (Houtzager, Grootenhuis and Last 2001). It was also speculated that psychoeducation to improve their knowledge of autism may help.

The impact upon the physiological well-being of siblings has yet to be fully established. Altered levels of cortisol, caused by prolonged stress, have been found in parents of children with autism (Bella, Garcia and Spadari-Bratfisch 2011; Seltzer *et al.* 2010) and it is likely that this may also be the case for the siblings of these children and young people.

With regard to the relationships that siblings of young people on the spectrum have with each other, Kaminsky and Dewey (2001) reported overall poorer quality relationships. Other studies have found fewer difficulties.

Recent research has focused upon the factors that may place some siblings at greater risk of negative outcomes than others. Benson and Karlof (2009) highlighted that the more severe the behavioural or emotional challenges experienced by the young person with autism, the higher the risk that siblings will also have difficulties, and this risk was even greater if the mother in the family was suffering from depression. Bailey *et al.* (1998) discussed high levels of what they referred to as 'sub-threshold' autism spectrum disorder-related symptoms (e.g. subtle social communication difficulties and a degree of behavioural rigidity) in many of the siblings of children with autism and cited this as an additional risk factor.

Walton and Ingersoll (2015) studied 163 mothers with two or more children under the age of 18 where at least one child had a diagnosis of autism. They found that although the siblings of children with autism tended to be somewhat more avoidant of them, overall their relationships were no better or worse than their relationships with typically developing siblings, but that there were differences. In terms of behavioural risk factors, they found that older brothers of children with autism were at higher risk of developing problems with both hyperactivity and peer problems, but they did acknowledge that there were limitations with the methodology of their study, namely they did not know how many of the siblings had sub-threshold autistic difficulties which could have accounted for the problems they identified. However, they did conclude that their study raised a number of important issues for clinicians working in this area, particularly in terms of offering whole-family support when there is a child in the family with autism. Also, they need to be aware of the needs of the siblings in terms of onward referrals for their own difficulties.

A paper by O'Connell, O'Halloran and Doody (2014), published in *The British Journal of Learning Disability,* gives a personal account of the first author's experience of living with a sibling with autism. She reported that 'everything was about' her sibling and recalls her teenage years as being the most challenging. She describes cancelled shopping trips and 'strange looks from the public' when her sibling was engaging in challenging behaviour. She also recalled being 'frustrated and angry' a lot of the time and noting that her sibling 'drained all of the energy' from her mother. Overall, however, in spite of this, she reported her childhood as 'relatively normal' and, on a positive note, stated that her relationship with her mother is now 'great' because of their shared experiences (pp.51–52). The authors of this paper do speculate that their story highlights the difference between the 'idealism' of public policies which purport to promote inclusion and community participation for those with disability and the actual lived experience of families who have a child with autism, who often isolate themselves from their families and community in order to avoid feelings of embarrassment and stigmatisation.

The impact of mental health difficulties on the family

The first part of this chapter has examined the impact of a family member having autism both upon parents and any siblings. However, as highlighted throughout this book, a significant number of individuals on the autism spectrum will also have additional mental health difficulties. Faust and Scior (2008) examined the impact of having both a developmental difficulty and a mental health problem on parents and carers. They cite the study by Berg *et al.* (2002) who concluded that child mental health difficulties are, on their own, a major stressor for families and have a significant impact upon both parenting ability and parental well-being. Faust and Scior (2008) speculated that the combination of both a developmental difficulty and a mental health problem in the child might be even more difficult.

In Faust and Scior (2008) parents reported struggling to understand the implications of any secondary mental health diagnoses given to their child. They also reported feeling that dealing with the mental health issues of their child with autism meant that their other children missed out even more on their time and attention. Some also reported feeling scared that either they or their other children could be at risk of being hurt if the young person became aggressive. One of the most commonly expressed feelings was that of self-blame and guilt and the feeling that they had somehow failed their child.

Whilst dealing with aggression is one area that has a profound impact upon families, for other families, the most troubling issue is that of managing self-harm. A study by Byrne *et al.* (2008), whilst not specifically focused upon the experiences of families of girls on the autism spectrum, did interview a number of families where their daughters had self-harmed and a number of themes emerged. The first was the need for support for the wider family. Parents were quoted as saying that after their children were discharged from the Accident and Emergency department, they had no idea how to access further support. The second theme focused upon the emotional impact on the family as a whole, including admitting to feeling anger towards the child who was self-harming, stating that it made the whole household unhappy. All agreed that it disrupted family life and stopped the family functioning as a unit. Some reported siblings feeling devastated and as if the rest of the family did not matter.

The key to managing self-harming behaviour was cited in Byrne *et al.* (2008) as good communication between the parents and the child. Parents reported being scared to discuss incidents of self-harm for fear of repetition. Uncertainty can lead parents to either withdraw from their child or attempt to gain control over the self-harming behaviour. Yip (2005) reported that adopting this approach was likely to lead to an escalation of the behaviour. Talking about self-harm with the young person and understanding why it has happened along with suggesting alternative coping strategies may be the most helpful.

Overall though, despite the level of family distress caused by self-harming, there appears to have been relatively little research that has specifically examined distress to others.

One mother interviewed for this book reported an incident when her daughter had run after her when she tried to leave the room. She described her daughter 'screaming and shouting' and said, 'She threw a table, a pair of trainers and boots with a heel on at me. The heel of the boot hit me in the eye. It was so painful.' This mother also reported repeated outbursts where she had been punched, kicked and bitten. On several occasions this had happened whilst they were driving in the car and her daughter was in the back seat. She also stated that she felt judged by others and that she had tried everything possible to help her daughter, with little or no external help.

Other parents reported getting very little sleep as a result of their child's mental health issues and described the stress of having to try to juggle work and care for the rest of the family whilst feeling tired. Some of the parents in the Faust and Scior study admitted to strong feelings of wanting to escape from their situation and talked about the many strategies they needed to adopt to avoid the escalation of anger, violence or other challenging behaviour. They also reported feelings of being trapped and admitting to having very little emotional space left for their other children. One mother interviewed in the course of research for this book stated, quite tearfully, that in some ways it would have been easier for the whole family if her child with autism had never been born. This was not to say that she did not love her child or want to do everything possible to help her, it was simply that, as a family, she could not recall a single occasion where they had been able to go out socially without the event being spoiled by having to meet the needs of their child with autism. Other mothers reported older siblings choosing to move away from home earlier than they would have liked to, just to avoid the disruption caused by the child with autism.

Participants in the Faust and Scior study also reported huge difficulties in accessing support and all talked about not knowing who to turn to for help, asking for services and receiving few. Many stated that they had to fight in order to receive any support at all. Parents also described feeling that their concerns and worries were not taken seriously and that they were perceived as neurotic.

In addition, on the occasions that the young people in this study became acutely unwell and needed admission to psychiatric units, these were often miles away from home and in their parents' words 'woefully inadequate' in terms of providing appropriate support or fully understanding the needs of their children.

Many of the parents interviewed in this study stated that the most important aspect of support as far as they were concerned was to feel 'listened to' and 'properly heard'. The findings from this paper mirror almost exactly the feelings of those parents seen by me in my clinical practice and maybe the most important message for fellow professionals is that sometimes the most effective support they can offer is to believe their stories.

Managing school refusal

Another area of potential stress for parents of children on the autism spectrum is the issue of school refusal. There is limited evidence in the research literature regarding either the causes of, or solutions for, this problem. Kurita (1991) cited the 'obsessive tendencies' of children on the spectrum as the underlying cause of school refusal.

School phobia, school refusal and school avoidance are all terms used in the literature to describe young people (not just those on the autism spectrum) who experience difficulty with attending school. The reasons cited for these difficulties include separation anxiety, problems with a particular teacher, social phobia, depression and anxiety, and learning difficulties. Berg, Nichols and Pritchard (1969) listed the following criteria for school refusal:

> » significant difficulty in going to school, often leading to long periods of absence

» severe emotional reactions around going to school which may include being scared, claims of feeling ill or angry outbursts

» absence from school with parents' permission.

Brand and O'Connor (2004) reported that 60 per cent of children who refused school had a primary anxiety disorder and that girls were more likely to school refuse than boys.

One aspect that may impact upon anxiety levels and willingness to attend school for children on the autism spectrum is cognitive ability. Many children with autism present with a 'spiky' profile of ability. Most children assessed with standard IQ tests such as the WISC-IV (Wechsler Intelligence Scale for Children, Version IV) will score equally well (or poorly) across all of the sub-tests. The WISC-IV measures verbal comprehension, perceptual reasoning, working memory and processing speed. Oliveras-Rentas *et al.* (2012) highlighted a pattern of difficulty they had observed in children with autism of slow visual processing speed and poor social language comprehension.

This finding has been replicated many times in my own clinical work. In addition, weaknesses in working memory are also often apparent, particularly in terms of holding multiple pieces of information in their head at any one time. This profile has implications for children on the autism spectrum in mainstream classrooms; first because they can often appear quite verbally able and their vocabulary and general word knowledge are often quite sound. However, the majority will struggle with more complex inferential language, so topics such as English become increasingly more challenging as the child moves through the school curriculum. In addition, poorer working memory means they may not always be able to recall what the teacher has asked them to do, and poor visual processing often makes it difficult for them to get their thoughts down on paper quickly or copy information from the board at speed.

It is not surprising, therefore, that if teachers are not aware of the implications of such a 'spiky' profile, they may, at times, feel that the child is not trying hard enough. Failure to understand or write down what is expected for homework tasks can lead to further anxiety.

Research has also shown that a number of individuals diagnosed with what was previously referred to as Asperger's syndrome have a similar cognitive profile to those diagnosed with a non-verbal learning disability (NLD) where their verbal IQ is significantly higher than their non-verbal IQ (less able individuals with autism often have a profile where their verbal IQ is significantly *lower* than their non-verbal IQ). Non-verbal learning difficulty is not officially recognised in the United Kingdom but is in the United States. It is believed to cause impairments in motor coordination, visual-perceptual abilities, pragmatics and social understanding and is defined as a learning disorder primarily affecting functions in the right hemisphere of the brain. In the classroom, this can cause significant difficulties in mathematics, visual memory and attention, which again is likely to impact upon school performance and anxiety levels.

Routinely testing children on the autism spectrum with IQ tests such as the WISC-IV could help to clarify a child's individual profile and might, at least in part, alleviate some of the anxiety around school attendance.

Identifying the right educational placement for the child on the autism spectrum

As can be seen from the evidence presented throughout this chapter, anxiety and challenging behaviour associated with school attendance are a major source of stress for parents and carers of children on the autism spectrum. Parental satisfaction with educational placements for children on the spectrum has been found to be higher when children are provided with the opportunity to attend a specialist autism provision (Barnard, Prior and Potter 2000; Batten *et al.* 2006) and also to be strongly affected by the overall knowledge of the teaching staff (Barnard *et al.* 2000; Whitaker 2007). The study by Barnard *et al.*, who surveyed members of the National Autistic Society in the United Kingdom, found that 50 per cent of young people with a diagnosis of autism were in a mainstream school. However, Treehouse (2009) reported that 43 per cent of children with autism had experienced at least one fixed-term exclusion from school and 55 per cent had from time to time been 'unofficially' excluded. In my own experience, parents often report being called in to school to pick their child up during the school day because of difficulties in managing his or her behaviour.

This clearly has an impact upon parents' ability to maintain employment. A study by Gore Langton and Frederickson (2015) of the educational experiences of children in general reported that children are most commonly excluded from the classroom for either non-compliance with teacher instructions or refusal to follow classroom rules. This is a particularly significant finding for those families who have a child with pathological demand avoidance. Debate continues as to whether pathological demand avoidance is a separate and distinct syndrome (under the autistic 'umbrella') or whether it represents a more 'female' phenotype. In the sample of young people surveyed in the Gore Langton and Frederickson study (aged from 4 years 9 months to 17 years 6 months), 33 per cent of those with a diagnosis of pathological demand avoidance (or those who scored above the cut-off on the EDA-Q, O'Nions *et al.* 2014) were female. Of the children with pathological demand avoidance, 57 per cent had one-to-one support within the classroom environment and 17 per cent were either receiving temporary home tuition or were wholly home-schooled. A high percentage (88%) had refused to attend school at some point. Parents in this study commented on what was important to them in an educational placement and cited lessening of anxiety, an environment where the child is 'safe, secure, happy, valued and cared for'. One also stated 'a place where [my daughter] could have at least one child she could call a friend' (p.259).

Successful school placements were also defined as those which were prepared to take a flexible and adaptable approach and those which were prepared to work in collaboration with families. This last point is possibly the most important issue for parents, as many report feeling blamed for their child's failure to attend school or for his or her behaviour when in school. However, it is fair to say that a large number of children, particularly girls, on the autism spectrum do manage to mask or hide their difficulties whilst at school. This was described by Attwood (1998) as a 'Jekyll and Hyde' phenomenon.

In my experience very few (if any) of the parents of children on the autism spectrum worked with clinically could be classed as 'bad', 'ineffective' or 'overindulgent' – all of which were labels reported in the course of research for this book. All, without exception, wanted the best for their child and for her to thrive and be happy, both at school and at home. Many reported the struggle they had on a daily basis trying to get their child to school on time and the criticism they were often faced with if they arrived late (or not at all). Several talked about the 'sinking feeling' when their phone rings and they are asked to pick their child up from school (again). All reported the huge impact upon finances, family life and career aspirations and many expressed concern about the future and whether their child would ever be able to function independently as an adult.

The ability to live independently for an individual on the autism spectrum is a very interesting debate, not least because this ability can wax and wane considerably depending upon the levels of anxiety experienced at any given time. Affording to live independently is probably more difficult for young people of today's generation (certainly in the United Kingdom) than for any previous generation. The high cost of rental property and an increasing trend towards 'zero hours' employment contracts (which guarantee little in the way of financial and emotional security) make it very hard, even for neuro-typical young people, to move away from home. The current young generation are often referred to as the 'boomerang generation' due to the frequency with which they need to return to live in the family home during their twenties and even thirties.

For young people on the autism spectrum this can be an even greater challenge. Social media sites and support groups for parents who have adult children with a diagnosis of autism are full of accounts of the dilemmas faced by parents who have a child who is creating havoc in the home environment but who receives no external support, and whose ability to manage even simple daily living tasks such as washing and keeping their living environment tidy varies from day to day. Combined with this is the issue of obtaining appropriate qualifications, attending college and ultimately securing and maintaining employment. Some individuals do manage to secure jobs only to lose them fairly quickly due to problems experienced in social interaction, organisation or even the willingness to follow instructions. Some, often at times of depression and high anxiety, lack the motivation to even get out of bed. Parents agonise over how best to support their children. Giving them an ultimatum or threatening to ask them to leave the family home is not really an option as the result of doing so would more than likely be homelessness.

Accessing financial support for themselves as carers or assisting the young person to access financial support can be problematic. Families report feeling desperate and hugely anxious about the future, particularly if they are no longer able to care for the young person.

Most young people with autism want their independence and are no different to their neuro-typical peers in their aspirations for the future. However, the lack of understanding about the debilitating impact of anxiety and the variable nature of daily living ability often means they (or their families) have to jump through hoops in order to access any form of support.

References

Allen, K.A., Bowles, T.V. and Weber, L.L. (2013) Mothers' and fathers' stress associated with parenting a child with autism spectrum disorder. *Autism Insights 5*, 1–11.

Attwood, T. (1998) *Asperger's Syndrome: A Guide for Parents and Professionals*. London: Jessica Kingsley Publishers.

Bailey, A., Palferman, S., Heavey, L. *et al.* (1998) Autism: The phenotype in relatives. *Journal of Autism and Developmental Disabilities 28*, 5, 369–392.

Barnard, J., Prior, A. and Potter, D. (2000) *Inclusion and Autism: Is It Working?* London: National Autistic Society.

Batten, A., Corbett, C., Rosenblatt, M., *et al.* (2006) *Make School Make Sense. Autism and Education: The Reality for Families Today.* London: National Autistic Society.

Bella, G.P., Garcia, M.C. and Spadari-Bratfisch, R.C. (2011) Salivary cortisol, stress and health in primary caregivers (mothers) of children with cerebral palsy. *Psychoneuroendocrinology 36*, 6, 834–842.

Benson, P.R. and Karlof, K.L. (2009) Anger, stress proliferation, and depressed mood among parents of children with ASD: A longitudinal replication. *Journal of Autism and Developmental Disorders 39*, 2, 350–362.

Berg, I., Nichols, K. and Pritchard, C. (1969) School phobia: Its classification and relationship to dependency. *Journal of Child Psychology and Psychiatry 10*, 2, 123–141.

Berg, N., Turid, S., Vikan, A. *et al.* (2002) Parenting related to child and parental psychopathology: A descriptive review of the literature. *Clinical Child Psychology and Psychiatry 7*, 529–552.

Brand, C. and O'Connor, L. (2004) School refusal: It takes a team. *Children and Schools 26*, 1, 54–64.

Byrne, S., Morgan, S., Fitzpatrick, C. *et al.* (2008) Deliberate self-harm in children and adolescents: A qualitative study exploring the needs of parents and carers. *Clinical Child Psychology and Psychiatry 13*, 4, 493–504.

Cidav, Z., Marcus, S.C. and Mandell, D.S. (2012) Implications of childhood autism for parental employment and earnings. *Pediatrics 129*, 4, 617–623.

Davis, N.O. and Carter, A.S. (2008) Parenting stress in mothers and fathers of toddlers with autism spectrum disorders: Associations with child characteristics. *Journal of Autism and Developmental Disorders 38*, 7, 1278–1291.

Dyke, P., Mulroy, S. and Leonard, H. (2009) Siblings of children with disabilities: Challenges and opportunities. *Acta Paediatrica 98*, 1, 23–24.

Ekas, N.V. and Whitman, T.L. (2011) Adaptation to daily stress among mothers of children with an autism spectrum disorder: The role of daily positive affect. *Journal of Autism and Developmental Disorders 41*, 1202–1213.

Estes, A., Munson, J., Dawson, G. *et al.* (2009) Parenting stress and psychological functioning among mothers of preschool children with autism and developmental delay. *Autism 13*, 4, 375–387.

Faust, H. and Scior, K. (2008) Mental health problems in young people with intellectual disabilities: The impact on parents. *Journal of Applied Research in Intellectual Disabilities 21*, 5, 414–424.

Fisman, S., Wolf, L., Ellison, D. *et al.* (2000) A longitudinal study of siblings of children with chronic disabilities. *Canadian Journal of Psychiatry 45*, 4, 369–375.

Gore-Langton, E. and Frederickson, N. (2015) Mapping the educational experiences of children with pathological demand avoidance. *Journal of Research into Special Educational Needs 11*, 4, 254–263.

Houtzager, B.A., Grootenhuis, M.A. and Last, B.F. (2001) Supportive groups for siblings of paediatric oncology patients: Impact on anxiety. *Psycho-oncology 10*, 4, 315–324.

Ingersoll, B. and Hambrick, D.Z. (2011) The relationship between the broader autism phenotype, child severity, and stress and depression in parents of children with autism spectrum disorders. *Research in Autism Spectrum Disorders 5*, 1, 337–344.

Kaminsky, L, and Dewey, D. (2001) Sibling relationships of children with autism. *Journal of Autism and Developmental Disorders 31*, 4, 399–410.

Kogan, M.D., Strickland, B.B., Blumberg, S.J. *et al.* (2008) A national profile of the health care experiences and family impact of autism spectrum disorder among children in the United States, 2005–2006. *Pediatrics 122*, 6, 1149–1158.

Karst, J.S. and Vaughan Von Hecke, A. (2012) Parent and family impact of autism spectrum disorders: A review and proposed model for intervention evaluation. *Clinical Child Family Psychological Review 15*, 3, 247–277.

Kurita, H. (1991) School refusal in pervasive developmental disorders. *Journal of Autism and Developmental Disorders 21*, 1, 1–15.

Lovell, B. and Weatherall, M.A. (2016) The psychophysiological impact of childhood autism spectrum disorder on siblings. *Research in Developmental Disabilities 49–50*, 226–234.

Macks, R.J. and Reeve, R.E. (2007) The adjustment of non-disabled siblings of children with autism. *Journal of Autism and Developmental Disorders 37*, 6, 1060–1067.

Meyer, K.A., Ingersoll, B. and Hambrick, D.Z. (2011) Factors influencing adjustment in siblings of children with autism spectrum disorders. *Research in Autism Spectrum Disorders 5*, 4, 1413–1420.

Morgan, S.B. (1988) The autistic child and family functioning: A developmental-family systems perspective. *Journal of Autism and Developmental Disorders 18*, 2, 263–280.

Neece, C.L., Blacher, J. and Baker, B.L. (2010) Impact on siblings of children with intellectual disability: The role of child behaviour problems. *American Journal of Intellectual and Developmental Disabilities 115*, 4, 291–306.

O'Connell, Z., O'Halloran, M.O. and Doody, O. (2014) Living with a brother who has an autism spectrum disorder: A sister's perspective. *British Journal of Learning Disability, 44*, 1, 49–55.

Oliveras-Rentas, R.E., Kenworthy, L., Robertson, R.B. *et al.* (2012) WISC-IV profile in high-functioning autism spectrum disorders: Impaired processing speed is associated with increased autism communication symptoms and decreased adaptive communication abilities. *Journal of Autism and Developmental Disorders 42*, 5, 655–661.

Olson, D.H. (2000) Circumplex model of marital and family systems. *Journal of Family Therapy 22*, 2, 144–167.

O'Nions, E., Christie, P., Gould, J. *et al.* (2014) Development of the 'Extreme Demand Avoidance Questionnaire' (EDA-Q): Preliminary observations on a trait measure for pathological demand avoidance. *Journal of Child Psychology and Psychiatry, and Allied Disciplines 55*, 7, 758–768.

Petalas, M.A., Hastings, R.P., Nash, S. *et al.* (2009) Emotional and behavioural adjustment in siblings of children with intellectual disability with and without autism. *Autism 13*, 5, 471–480.

Pozo, P., Sarria, E. and Brioso, A. (2013) Family quality of life and psychological well-being in parents of children with autism spectrum disorders: A double ABCX model. *Journal of Intellectual Disability Research 58*, 5, 442–458.

Pruitt, M., Willis, K., Timmins, L. *et al.* (2016) The impact of maternal, child and family characteristics on the daily wellbeing and parenting experiences of mothers of children with autism spectrum disorders. *Autism 20*, 8, 973–985.

Rivard, M., Terroux, A., Parent-Boursier, C. *et al.* (2014) Determinants of stress in parents of children with autism spectrum disorders. *Journal of Autism and Developmental Disorders 44*, 7, 1609–1612.

Seltzer, M.M., Greenberg, J.S., Floyd, F. *et al.* (2001) Life course impacts of parenting a child with a disability. *American Journal of Mental Retardation 106*, 3, 265–286.

Seltzer, M.M., Greenberg, J.S., Hong, J. *et al.* (2010) Maternal cortisol levels and behaviour problems in adolescents and adults with autism spectrum disorder. *Journal of Autism and Developmental Disorders 40*, 4, 457–469.

Treehouse (2009) *Disobedience or Disability? The Exclusion of Children with Autism from Education. Report 3*. London: Treehouse.

Vohra, R., Madavan, S., Sambamoorthi, V. *et al.* (2014) Access to services, quality of care and family impact for children with autism, other developmental disabilities and other mental health conditions. *Autism 18*, 7, 815–826.

Walton, K.M. and Ingersoll, B.R. (2015) Psychosocial adjustment and sibling relationships in siblings of children with autism spectrum disorders: Risk and protective factors. *Journal of Autism and Developmental Disorders 45*, 9, 2764–2778.

Wang, L. and Leslie, D.L. (2010) Health care expenditures for children with autism spectrum disorders in Medicaid. *Journal of the American Academy of Child and Adolescent Psychiatry 49*, 11, 1165–1171.

Whitaker, P. (2007) Provision for youngsters with autistic spectrum disorders in mainstream schools: What parents say – and what parents want. *British Journal of Special Education 34*, 3, 170–178.

Yip, K. (2005) A multi-dimensional perspective of adolescents' self-cutting. *Child and Adolescent Mental Health 10*, 2, 80–86.

Chapter 10

The Women and Girls' Own Stories

This chapter consists of case studies and anecdotal evidence from girls and women on the autism spectrum who have experienced mental health difficulties, and explores how they have learned to manage their difficulties and anxiety, and build a future for themselves. It also includes the stories of some of the mothers who have gone through the diagnostic process.

What has emerged as a common theme throughout the writing of this book and many years of clinical practice, either as part of an assessment team or working with individuals in a one-to-one therapeutic capacity, is the sheer determination and resilience shown by the girls and young women on the autism spectrum.

As one of the women who have been kind enough to provide their stories so aptly puts it, 'Having the kind of challenges that inevitably face a woman with autism helps you to develop a real "kick-ass" approach to life.' Although many of them had faced quite significant mental health and personal challenges throughout their lives, the majority felt that having a diagnosis had allowed them to put their lives in perspective and understand why so many things had been difficult for them over the years. They were able to appreciate that their behaviour made them neither 'bad' nor 'mad'.

What also became clear was the rollercoaster nature of their lives; a frequently repeated pattern of things going well for a certain time, or at certain points in their lives, followed by an inevitable 'crash' emerged.

This does raise the issue of early and accurate diagnosis for girls and women. As stated back at the beginning of the book, the most common age for girls to receive a diagnosis appears to be during their early teens. For many of the young women interviewed for this book, the age at which they received their diagnoses was significantly later. This has to change. Professionals and teams working with children need to become aware of the ways in which girls can mask their difficulties, and need to move away from using the DSM as a 'bible'. Stating that someone does not fulfil criteria, when these criteria are based upon a 'male' presentation of a disorder, is short sighted in the extreme. This is before clinicians even begin to consider the issues of gender identity and gender dysphoria. In the course of many years working in assessment teams, I have come across girls who present in a very typically female autistic way, through to girls who present in a more typical male way (obsessive and very restrictive interests, less interest in socialising or peers), and amongst these are girls who identify themselves as 'gender non-binary', in that they do not relate particularly to either gender or consider themselves 'asexual'. A small number have actually chosen to live as the opposite gender. Assessment and diagnosis of autism cannot and should not be based upon a tick-box approach. Spending time talking to the young women (and their families) can often reveal more than standardised assessments. Perhaps rather than relying on rigid 'criteria' that determine the degree of impairment needed in order for a diagnosis to be given, a better way would be to start with the areas of impairment seen in all individuals on the autism spectrum, namely social communication, social interaction and social imagination/flexibility of thought, and examine the very different ways these impairments present in women and girls.

Girls may chatter away and appear to have very good communication skills. However, when you dig deeper, like their male counterparts, they too struggle with the pragmatics of language – when to join in with a conversation, what to say, how to tell when someone is being insincere, teasing or even bullying them, reading body language, facial expression and tone of voice.

At first glance, girls may also appear to have good social skills, but again, look closely and often these will be intense, short-lived friendships that often go wrong or inexplicably fizzle out. Alternatively, a girl may become totally obsessed by a friend and insist upon dominating all of her time and be devastated if she wants to spend time with someone else. Their need for control can often make them appear bossy and forthright. Quantifying and identifying difficulties with imagination can also be difficult in a formal assessment situation. Girls with autism can demonstrate good imaginative ability, again superficially. They can be excellent at creating fantasy worlds existing of unicorns and wonderful creatures. However, their imaginative play with dolls, although it looks fine, is often stilted, scripted or involves acting out things that have happened at school.

The other area that often causes confusion is the incredible ability of girls (and young women) on the autism spectrum to observe and copy their peers, not to mention the ability of many to become excellent actresses. Two of the ladies interviewed, whose stories appear below, reported 'putting on a mask' and 'playing different parts': changing themselves and their personas with chameleon-like speed in order to either do what they thought was expected of them or fit in with their peers. This type of 'imagination' is very different from social imagination. Imitating, copying and acting out scenarios is very different from being able to visualise what might happen as a consequence of a particular action or of something happening or not happening. One woman stated that she had read recently about aphantasia and felt that this was something that could describe her difficulties with social imagination. Aphantasia is described as an inability to create visual mental images in your mind, or in other words to see something in your 'mind's eye'. This difficulty, if indeed it proves to be common in individuals with autism, may go some way to explaining the inflexible thinking style and anxiety about change and uncertainty that affects most people on the spectrum. Identifying signs of autism in girls is about much more than asking whether they engage in repetitive routines or have fixed, obsessive interests. Many do not.

Another area that can be helpful in unpicking underlying autism spectrum disorders and which, in fact, now forms part of the DSM-5 diagnostic criteria (APA 2013) is sensory processing difficulties. Sensory processing disorder is a neurological disorder that affects the processing of information from the five senses – touch, vision, auditory, olfaction and taste – as well as affecting the sense of movement (the vestibular system) and proprioception (the awareness of one's body in space). In people with sensory processing disorder, it appears that the sensory information is received and 'sensed' in the usual way – there is no impairment in sight or hearing, for example. However, it is perceived very differently and can cause extreme distress and discomfort and leads to a feeling of being overwhelmed (often accompanied by a fight, flight or freeze response).

There has been considerable debate about where sensory processing difficulties stand in terms of a diagnosis of autism. Almost without exception, people who receive a diagnosis of autism will report experiencing sensory processing difficulties. What is less clear is the extent to which sensory processing disorders exist as a distinct entity within the general population (i.e. without any features of autism or another disorder). What is clear from the stories below is the huge impact that this type of difficulty can have upon an individual – how it can make it difficult to cope with a busy, noisy work or school environment, how certain social events can prove stressful, how it impacts upon eating and hunger perception. All of these areas present challenges but at least there is an element of choice. The individual can choose to avoid certain situations and places (and women and girls on the spectrum often do choose to avoid certain situations, or feel so overwhelmed that they have to distance themselves from overwhelming stimuli). What is perhaps most distressing are the accounts from the young women who have found themselves in the situation of needing to be held or restrained.

The other key area to consider is the impact upon a young woman's self-esteem and sense of worth. A common theme when working with young women, particularly those who have received a late diagnosis, is low self-esteem combined with huge feelings of shame and guilt, particularly those who have been prone to emotional outbursts or perhaps even aggression. Some have even reported struggling with suicidal thoughts because they have felt so bad about the way they have behaved in the past. It colours every aspect of their lives. This is often combined with a long history of difficulties with relationships, either becoming obsessive or domineering within a relationship or, as appears to be more often the case, allowing themselves to be sucked into abusive and unhelpful relationships because they feel that is all they deserve.

Another area of particular interest is the number of mothers who, when they bring their children for assessment and go through the diagnostic process, suddenly realise that many of the issues raised resonate with their own experiences and history. This raises important questions about nature and nurture. It is well documented that autism has a strong genetic link and the variety of different presentations of autism, ranging from the multitude of syndromes associated with autistic features through to the differing behavioural profiles (Asperger's syndrome, pathological demand avoidance, etc.), reflects the complexity of its genetic profile. What is less well researched appears to be the impact of a child having a mother with undiagnosed (or for that matter diagnosed) autism.

In the course of clinical work, I have often been approached to provide an expert witness report for a mother who has autism. Often these mothers are very young and are either in specialist mother and baby units or have had their children removed from them. The request from the authority commissioning the report is often in two parts: first, to comment upon the parenting style of the mother and second, and perhaps more importantly, to comment upon their 'capacity to change' within a reasonable timescale. These mothers are often highly anxious, with low self-esteem, and frequently have other mental health issues. Some have experimented with both alcohol and drugs and all stated that the reason for doing so was because they struggled to cope, practically and emotionally. This led to me carrying out research and writing a chapter in a book used primarily by legal teams which aimed to clarify the extent to which changes to parenting style were possible and what type of support these mothers were likely to need in order to achieve this (see Eaton 2015). Two issues arose from this research, the first being the mental health issues and general low self-esteem, the second focusing upon the core neurocognitive deficits associated with autism (namely weak central coherence, poor cognitive shifting and poor theory of mind). These difficulties can (but do not always) lead to difficulties in parenting effectively. There are obviously many mothers with autism who are very good parents and there is absolutely no doubt that they love and care for their children very deeply. However, what was clear was that sometimes mothers on the spectrum are slightly 'out of time' when responding to their children. It is very difficult to clearly explain the subtle timing difficulties observed in some mothers with autism, and perhaps the best way to describe it is in terms of a slight feeling of discomfort. I very clearly recall this feeling when working with a mother on the spectrum who was in full flow, discussing issues that were important to her, as her six-month-old baby daughter became increasingly distressed whilst sitting at her feet. This appeared to be a good example of the 'mono processing' or ability to focus upon only one task at a time that is both a strength and a weakness of autism. It also clearly outlines the challenge of unpicking the nature-versus-nurture aspects of the types of presentation seen in autism and highlights the need for a systemic family formulation when carrying out autism assessments.

In addition to assessment, there is also the issue, particularly in the United Kingdom, of how mothers with autism access appropriate support for their parenting. One mother (with a diagnosis of autism who has two children on the autism spectrum, one boy and one girl) reported that she desperately wants to be a good mother but knows that she is struggling with the day-to-day parenting of her two children. In part, it would appear that this is due to her not really knowing what 'normal' or more accurately 'typical' child development looks like.

Another aspect which became very apparent when pulling together the stories from the girls and women who were kind enough to share their experiences is the aspect of daily living ability, and the impact of mental health difficulties and high levels of anxiety upon the ability to cope with day-to-day activities. This clearly impacts the women both with and without children.

There are a range of financial benefits available (in the United Kingdom) for those who are unable to work because of long-term ill health or disability. However, what is often required is that the individual who is in need of support has to demonstrate to others exactly how their difficulties impact upon their ability to carry out everyday activities and how often they are affected. The women who have contributed to this book outlined this as one of the most challenging aspects of their mental health difficulties. What appears to be less than well understood is the often fluctuating nature of their ability to manage from one day to the next.

All described the overwhelming and crippling anxiety that often stops them from getting dressed, washed and managing household tasks, not to mention the impact upon their ability to perform at, or even attend, work. This is often poorly understood by those responsible for making these assessments, especially if the individual is good at masking their difficulties.

The stories and individual accounts of living with autism that make up the remainder of this book will, it is hoped, provide an insight into the struggles, challenges and occasional high points that are experienced by women on the spectrum. These stories are divided by category – accounts from women and girls with autism telling their own stories, including their challenges in accessing the right kind of support, both emotional and financial, and a number of accounts of the journey to a diagnosis, both in the United Kingdom and in the United States, including an account from a mother who was accused of fabricating her child's difficulties.

Stories from women and girls with autism

All names have been changed to protect the identities of those kind enough to share their stories.

CLAIRE'S STORY

Claire and her mother approached me with a view to obtaining an assessment for autism. There was no family history of autism and this possibility had not occurred to either of them until counsellors working with her following a traumatic imprisonment and rape suggested that this could be a possibility.

After a full assessment by a multi-disciplinary team, it was agreed that this was an appropriate diagnosis. Claire was also provided with a full sensory screen and it was identified that in addition to her social communication difficulties she also had significant sensory processing issues. She has very bravely agreed to allow her story to be shared as an example of how having an undiagnosed autism spectrum disorder can impact so massively on a person's life.

Her experiences clearly demonstrate how using the traditional 'male' model of how autism presents would have meant that Claire would have been unlikely to get a diagnosis when she was younger. She had friends. She is chatty and very articulate. She makes excellent eye contact and uses gestures and facial expression to convey her feelings (although to the trained eye these do appear a little 'learned'). However, her social imagination is effectively broken. She cannot 'read' people or envisage what their motives might be. She puts herself into incredibly risky situations without any concept of the possible consequences. She is a very beautiful, intelligent and charismatic young woman who has been traumatised and broken both by those who have bullied and teased her in the past and physically and sexually abused her as she has grown up.

The experience of being sectioned twice under the Mental Health Act has further traumatised her, as when she was restrained and placed in a police cell, not only did this trigger traumatic memories of her imprisonment and rape, she also had to manage huge sensory integration difficulties. The smells, noise and experience of being held were all an additional challenge. Is it any wonder that, as she admits, she completely 'lost control' in this situation?

Her nightmare is not over yet. She continues to experience flashbacks and intrusive thoughts. She has admitted to suicidal ideation and is currently on medication for anxiety. In addition, she still faces the potential of a further trial. Given her ability to mask and take on a role, it is very hard for professionals within the criminal justice system to appreciate the level of difficulty she has with social communication.

Claire is now 21 and is the eldest child of four born into a loving and involved professional family. From an early age she was seen as a 'difficult' baby who was never happy being cuddled or held. It was always hard to find anyone who was prepared to look after her and even her grandparents struggled. By around 18 months she was regularly having extreme emotional outbursts where she would roll around screaming, biting and scratching and would often try to wedge herself under furniture or into small spaces. She developed speech early and experienced no delay in other developmental areas.

At two she was taken to a small 'mums and toddlers' group but was asked to leave because she often became physically aggressive when the other children tried to approach her.

When she started school she found it difficult to settle and make friends. It was at this early age that her pattern of short-lived, but intense friendships began. She frequently switched between being controlled by her peers and attempting to control them. Her mother described Claire's life at this time as an 'emotional rollercoaster'.

By the time she went to high school, things appeared to have settled a little. For the first three years she was very well behaved and worked hard at not drawing attention to herself. However, she began to be accused of being a 'goody two shoes' and her peers began to tease her. Relationships within her small friendship group became more complex and she often found herself 'dumped' or isolated from the rest of the group. At this time, although she was presenting a brave face to the world, she continued to have what her mother referred to as 'raging tantrums' when she got home. She used to seem completely emotionally overloaded when she got home from school and would often be inconsolable and could not be comforted. Her parents reported handling this by walking away and allowing her to calm down in her own time.

Academically Claire continued to perform extremely well and was placed in top sets in most subjects.

One of her key abilities is that she can be an incredible mimic. She is referred to as being 'hypervigilant' and was always watching carefully to see how people reacted in particular situations. In an attempt to fit in socially and reduce the potential for bullying she used this ability to become a 'social chameleon' and effectively 'became' whoever she was mixing with at that time.

Her interest in and need for social contact meant that whenever she met a new person who responded to her in a friendly way, she seemed to dive into friendships with a determined intensity and passion. Unfortunately though, her inability to read emotional cues and judge personal distance often meant that the person was effectively frightened off, leaving Claire 'utterly rejected and devastated' when they backed off from her.

Around this time, she also began to tell lies to try to reinvent herself and make herself appear more attractive and this, unfortunately, has become a pattern of behaviour she has struggled to shake off. She often exhausts herself trying to keep up the latest persona she has adopted.

In her later teens, she developed an obsession with acting and drama and showed a real flair for it. She was offered a place at the National Youth Theatre (there were 200 applicants for each place). She did not ultimately pursue this for a variety of reasons. One of these was that her mother became extremely unwell and spent a period of time in hospital. At this time, Claire's behaviour at school changed dramatically. She stopped being well behaved and began to be disruptive in class. Clearly struggling with the dual challenge of difficulties at home and friendship problems at school, she withdrew from her female peers and escaped into a fantasy world that she had created. When her peers found out that much of what she said was not true, they rejected her even more. She did not appear to share the typical interests of her peers and was not interested at that time in having a boyfriend.

Claire stated that she has always described herself as 'odd', 'different', an 'outsider' and a 'misfit'. However, following her mother's eventual recovery, she did settle down and managed to achieve well in her school work. She subsequently went on to college to complete further study.

She became involved with her first boyfriend at 16 whom her mother described as a 'very accepting and placid person who adored Claire and accepted her variable moods and meltdowns'. He came to live with Claire in the family home and the relationship continued for two years. She also found a great deal of comfort in her relationship with the family pets, bringing home a stray puppy whom she became devoted to.

She continued to enjoy drama and literature and developed a deep fascination with Shakespeare, learning many sonnets and speeches off by heart. Whilst at college, she was selected to play Rosalind in *As You Like It* and performed exceptionally, to great acclaim from the audience. However, as it was unusual for one of the younger girls to be chosen to play the lead, this caused resentment from her peers. She did well at college and did consider auditioning for RADA (the Royal Academy of Dramatic Arts in London, UK) but decided not to because she feared rejection.

After leaving college, she managed to find employment. She has always been able to adopt a role and appears able to talk her way into any job. These do, however, tend to be fairly short-lived as she is unable to keep this up over time. In addition, her tendency to form close and very intense friendships with girls continued and these often ended in dramatic arguments.

At this time, a rather traumatic event occurred which resulted in Claire developing panic attacks and high levels of anxiety. She was out walking with a friend when the friend was attacked and badly bitten by a dog and was hospitalised as a result. She also moved away from home and into a house share with three older men who 'looked after her'.

At 19, Claire decided to move to London and managed to secure a job and lodged with a family friend. She had only been in the city for a couple of weeks when she became lost late one evening. She was alone, her mobile phone battery was flat and she was clearly anxious.

A young man asked her if she was all right and she told him she was lost. What followed clearly outlines her vulnerability and difficulty with reading situations. The man persuaded her to come into his flat, saying that he would call her a taxi. Over the course of the nightmare that followed, Claire was falsely imprisoned, threatened with death and raped. She was also pressurised into taking drugs. She managed to escape the next morning by pushing one of her captors down the stairs. She was subsequently picked up by a security guard as she ran into the high street. The police were called and used her information to track the perpetrators. In addition to being horrendously traumatised by these events, she was also asked by the family friend to leave the place she was staying at due to fears of reprisals (the young men were part of a known drugs gang).

Her parents found her a place to live and took it in turns to stay with her. However, her mental health declined and she was ultimately sectioned under the Mental Health Act in a public house after paramedics were called when she began to have a panic attack and she became (unsurprisingly) hostile and aggressive when they tried to assist her. She was taken to a local police station which served as an s136 suite (place of safety) where she was detained until she was deemed calm enough to leave.

She then returned to the family home, but remained distressed for much of the time. She received private counselling whilst the rape trial continued and had to face being the main witness in the young man's trial. She now reports the trauma of being in the courtroom as almost as bad as the rape itself.

She was ultimately able to move back into her own flat, in her home town, and very soon afterwards started a relationship with a young student. This caused her extreme distress as this young man was very controlling and physically abused her. One evening, she became so upset that she tried to stab herself in the stomach. She called the police and asked them to detain her under the Mental Health Act. Later, the young man beat her up badly and the police were ultimately called to her flat. When they arrived, she continued to attempt to protect him. She asked to be left alone and not touched. They ignored this request and she recalls going 'berserk' and ended up being arrested, handcuffed and taken to the local police station and kept overnight in the cells. Claire's mother ultimately made an official complaint against the police officers involved as they had failed to act upon the information that she was considered a 'vulnerable' adult and that she would more than likely react adversely to being touched.

Not long after she terminated this particular relationship, she befriended another young drug dealer who persuaded her to allow him to store cannabis in her flat. Shortly after, the police raided her flat and arrested her (and her younger brother who was staying with her) on possession of Class A drugs. The young man had secreted cocaine in her flat. She was once again arrested and detained in a police cell and now faces a trial.

Claire's mother remains extremely concerned that Claire appears to be drawn to this particular type of young man. Claire continues to believe that the man who secreted drugs in her flat is a kind, decent young man. Her struggle to read people combined with her desire for relationships seems to have led her into a pattern of abusive and unhelpful relationships.

She struggles to look after herself and take care of daily living tasks. Often she will forget to eat for long periods of time.

As stated, she is an extremely attractive, articulate and intelligent young woman, with a loving and caring family who do everything possible to help and support her. Her story raises the important question of how different her life could have been if she had been assessed and received a diagnosis earlier. She is now receiving more appropriate support and is hoping to access therapy.

LIBBY'S STORY

Libby is a 47-year-old woman, who also received her diagnosis of autism later in life. She has also been kind enough to share her story.

She stated that getting a diagnosis of high-functioning autism was helpful but it was when she became aware of the difficulties faced by children with the pathological demand avoidance profile that she had her 'lightbulb' moment where she completely identified with the challenges outlined in the description. She described this as suddenly realising 'this is me' and being 'the last piece of the jigsaw puzzle'. She describes her story as one of 'paralysing exhaustion' which has resulted from her constant and ongoing struggle to manage her anxiety, and Libby wanted to share her story to help parents of children, particularly girls, with this profile to understand the issues that face them, especially as they may be unable to verbalise these feelings when younger.

Libby was diagnosed with both dyslexia and dyspraxia at the age of 45 when she was in the second year of a Master's degree, and prior to this a psychiatrist had observed 'autistic traits'.

However, having been referred to her local adult team for a full assessment, she failed to get her diagnosis confirmed, because she believed that the team were obsessed by the fact that her parents were unable to give a good account of her childhood. This she attributes to the fact that she believes that both of her parents were also somewhere on the autism spectrum and neither realised that Libby's behaviour was not typical or normal.

Libby describes herself as 'carrying two psyches' and reported experiencing a physical 'crash' shortly before her eventual diagnosis at the Lorna Wing Centre for Autism in London. She believes this crash was precipitated by chronic anxiety and stress.

She believes she was missed in terms of a diagnosis because she appeared capable. She went to boarding school where she was bullied for being 'weird'. She also challenged the assumption that people on the autism spectrum lack empathy. She stated that, if anything, she is hyper-empathetic – she almost feels too much. The distress of others affects her 'ridiculously'. It is almost as if she feels it herself. She is also creative and has a wonderful imagination and has built a career in design. Like Claire in the previous story, Libby also gets great pleasure out of acting and being on stage.

She has had problems maintaining employment because her employers have not realised that, although she is extremely capable in some areas, she needs support in others, for example, in the scheduling of activities and jobs. She reported times where she was supposed to have met a strict deadline and she would find herself paralysed by anxiety and the only way to calm herself down was to watch YouTube videos of cats. Of course, this was not well received by her employers. Libby was devastated by losing this job. She loved her work and said that all it would have taken was a brief meeting each morning to discuss what her priorities should have been and she would have been fine.

She explained clearly and coherently how it feels to be 'locked in' by anxiety and constantly feeling like she was in fight or flight mode. She also explained that because of this she would often seek to impose her own structure on activities and people in order to reduce these feelings. She describes her brain as being like an ocean liner – it cannot change direction quickly or easily. She discussed the concept of masking and said that rather than masking she actually wears 'multiple hats', adjusting her behaviour and taking on a role depending upon who she is with. She admitted that, during the interview with me, she was 'playing the part of the academic, discussing research'. She did not, however, feel that she has been especially vulnerable to pressure from others, describing her difficulties as predominantly not having a 'stable sense' of who she is, although she did admit to an abusive relationship with an ex-partner who she felt had similar difficulties to herself.

She also described having been diagnosed with a borderline personality disorder, following a meltdown in front of a health professional, as the 'ultimate insult', although she does acknowledge that even though she is in her forties, she thinks she has the emotional maturity of someone in their twenties. She expressed sadness at only having become ready to have children at a time when it was probably too late for her.

She talks about 'craving structure and intimacy' in her life, but 'struggling with the demands of it'. She also discussed the strong feelings of rejection that she has experienced when people have promised to get in touch with her 'within two weeks' and then have not.

When asked about her experiences as a child, Libby explains demand avoidance very well. She said she can understand why children have meltdowns. She recalls understanding quite clearly what was asked of her. It was not that she could not understand or was not able to internalise principles and rules, it was just that she could not understand how other people's rules and directions could be so different to what she was thinking or hoping to do. This, of course, can be attributed to poor theory of mind (the ability to attribute thoughts, feelings and intentions to others that might be different from your own). She also recalled acute feelings of people being angry and disappointed in her because she did not behave the way they thought she should do. This further raised her anxiety levels. She remembers being 'constantly on the edge' and being aware that she could 'tip either way' at any time. Parents of children with this type of profile have likened this to constantly walking on eggshells. They report constantly being on high alert and aware that a meltdown could be triggered at any moment.

Libby also described her experiences of therapy, specifically CBT, as 'hideous'. She felt that CBT is a good tool, but that it creates expectations – expectations that people have the ability to 'fix themselves'. She perceived this as a demand and found that it raised her anxiety even further. She stated that the most helpful tool she personally had come across was a decision tree. A decision tree is described as a decision support tool and is most commonly used in business contexts to help identify the most appropriate strategy to achieve a particular outcome or goal. Decision trees are flowcharts which represent visually the process of making a decision or series of decisions. It seems that this appealed to her need for structure and a logical, linear thinking process whilst at the same time allowing her an element of control. She uses these to map out possible scenarios that may occur depending upon the decisions she makes.

Libby is currently going through the process of obtaining care support for herself. In the United Kingdom this involves a long and drawn out process of the applicant (or applicant's advocate) detailing how and why support with tasks such as cleaning, dressing, washing and so on is needed. She talked at length about her frustration with the process, her anxiety, and how it was a real challenge to explain to people who are not aware of autism how someone who is apparently capable and articulate can be crippled by anxiety to the point that daily living tasks become impossible. This reflects similar frustration expressed by parents of children with autism who are trying to explain to people why, at times, their child's self-care skills may suddenly deteriorate or they may simply be unable to get out of bed and face going to school.

Libby did express some positive aspects of her condition. She feels that ultimately her struggles have given her 'kick-ass strength' as a person and that her knowledge, now, that she is 'different not broken' has helped her immensely. She now focuses on calmness and standing up for herself.

JACKIE'S STORY

Jackie is a young woman in her thirties who has a diagnosis of autism, ADHD and pathological demand avoidance. She was diagnosed as a child and continues to have difficulties now. She was also kind enough to share her story. She described the types of issues she faces on a daily basis and the struggles that she has also had in accessing financial support.

She is described as high functioning and has above-average intelligence levels but on some days is completely unable to function due to crippling levels of anxiety. On a 'good' day she reported that she is able to check and reply to emails, eat the meals that have been prepared for her, get dressed and enjoy some social interaction. On a bad day, she may not be able to do any of these things.

She has a supportive partner who she stated helps her with 90 per cent of tasks. Although intelligent, Jackie has specific difficulties with spelling and mathematics. She said that if she handed someone a £20 note for some shopping, she would have no idea how much change she could expect back. In the past, she would have tried various strategies to avoid letting people see her difficulties, but now she is more honest about them.

She is also very aware of exhausting her 'social energy'. If she takes on too much in one week, she may need to withdraw totally for a period of time in order to recharge her social batteries. During this time, she may be incapable of managing any significant social interaction and may not even be able to get washed and dressed.

She discussed her difficulty with going to places like busy supermarkets and how she quickly becomes overwhelmed. She said, with some amusement, that her local supermarket had recently started having 'autism-friendly' shopping times. She stated that this was helpful to some extent because they had at least turned off the music within the store and stopped loud announcements. However, she did observe that it now meant that the shop was full of parents with children on the spectrum, so, if anything, it was even more busy and noisy than usual!

When discussing her levels of anxiety, Jackie described not knowing what it feels like to not have anxiety. She stated that it is always with her, all of the time. Much of the time, this makes her feel angry and upset, but this is mostly anger at herself for not being able to do things. She can also feel sick and dizzy and her thoughts race constantly. She feels bad about herself because she is so scared of everything and, even though she knows it is not logical, she worries endlessly about what might happen.

She also described how demands become difficult the more anxious she gets. She talked about how even simple things like following a recipe can become impossible because it feels like a 'tirade of instructions'.

She also worries greatly about being perceived as volatile and losing control. She does care about what people think of her when she is out socially and expressed concern that one day she might 'flip and never come back from it'.

She also has huge worries about the public perception of autism and is often embarrassed to admit that she is on the spectrum. She does, however, carry an Autism Attention Card (this is a card for people with autism which is available from the National Autistic Society in the United Kingdom). She is always concerned that people might think she is 'odd' or 'weird' and also thinks that many people automatically associate autism with a lack of intelligence, and described how humiliating it can be at times when she does admit to someone (she gave the example of a train guard at the railway station) that she has autism and they begin talking to her as if she has a learning difficulty.

She feels that she has, at times, experienced prejudice as a result of acknowledging she has autism. She has had people say to her that she can't be autistic because she is 'too intelligent' or because she is female.

Jackie also talked about being given a diagnosis of borderline personality disorder, which she described as insulting and which she has insisted upon having removed from her medical notes.

Jackie was also kind enough to talk about her relationship with her boyfriend. She has been in a monogamous relationship for several years. She feels that her partner understands her and is a big support in her life. She did say though that she did not feel that she would be able to manage having both a job and a relationship, as she did not think that she would be able to give enough to both. She talked a great deal about how supportive her partner is. However, when asked about how easy it is for her to provide the same level of support to him, she did admit that it can be difficult. She said that even when she is having a good day, she will still need to remind herself to check if he is all right. On a bad day, she described his needs as being 'invisible'. Although she loves her partner very much, she said that being in a relationship 'does not come naturally' to her. However, she stated she does believe strongly in monogamy as she is a 'stickler for rules'.

She did not describe any difficulties in having an intimate relationship with her partner, other than the problems she reported experiencing when trying to share a bed with him. She stated that she has not slept well in a bed for many years and usually sleeps on the sofa.

Her biggest challenge at the moment has been trying to access support through the United Kingdom benefit system. Her current claim has been turned down and she now faces a stressful appeals process. The reason given for rejecting her claim was that on a 'good day' she can manage a number of tasks for herself. It would appear that the staff evaluating her claim do not understand the variable nature of skill level experienced by those on the autism spectrum or the impact of high levels of anxiety.

REBECCA'S STORY

Rebecca had always felt strongly that we don't get taught how to 'do' life and described herself as a long-term seeker of information, hanging around self-help bookshelves since her early twenties. Before that she reported being passionate about the theatre and acting as it gave her a space within which to experiment with different ways to be; importantly, it gave her somewhere to put her 'big feelings' – the more tortured the heroine she played the better. It also gave her a script to follow – guidance that strongly attracted her. She loved the freedom that came with acting as it made it 'safe' to express herself, something that only really came comfortably to her as a teenager and adult when she was drunk, or on drugs at a festival atop a podium. She described herself as an extrovert, happiest when she was the centre of attention.

However, she reported that when she looks back now, the early signs of anxiety were always there. She noted that she has been a nail biter since she was five years old, and suffered with nervous tension stomach aches that kept her doubled up for days. She also struggled to settle to sleep at night. In the family she developed a reputation for being bossy and reported being so certain that she knew the 'right' way of doing things that she would always take charge. This has followed her throughout her life and was put to good use when she took roles on whatever council or committee she could be a part of.

She also described being a fussy eater and only eating from a very restricted range of food groups yet also being strongly drawn to sweet foods. She recalled her brother taking a whole week to eat his weekly allowance of sweets as she gorged on them in one sitting. Later she took to stealing sweets at a newsagent's she worked for and binging on them on the way home before Sunday lunch.

Rebecca reported becoming aware of the 'hole in her soul' when she suffered a number of close family bereavements in her early twenties. She commenced counselling and described a sense of emptiness inside, alongside hurling herself whole-heartedly into the social scene – she became determined to say yes to everything because it felt like a very real possibility that life was going to be cut short. She now believes that, at some level, she was finding a sense of freedom in the feeling of losing control. She now appreciates that this was the freedom from the endless fear and self-hatred-focused thinking she had struggled with her whole life.

Rebecca's story includes numerous incidents of being bullied, by school mates, work colleagues, housemates. The only conclusion she was able to come to was that it must be her fault. That belief was the automatic answer she came up with for most things that went wrong in life. This tendency to be really hard on herself is something she has been given feedback about again and again from every angle. She wonders now if all along she has simply been unaware of some unwritten but widely understood social code of conduct, and her ignorance of this primed her to become a scapegoat. Rebecca is very thankful that she has been blessed with a small number of lifelong friends who she feels really connected with her and kept her from completely losing the plot, and later a husband who she states 'endures my difficulties with great patience'.

Thinking back on her experiences of so much loss at a young age, Rebecca now feels that this may have contributed to her slowly progressive obsession about gaining perfect health. After a great deal of lower back inflammation in her twenties and an ever-increasing list of symptoms that could not be 'sorted' by a trip to her GP, she describes herself as 'leaping' into the alternative therapy world and being quickly swept along by a combination of treatments, practitioners, supplements, laboratory tests and advice on cutting out food groups. She managed to achieve her goal of perfection once, for a few short months, which unfortunately was an experience that locked her into a pattern of behaviour that eventually led to a full-blown eating disorder spanning some 15 years.

At the time she described herself as believing that she wasn't 'good enough' to follow the guidelines suggested, that if she could do whatever it was for just one more month – see one more practitioner, or cut out one more food group – then maybe she could be 'well' again. She recalls spending much of that time being aware of and resentful about being different to everyone else, feeling deprived and full of self-pity. She recalls an increasing sense of alienation and isolation as those around her looked on in despair. It was a very lonely place and, true to the nature of denial, she had no idea what she was battling.

Rebecca recalls her relief at this point at having been introduced to a 12-step fellowship who offer a spiritual programme of recovery. As soon as she joined the group, she reported identifying with the recovered fellows who shared their stories about being 'self-critical perfectionist control freaks running on a hundred different forms of fear'. As a member of this fellowship, participants believe that instead of being addicted to the compulsive behaviours around food and exercise, the 'drug' to which they are addicted to is just an illusion of control. Rebecca now feels that she has gained freedom from food obsession and needing to be in control in order to feel safe by following this programme, and feels that she is slowly being introduced, finally, to a way of 'doing life'.

Rebecca then moved her story forward several years to the time when she witnessed her daughter have a breakdown at the age of seven. At first there was no explanation but Rebecca eventually found a description of pathological demand avoidance online. She then read up on autism in general and realised that everything she was reading about high-functioning autism fitted exactly with how she had experienced the world. Up to that point she had come up with several different names for what she was experiencing: trauma, co-dependency or addiction.

On the day that Rebecca's daughter was finally diagnosed with autism with a pathological demand avoidance profile, she received a professional opinion that she too had high-functioning autism. She describes this as being like the final piece in a jigsaw puzzle she had been doing her whole life and reported going outside the building and weeping. In her own words she recalls 'looking up in the sky, and seeing a rainbow as if it had been put there just for me'.

Rebecca is keen to point out that this is not where her story ends. In fact, to her it feels like it has only just started. Over her many years of searching for an answer for her difficulties, she has acquired huge amounts of knowledge and this has enabled her to train as a transpersonal integrative psychotherapist. She feels that she has found her way intuitively to a 'peaceful way' of being a parent and hopes and trusts that this has enabled her to help and support her own daughter. She now feels that it is time to begin to integrate that knowledge on the ground, to adjust and learn alongside her daughter, as with every day she finds herself challenged to drop her expectations, become more honest and separate her needs from her wants. Most importantly, she is working on it being okay to be 'good enough' and to trust that she can ask for help when she needs it.

Rebecca's favourite mantra from her autism coach is 'you're still learning', something which she uses both for her daughter and herself. She reports that the day she received her own diagnostic opinion she 'got a fresh delivery of self-compassion'. She let go of the shame she carried for needing so much support, and felt proud that she has managed to achieve so much whilst suffering with an undiagnosed invisible 'illness'. She reports that she is still learning to manage her strong sense of intuition, her acute sensitivity and deep thinking, which she has always believed to be both a blessing and a curse. She also hopes that this will provide her with the opportunity to help her daughter 'meet the world in a way that enables her to know and express herself more lovingly'.

ELEANOR'S STORY

Eleanor is nearly ten years of age. Her parents had experienced longstanding concerns about her high levels of anxiety and sometimes aggressive behaviour towards members of the family. She was also suffering from extremely low self-esteem and would spend many hours before going to bed each night going through all of the things that had gone wrong for her.

The family sought help and support from their local CAMHS and Eleanor was ultimately assessed for autism. At that time, the team did not feel that she met criteria for a diagnosis and were not able to offer any other form of support for the family. Ultimately Eleanor's parents made the decision to seek an independent diagnosis and eventually she was diagnosed with autism with a pathological demand avoidance profile.

Eleanor was asked what her life was like before she had her assessment. She replied that it was 'strange, because I got stressed but didn't know why'. She was also asked how she felt after she eventually got a diagnosis of autism and she said that she felt better because she now understood herself, and other people also understood why she becomes so anxious. Before her assessment she said that she felt sad, lonely and 'so stressed'. She also felt that she did not fit in. She said that she was happy because the (cognitive) assessment had also shown that she is very clever. Eleanor was then asked about her self-esteem and general confidence. She admitted that this was still a problem for her but that she was 'working on it'. She also said that at one time, because of her issue with anger, she used to worry that she might end up in prison but that she does not think that this will happen now.

Eleanor also said that she thinks that things have improved at home for all the family.

When asked how she would describe how it feels to have autism and pathological demand avoidance, she said that it is 'stressful, because everything seems like a demand and you can't even boss yourself around'.

Eleanor was also asked what tips she would give to a teacher or someone who works with children who have this profile and she said, 'Always have options, and if you do have to give someone work to do, try and combine it with something fun, like an art activity.'

When asked for what she thinks is the best advice for parents of children with autism and pathological demand avoidance, she stated that the most important thing is to listen and 'don't try any stupid reward systems as that just makes things worse!'

Eleanor was also kind enough to provide the following advice for parents regarding 'meltdowns'.

A few tips if your child is having a meltdown

- Don't take it personally.

- Leave them alone to calm down.

- Write on a notebook what the problem is (e.g. 'We have to go shopping because we have nothing for tea') and pass it back and forth until they decide to talk to you.

She also had some helpful tips for brothers and sisters of children on the spectrum, particularly with regard to when things go wrong when playing a game. Her advice was 'to walk away and give [the person] some space'.

Finally Eleanor advises other girls with the same difficulties to 'accept themselves' because 'life is too short not to like yourself'. Her final piece of advice was, 'Remember be proud of who you are – you are amazing!!!'

The mothers' stories

During research for this book, in addition to the stories bravely shared by women and girls on the autism spectrum about their own experiences, I was also approached by a number of mothers of girls on the autism spectrum who had their own stories to tell – stories about their challenges of getting a diagnosis, stories about their daughters' experiences of being an inpatient, and what life is like for them as parents and for their child's siblings.

In the course of writing, I took a break and read a book by a British author, Amanda Prowse, entitled *The Food of Love* (Prowse 2016). Although this is a work of fiction and not about a child with autism, it describes beautifully the impact of having a daughter with a mental illness upon the whole family, describing the journey from a growing awareness that there was a problem through to the eventual decision to agree to a psychiatric admission. This story reflects the experiences of the families interviewed for this book and encountered during years of work in inpatient units incredibly well.

Many of the parents who came forward to share their stories had daughters diagnosed with pathological demand avoidance. Pathological demand avoidance, despite its acceptance by the National Autistic Society as part of the spectrum of autism, is still highly controversial. This may be, in part, due to the term 'pathological'. This is deemed by many professionals, myself included, to be a derogatory and unhelpful name for such a debilitating condition. Extreme anxiety or extreme demand avoidance might be better. Quite possibly, this dislike of the name 'pathological demand avoidance' might be contributing towards the sometimes angry response that parents feel they get from CAMHS professionals and doctors when they raise this as a possibility. All too frequently any mention of demand avoidance seems to provoke the response that the child has attachment issues and needs clearer boundaries or even that avoiding demands is a child's way of getting attention in a busy household.

Outlined in the rest of the chapter are some of the stories from mothers who have gone through a long, and sometimes quite traumatic, journey in their attempt to secure an appropriate assessment and diagnosis for their daughter. One describes her experience of having been faced with accusations of fabricated and induced illness (FII) and who has had to go through extensive social services investigations before ultimately obtaining the appropriate diagnosis and support for her child. Others describe the daily issues they face as parents of a child who presents with high levels of anxiety and challenging behaviour. There are also accounts of how difficult it is to juggle the needs of these children alongside those of siblings. As the author of this book and as a psychologist who has been involved in quite literally hundreds of assessments and who has heard stories like the ones below over and over again, I would strongly urge any professional to read them, hear the voices of both the individuals who have shared their stories and their families, think about the impact of not recognising the common features in these stories, and accept that there just might be a case for re-writing the diagnostic manuals in order that future professionals can learn about the way in which autism presents in girls, not to mention the impact of mental health difficulties on the young women and their families, which are clearly not helped by lack of understanding and compassion.

ANGELA AND NATALIE'S STORY

In her story, Angela, a mother of three children (two of whom are on the autism spectrum), describes her experience, over a number of years, of trying to get an appropriate diagnosis for her daughter Natalie.

Angela describes that when her first daughter, Natalie, was born, she was 'bursting with broodiness', but had waited some time to have her so that she could afford to stay at home with her. Natalie had a very difficult delivery, being a posterior presentation and not turning. She was blue on delivery but achieved high scores on all her Apgar tests.

Natalie was reported to have not been able to latch on and suckle easily and Angela recalls being told by the midwives that Natalie had poor muscle tone and was floppy, especially with regard to the way she held her head during the early days. Later Angela realised they may have been hinting that she may have cerebral palsy. Natalie was a very 'colicky' baby and only slept very briefly. She was woken by the slightest sound and had acute startle reflexes. She was given a dummy (pacifier) which seemed to frustrate more than comfort her.

When she was about four months old Angela recalled attempting to pull her by the arms into a sitting position and noticing that she still didn't hold her head up. Her peers all seemed to sit without support at around six months, but it was eight months before Natalie could manage this. She seemed to love imaginative play and music but as she got older it became clear how difficult she found completing even simple jigsaw puzzles or shape matching.

When Natalie was about nine months old the family went on holiday to Wales and some friendly strangers remarked on how she didn't seem to be at all worried when being held by them and weren't they concerned about this from a safety point of view? At about this time they also noticed that she was picking up certain shapes and patterns very quickly. For example, she quickly recognised the McDonald's golden arches.

During that break to Wales Angela recalled with some sadness that she had to suddenly stop breastfeeding as Natalie's biting had turned into drawing blood. Angela said that she was really sad about this – heartbroken in fact – as she had planned to carry on for at least a year. She recalled having to quickly trawl the local shops for formula and bottles.

Natalie learned to wave early, crawled beautifully and walked at a year. She was a whirlwind of fun and changing moods with lots of painful ear infections. On stripping her down to a nappy (diaper) in the summer with her peers, her poor muscle tone was very apparent.

She disliked the feel of grass and sand and appeared to have very sensitive feet. She enjoyed being hugged and seemed to find water very calming. She was puzzled by her Jack-in-the-box and jumped terribly when he came out of the box – as if each time was the very first time she saw it and she didn't remember for the next time.

Angela recalled Natalie's vocabulary developing amazingly quickly. She was speaking fluently at a much younger age than her peers – they thought they had a gifted child!

Natalie began to attend a playgroup and it was clear that she loved the social interaction and was a natural extrovert – a loud and bossy, fun-loving little girl. However, she never spent much time on any activity. One day Angela recalled that she was having a coffee with a friend and turned round and saw that Natalie had covered herself in red paint, right up to her elbows like she was having a wash in it! Her natural exuberance was like Marmite – people, both her peers and the other mothers, either loved or hated her – it seemed like they were already starting to notice her differences.

Natalie would fall asleep in the strangest of places and positions. She could be in the middle of singing a nursery rhyme in the car and halfway through she'd be gone! She was very loving and frequently said she loved her family with 'all her heart and tummy'.

Natalie's first sibling was born just before her second birthday and she was so lovely with her from the first time she met her. She was speaking fluently by this age and loved singing and when she first met her at a few hours old she exploded towards her, crying, 'Baby bundy, little sweetheart!' Her present from 'the bump' was an electronic toy Barney – an American TV character she loved – but to Angela's horror she was immediately terrified of it, expecting it to explode into a much bigger version of itself, like it did on TV.

The whole family went to a garden party a few weeks later and Natalie met a little girl for the first time. A year later Angela recalled that when they were out and about, by chance Natalie spotted this little girl again and somehow had remembered the little girl's name.

At this time Angela was also trying to toilet train her. She was dry by day at two and a half and by night at three, but Angela noticed that when she was changing Natalie's baby sister, Natalie used to lay down in the changing position and anxiously put one of her nappies around her as if she missed the attention of being changed. She appeared very 'needy'.

When she was three years and eight months her baby brother was born and the family was complete.

When it came to her going alone to playschool in preparation for big school she found separating from Angela incredibly hard. She hated it – yet she had been fine being left with her maternal grandmother before this. Angela found this heartbreaking.

When she had her pre-school assessment by the health visitor, Natalie was asked to make a bridge from three bricks, placing two side by side with a gap between and one on top. She struggled and it took about three goes to get it right but the health visitor passed her anyway.

Although she loved dancing and moving to music she found a lot of physical things difficult, like hopping, balancing and standing still. She had been to baby gym, swimming, Tumble Tots and ballet and had found concentrating on instructions, keeping quiet and copying movements difficult. Body awareness in space was obviously difficult.

At Christmas when Santa came to visit with his sack of presents for all the children Natalie hovered round him excitedly the whole time, impatiently waiting and thinking each was her present from the very first one and showing her disappointment every time it wasn't. Hers was last out of the sack. The other children barely noticed theirs. Angela analysed this after the event and wondered if the staff were trying to teach her how to take turns.

In the Christmas play during her first term at nursery, Natalie was put in the centre, holding a large star and wearing a crown, as if to help her natural eccentricity seem part of the performance, as she didn't blend in with the quieter children.

The family had a wonderful break to Disneyland Paris in the spring, just before Natalie started full-time school. Angela recalls making a number of video recordings of this holiday and it was becoming clear that Natalie's younger sister was displaying far superior motor skills, for example, how she managed to play on the equipment at the playground and manipulated the straw through the little hole in the juice carton.

When it came to attending school full time, during the term (semester) she became five, Angela stated that she really didn't feel that Natalie was ready – developmentally she was quite forward in some ways, she didn't have a daytime nap like some of her peers – but it was her emotional development that Angela was most concerned about. She simply didn't feel that Natalie was emotionally ready to leave her or her siblings yet.

When Natalie started in the reception class, she was one of the youngest in the year. The children initially attended in the mornings only and were collected by parents from their little playground at lunchtime. On the first day most children were crying and clinging to staff as a result of being left for the first time. However, to Angela's relief Natalie appeared fine and excited to be there in her new school uniform. However, after the first PE lesson when they had to change independently into their kit, when Angela went to collect her, the teacher – in front of all the other parents and children, including Natalie – announced loudly, 'Can you please, please, please teach her to dress herself... She's HOOOPELESS!!!!'

Angela stated that she *had* tried to teach her, but Natalie found it so hard. She would hold a sock against her foot as if she expected it to hop on, she would hold her foot out for Angela to put her shoe on and hold her button near the hole as if she expected it to jump in.

After the event, Angela wrote a letter explaining how embarrassing this had been in front of her little girl and how unprofessional she thought this was. Angela recalls that the teacher was near retirement age and obviously knew all the tricks in the book. She called her into school to meet with her. She said that Angela's letter sounded 'very sad' and that she knew that she had recently had a baby – Angela felt that the teacher was suggesting that she may have postnatal depression.

The next criticism Angela received was how Natalie didn't like sitting for long periods at the table in class and how her handwriting wasn't up to scratch. She entered a colouring competition at school and exuberantly coloured the page – all outside the lines. When Angela handed this into the student teacher she looked at it in disbelief and said, 'Wow.'

At parents' evening Angela and her husband dared to mention to the student teacher that they thought she was bright, but the teacher replied that she was 'just average'. Angela remembers thinking if there was one word that you just couldn't describe her as, it was 'average'! The teacher did say that Natalie was good at sharing, which was unusual for her age group, which they thought was lovely. However, they put this down to her having close siblings, whom she shared with every day.

At this point, Angela recalls that her intuition that Natalie may have some kind of difficulty was starting to kick in. She became increasingly aware of the feeling that they were somehow trying to 'bash a square peg into a round hole'.

Angela and her husband were told by the student teacher that the school prided themselves in achieving 'excellent results'. Yet they were already asking themselves, 'but at what cost?'

At that time, one thing she did excel at was reading. She always enjoyed being read to, looking at books and going to the library. She always got so into the characters, and Angela felt that it was great that she picked up reading.

At that time, she appeared full of confidence and enthusiasm.

The whole family had made lots of friends in the little town they had moved to three years before. It had a great network of nurseries and schools. Angela recalls feeling that they were such a happy family and felt so blessed to have her three beautiful children. As a family, they walked miles with the pushchair, meeting lots of people and doing lots of activities every day. But suddenly everything changed.

When Natalie was five her younger sister became ill with a polio-like illness. Natalie had been used to her being regularly in and out of hospital with asthma needing inpatient treatment, but this was much more serious and meant Angela had to leave Natalie and her brother with their grandparents for a long weekend whilst they were at Great Ormond Street Hospital with Natalie's sister, undergoing tests.

Natalie's sister remained unwell for some time and Angela became increasingly depressed and anxious. She became aware that rumours were spreading in the small town they lived in about Natalie's behaviour. Apparently it had been reported that Natalie had tried to strangle her little sister. People who Angela had thought were her friends crossed the road rather than speak to her. It was very distressing.

In addition, it was becoming more and more obvious to Angela that Natalie was now being bullied at school. She was constantly contacting the staff at the school, but nothing was ever done about it. Natalie's sleep became affected. By the time she was in year two, Angela began having huge trouble getting her to school in the morning. At parents' evening Natalie's teacher said she was thinking of putting her in a lower maths group but had decided to give it a little more time as, on one occasion, when she was trying to explain how to do a complicated sum on the board, Natalie suddenly shouted out the right answer!

Angela and her husband ultimately decided to move Natalie to another school. The headmaster of the new school was 'lovely', and the school had a real nurturing ethos. It was believed at the time that all of Natalie's difficult behaviour was due to the impact of the trauma on the whole family following the serious illness of her younger sister.

In the first week or two at the new school, Angela recalls speaking to Natalie's form teacher about her anxiety and the fact that she was having trouble finding her way around the corridors; she said it seemed like a maze.

Some time later, Angela recalls that when her younger son began displaying certain features that could be consistent with him having autism, he was sent for a pre-assessment with a paediatrician. She stated that every question that the paediatrician asked could also apply to Natalie. Angela questioned the paediatrician about this and she told Angela that this was unlikely as 'autism is very rare in girls'.

At the same time, Natalie's teacher said she continued to be worried about her coordination, and referred her to the child development centre for assessment. When Natalie was seen by an occupational therapist, Angela and her husband were initially told that her motor planning and proprioception were poor for her age, as were her fine and gross motor skills. At the second appointment they asked if Natalie might have dyspraxia. When the eventual report was sent out, they found that her development was actually more in line with a three-year-old than a five-year-old. However, Angela stated that they were not offered any further advice or follow-up therapy to support Natalie with this.

At about this time, Natalie started Brownies. She was quite anxious about going and when Angela was invited to stay a while at one session, she recalls noticing the body language between the girls around her and how unaware Natalie was of it all.

Natalie had put on quite a bit of weight over the previous year or two and was heavier-made than some of her peers. In Christmas plays she was often chosen as an angel because of her flowing blonde hair and gentle nurturing nature. Angela remembers going to a private swimming pool for a session with Natalie and her younger siblings. Angela and Natalie were sitting out whilst the younger two were swimming. Natalie was fussing over all the babies; the mothers loved her and said how maternal she seemed to be.

Natalie continued to be uncoordinated and this was painfully obvious when she was taken to ballet lessons, and Angela recalled feeling that this was so sad because Natalie loved music and dancing; one school report had stated that she 'felt music in every cell of her body' when she danced.

The family had also noticed that from a young age, Natalie was unable to keep her body heat comfortably controlled and she very easily became overheated. Angela regularly wondered if she had thyroid problems but was told not.

Learning to ride a bicycle was yet another challenge. Natalie did not manage this until she was eight.

The difference in independence skills between her and her, now physically disabled, sister who was two years younger were always obvious, but as the years progressed, it became glaringly so. Angela and her husband tried not to compare their children but it was difficult.

Natalie had learnt to swim, albeit slowly – she had always enjoyed water – and they regularly visited a private pool on Friday evenings. Angela began to notice how overwhelmed and distracted Natalie became in the shower afterwards. She found it hard to shampoo her hair and found it a struggle to get dressed. This started to attract unwanted glances from other families so eventually they stopped going to the pool.

At the age of ten Natalie suddenly had a growth spurt and, after a few signs the year before of puberty beckoning, she started her periods. Sadly she was the first in her class – another difference in her young life she has had to cope with. Angela remembers watching her in the queue at the supermarket checkout, being slightly loud and disagreeable. She looked much too grown up for her age and was attracting a mix of admiring glances because she was so pretty, and less positive looks because her behaviour was outside of the norm for her age.

It was becoming obvious how much younger 'in her head' she was than most of her peers. At a time where they were becoming more independent, almost as if they couldn't wait to grow up, Natalie was, if anything, becoming more emotionally needy than ever. She was suffering really badly with premenstrual symptoms, which was not a shock because it was something that both Angela and her maternal grandmother had also suffered from. However, it was causing huge disruption at home.

The combination of premenstrual syndrome (PMS) and headaches meant low energy and it became increasingly hard to get Natalie to school. There were many explosive fights and school refusal. She had a short cycle of only 26 days, so the mood swings seemed to come round very regularly.

She suffered greatly from pain and appeared in sensory overload. This often led to blackouts on the toilet and days off school. Angela reported that she was keen to help Natalie to develop the necessary independence in this area, but it was difficult and seemed a cruel joke that her body and mind were so out of sync.

At the time, the family lived a ten-minute walk away from school in a small town where early independence was encouraged in children. Many of Natalie's peers walked to school in groups, calling for each other on the way. A couple of girls who lived just around the corner, whom Natalie classed as her friends, walked together – but for some reason they never included her. Instead Angela, Natalie and the younger children walked as a family together. Sometimes Angela recalled taking the initiative and calling on a friend on the way, but she could see that the friend was becoming less and less interested.

There were some positives though. As she moved through to upper school, her ability in language and science subjects shone through and her music teacher discovered when she was about 12 that she had a lovely singing voice and gave her a solo part in the school production.

Natalie loved dressing up for school discos and wearing dresses and heels. It seemed to give her new-found confidence. However, Angela now realises that this was a form of masking.

Natalie was given some tests of her cognitive ability and was given extra time in her examinations.

At this time, she was part of a group of friends who were all 'quirky' and started going through a 'Goth' stage. Her whole wardrobe was black.

However, by the age of 14, problems were beginning to emerge again. The bullying had started again and, following numerous talks with her head of year, Angela was told that the school were sure she was not being bullied and that it was just Natalie taking things too seriously and not realising when her peers were fooling around and having fun.

Her mood became very low and at the age of 14 she was referred to CAMHS and was put on citalopram (an anti-anxiety medication). Life was also becoming more difficult at home. There were lots of arguments and shouting at her siblings. She even began to have outbursts in the middle of the shopping centre. This escalated to the point that she was pointing and shouting loudly at innocent bystanders and accusing them of staring at her or talking about her.

Natalie took her GCSEs (examinations taken by children in the United Kingdom at age 15/16) having missed a whole term in her first year of GCSE study with a kidney infection. She had remained under the care of the local mental health team, following her contact with them at age 14. Apart from that the only extra help she received was a little additional time in examinations and being allocated to a special needs group. Grouping her with these children was not helpful for her. She wanted to work, learn and to achieve, but her highly sensitive system made it difficult for her to focus in this rowdy group, who were labelled as 'naughty' children.

Her determination to do well meant that she spent many, many hours at home 'hyper focusing' on her homework. Her urge to produce 'too much' work could not be quenched. It may be that she simply struggled to pick out what details were essential.

In terms of her personal development, she was still going through her 'Goth' phase. All her clothes were black and she was still trying hard to fit in with her peers. She copied hair and make-up styles from celebrities and picked up their accents and mannerisms.

She still felt bullied at school. However, at numerous parents' evenings and extra meetings organised at her family's request, they were simply told that any bullying was simply her perception, or that she had brought it on herself.

A school trip to Thorpe Park (a large theme park) ended in a public meltdown which was interpreted as 'spoiled behaviour' by the teachers in charge. The deputy head appeared particularly baffled by this, especially as shortly afterwards she was able to sit with the other girls and was observed laughing and giggling. Apparently Natalie was the 'worst behaved student ever' on a school trip and was promptly excluded from all future trips. She was unable to complete a planned work experience in a hospital nursery as she had insisted on adding 'anxiety' to her self-descriptors on the application form.

At this time Natalie joined her mother, Angela, in an evening course in hairdressing at a local college. This allowed her to mix with a group of people of a range of different ages and backgrounds, who really seemed to take to her innocent warmth and sense of humour. She was popular in the class if not a natural hairdresser! As the class progressed into more complex skills it became obvious how hard she found the practical side, despite sailing through the theory. This highlighted some painfully obvious difficulties with proprioception and fine motor coordination which had been discovered in her past but, sadly, neglectfully ignored by professionals.

Later that summer, the results from her GCSEs were published; it emerged that Natalie had done much better than expected, including in mathematics, which was an amazing achievement considering she found it so hard and could not even read an analogue clock face!

The family's local CAMHS discharged Natalie at age 16, stating that she no longer required their services. This was worrying and Angela went with her to visit her GP to request that he write to the team with a view to providing ongoing support. This was not effective and no further support was forthcoming. This meant that ultimately Natalie was without support services for the next two years. The antidepressants she had been prescribed had caused an unwelcome weight gain and little improvement in symptoms, so were stopped.

Over the school holidays, a friend she had known platonically for years started contacting Natalie more frequently. He asked her to meet him at the cinema, not as a friend but as a girlfriend. Angela was slightly concerned about this, but cautiously agreed. Their relationship quickly developed and became very intense, and Angela now acknowledges that, looking back, she was 'devastatingly' unaware of just how dangerously naive and vulnerable Natalie was. She recalls giving Natalie the usual 'mum's advice' which she mistakenly thought meant the same as it did to her – that she would be able to put down boundaries and say 'no' if things moved too fast or got uncomfortable. Over the next few months they appeared so happy together. However, shockingly, it appeared that the boy had been emotionally and physically abusing Natalie. She kept all of this to herself and appeared blissfully happy, both at home and at school. A subsequent trip to see a doctor revealed the level of abuse and resulted in police involvement and a downwards spiral affecting the whole family. Angela reports that it is still 'incredibly painful' for the whole family to reflect on and Natalie has not had another relationship since. Angela said that she finds it hard to forgive herself for the pain Natalie went through. She masked her difficulties so well.

A few weeks after the police involvement, the whole family went on holiday to Morocco. The first night ended in a massive full-on meltdown, but after this, she was fine for the rest of the holiday, enjoying the attention from the local boys who called her 'princess'.

Natalie did not continue with the hairdressing course with her mother as the tutor stated that she was reluctant to 'set her up to fail'. However, amazingly, even with everything going on for her, she did manage to complete one year of the sixth form (age 16–17 in the United Kingdom).

She was still struggling to come to terms with the after-effects of being in an abusive relationship and became obsessed with blaming Angela. She also began self-harming.

When she was 18, she received a letter out of the blue inviting her to attend an appointment at her local Adult Community Mental Health Service. Angela attended these appointments with Natalie and, after a few visits, the psychiatrist queried whether Natalie may have a mood disorder or even a borderline personality disorder, but stated that, at the time, she was too young to diagnose formally.

When he asked Natalie if she felt 'empty inside', she was confused and said she did not know what she felt. In fact, describing her as feeling empty inside could not have been further from the truth. If anything, she felt too much. She was prescribed a different antidepressant medication from the one she had been taking previously and, at each appointment, the dose was increased. Angela reported feeling suspicious and anxious about this and began to try to find out for herself what was really going on for her daughter. Every search she made came up with the possibility that Natalie may have Asperger's syndrome. Angela described this as her 'eureka' moment. She became sure that this provided the best explanation for her daughter's difficulties throughout her life.

At the next appointment with the psychiatrist, Angela mentioned this as a possibility. He searched for it on the internet via his mobile phone as if he had never heard of it before. He umm-ed and ahh-ed and finally nodded his head. Angela reported being completely taken aback at his lack of knowledge of neurodevelopmental disorders as a mental health professional. She then contacted the first specialist whose name came up when she searched for someone to assess Natalie and was offered a quick appointment. This woman had written books on the subject. Angela also rang another woman who was setting up a new charity in a nearby town and spoke to her for hours.

At the assessment Natalie had not been in the room for five minutes before the conclusion was drawn that she definitely had Asperger's syndrome. A report was written which was then passed on to her GP who expressed concern about the high dose of antidepressant she was being prescribed.

At the same time, the family were also going through child protection proceedings as Angela had been accused of fabricating and pathologising illness in her children. The assessment that confirmed that Natalie had Asperger's syndrome was 'thrown out' by the social worker who did not believe that she was on the autism spectrum. This sparked further investigation and finally, with a letter of support from a different social worker on her Community Mental Health Team, the family were awarded funding to send Natalie for an assessment at the Maudesley Hospital (who carry out complex assessments). At this point Natalie had lost a great deal of weight.

During this assessment, a very detailed history of Natalie's development was taken including a three-hour conversation with Angela on the telephone. In addition, several further appointments and visits to meet the team were made. Whilst this was taking place, Natalie's behaviour suddenly became very unusual. The family asked for a home visit from a community psychiatric nurse, who as soon as she saw Natalie declared, in an inappropriately loud and insensitive voice, 'SHE'S PSYCHOTIC.' Angela vividly recalls her shock at hearing someone dear to her described in this way. She reports that the words 'seared through her'.

The crisis team were called in. They could not believe that the consultant psychiatrist on the Community Mental Health Team had not even met Natalie and that, it appeared, she had been left in the care of a very junior colleague. They prescribed her a very small dose of risperidone (an anti-psychotic drug) which worked very quickly to settle her. However, she did experience very profound side-effects. Eventually, she became so unwell that the family decided to take Natalie to the Accident and Emergency department at her local hospital in the middle of the night. A special meeting was called early the following morning with the team and it was decided to admit her to the psychiatric assessment ward. The security guards were called and they had to pull Natalie from her mother's arms as Natalie was so reluctant to let her go.

A few hours later, her condition had deteriorated still further and another meeting was called where it was decided to admit her. She had agreed to be admitted as a voluntary patient, so it was not necessary to section her under the Mental Health Act.

What the family were not aware of at that time was that this would turn into a 'horrible six months' of trial and error, with many different drugs tried and many different 'working diagnoses' being given to Natalie. What she went through during this time Angela describes as 'just short of torture, both mentally and physically'. Natalie did eventually need to be sectioned under the Mental Health Act as she kept 'trying to escape the locked ward every time the door was opened to let other people in and out'. Her physical health deteriorated and she gained a lot of weight.

Angela reported that the hardest thing of all was to see their 'little girl' with all her naivety and vulnerability being placed on a mixed adult ward that had dormitories (as opposed to the individual rooms that are the norm). The ward was eventually deemed unfit for purpose and ultimately closed.

During this time, the family were fortunate that they were able to see Natalie almost every day and did manage to build some good relationships with the staff who were treating her.

Thank goodness, the consultant psychiatrist who was treating her did manage to spot the autism that was 'unmasked' by her illness. However, he was not qualified to diagnose autism and chose what he referred to as the 'closest fit', namely childhood schizophrenia. This did at least mean that she would be entitled to lifelong services. He formed a professional relationship with the team at the Maudsley Hospital and arranged an appointment for her to go back once well enough to be discharged from the psychiatric unit.

The Social Services team were reluctant to allow Natalie to return home as they deemed that she could be a risk to the other children in the family. Fortunately, the consultant psychiatrist working with her managed to persuade them that she was not a danger to anyone and the family were taken off the Child Protection Register.

In May 2013, by this time bloated with olanzapine (an atypical anti-psychotic), during the month the new DSM-5 came out, Natalie was finally, and correctly, diagnosed with autism.

ANNABELLE'S STORY

Annabelle is the mother of a child with autism and pathological demand avoidance. In her story she describes her experiences of getting a diagnosis, trying to manage her child's difficult behaviour and ultimately having her own parenting questioned to the extent that her children were placed on a Child Protection Plan. She found herself being accused of fabricated and induced illness and describes her fight to clear her and her husband's name, and her subsequent mental health difficulties. Finally, she describes her own journey towards a diagnosis of autism for herself.

Her story started when her older child was around two and a half. She recalled going to her GP and asking for support with her child's behaviour. She described her child as 'over-emotional' and as massively over-reacting to everyday events. At this point she was not aware of autism or pathological demand avoidance and was simply asking for help. The GP referred her to her local consultant paediatrician and also made the health visitor aware that Annabelle was experiencing some difficulties managing her child.

The paediatrician saw her and agreed that there were some difficulties. He then referred her on to an occupational therapist and a speech and language therapist. Her child at this point was banging his head on the wall and running around a great deal. Annabelle now realises that these difficulties were related to sensory processing difficulties and sensory overload.

At this point, it became clear that some of the professionals involved with Annabelle were beginning to question her parenting. Comments were made about 'letting him cry it out' and her 'not giving him enough freedom'. At this point Annabelle's child was becoming more distressed about certain things in the house. Annabelle recalls moving things away into a spare room which they jokingly referred to as the 'wrong room' (this was meant in the context of her child not being able to tolerate the items because they were different or not quite 'right'). When this was mentioned to the professionals working with him, this was interpreted as her being overprotective and not allowing him to experience a full range of emotions, when in fact, it was a reflection of his (then undiagnosed) inflexibility of thought and sensory difficulties.

These concerns continued to be raised, without Annabelle's knowledge. Thinking that she was being honest in acknowledging how difficult her little boy was, she continued to try to explain how challenging it was trying to manage him. When she expressed concern that the local nursery and school were not in a good area and that she did not feel it would benefit him to attend because of his communication difficulties, this was recorded as her having a 'distorted sense of social class'.

At the same time, it was becoming increasingly difficult to manage her little boy out of the family home. Shopping trips to local supermarkets were especially challenging. As a result she applied for a 'blue badge' (this is a badge given to people with disabilities or parents of children with disabilities which enables parents to park very near to a shop entrance).

Annabelle was then asked by her paediatrician to put together 'evidence' in the form of photographs and so on that demonstrated the degree of difficulty she was experiencing with her son. One picture was taken after her son had bitten his arm and was smiling (this was due to his exceptionally high pain threshold). She then asked for a referral to her local CAMHS. At this point, she was told that it was felt that his problems were due to her own levels of anxiety. She has subsequently discovered, after requesting full disclosure of all emails and correspondence, that her son's nursery nurse had accessed Annabelle's professional art site on the internet. Annabelle acknowledges that she creates quite graphic and 'emotive' art and now realises that she used this to express her own internal struggle with trying to make sense of her own emotions. However, this was interpreted as indicating that her psychological well-being was not good and that it was she, and not her son, who needed support.

Following this, concerns were escalated to the point of the professionals working with the family deciding that there were 'safeguarding' concerns. Once again, Annabelle and her husband attempted to be very honest about their own struggles (her husband had experienced behavioural difficulties as a child and felt that he may be on the autism spectrum). Annabelle also described the issues she had faced as a child. None of the professionals involved with the case considered that this might be helpful to explore further. Over time it was suggested that parental anxiety might be the issue and this eventually changed to suggestions of fabricated or induced illness and a desire to seek benefit payments.

At this point Annabelle was pregnant with her second child and her son had become increasingly aggressive to the point that her husband eventually gave up work so that he could help to protect her from being kicked because of the risk this would pose to the unborn baby.

Annabelle then described how, shortly before one Christmas, when the family were at home making decorations, they received an unannounced visit from Social Services. They were not aware at this point that this was as a result of a child protection concern having been raised. Once again, they were very honest about their struggles in the hope they might receive some support. Following this visit Annabelle then saw a report which stated, 'Mum shouts at professionals and gets very irate when she does not get what she wants.' She was also referred to as 'manipulative'. She was also told that there was 'nothing wrong' with her son. Annabelle refers to the report as being 'vile' and describes feeling 'ripped apart'.

The family were then placed on Section 47 of the Children's Act 1989 (this indicated that professionals working with the family believed that they have 'reasonable cause to suspect children are suffering or likely to suffer significant harm'). The term 'fabricated and induced illness' was also mentioned. Annabelle reported having no idea at that time what this term meant. She then went on the internet to find out and was 'terrified' as she could see that it could be easy for others to misinterpret some of the behaviours she had reported.

Following this, Annabelle reported having a 'huge meltdown' because she felt so overwhelmed by everything. She banged her head on the floor and became almost catatonic. Following this, she visited her doctor and was referred to her local mental health team who subsequently diagnosed her with a borderline personality disorder. At first, Annabelle was happy with this as she felt that it might mean that she was no longer judged and that people would understand that she was struggling.

At this point, she also decided to seek an independent assessment of her son. He was diagnosed with autism and pathological demand avoidance. Once the professional report was received, the child protection concerns were dropped and there has been no further social services contact.

This experience has made Annabelle look seriously at her own difficulties and she is now pursuing a diagnosis for herself. She is aware that she is very anxious. She shared a comment that she had written as a statement to describe some of her artwork (she is a successful and talented artist who has exhibited her work at major art galleries in the past): 'I cannot control my emotions. I cannot understand. I love, I hate, I binge, I purge.' She acknowledges that she is a very literal black and white thinker and that she is someone who becomes very angry and anxious when other people cannot see her point of view. She also reported 'speaking as she finds', sometimes to the point of appearing blunt and rude. She is also aware that she is very vulnerable and sees 'everyone as her friend'. At 18 she developed bulimia and used to self-harm 'out of frustration'. She recalls not fitting in at school and not doing well academically. In terms of a career, she reported having 'chopped and changed' direction many times and moving frequently from job to job.

She stated that she has very few friends (apart from one woman who has a diagnosis of Asperger's syndrome). She is very aware that she struggles to cope with pressure and can be self-destructive. She admits to drinking to excess as a 'way of fitting in'.

She also stated that her experience of trying to get support for her son and the subsequent criticism of her parenting has had a huge impact on her. She struggles to trust people now and prefers everything to be put in an email so that there is less danger of her misinterpreting what is said to her.

JENNY'S STORY

Jenny is the mother of two children on the autism spectrum. She too describes the struggle she had in accessing an appropriate assessment and diagnosis for her daughter.

Jenny reported that, following significant concerns about the development and behaviour of their son, they were referred to a child and family unit which offered specialist inpatient and outpatient mental health treatment for children with their parents and siblings using a whole-family approach. The unit provided assessment and treatment for children with complex developmental and/or psychiatric disorders and children presenting with severe emotional and behavioural problems. They carried out a number of assessments with Jenny's son. However, whilst they were there, Jenny recalls mentioning to the team that her daughter was also displaying difficulties. She was very demanding and refusing to do anything they asked her to. This was when she was about six. The centre agreed to have a look at her at the same time as they assessed her son. After spending some time with her, Jenny recalls that she was told, 'Oh, she's just like a lot of siblings of children with autism,' and diagnosed her with an attachment disorder. They carried on seeing her for a further six weeks and, at the end of this time, Jenny's daughter was extremely distressed – the methods they were using just didn't seem to be working. However, in spite of this, Jenny was told to carry on with these methods once the family returned home. Jenny tried this but her daughter remained extremely distressed and it took several weeks before she was calm again.

Her behaviour did not improve and after several years going backwards and forwards to their local CAMHS with various support workers coming and going, being sent on a variety of parenting courses, being given all sorts of reasons and being blamed for how her daughter presented, Jenny finally decided to go back to her doctor.

At this point Jenny's daughter was reported to be 'really struggling' (she was now 12) so Jenny asked for a second opinion on her diagnosis. She reported that her local CAMHS team refused to reassess her, simply saying she was 'very complex'. In the end Jenny's GP wrote to CAMHS to ask for funding to have her assessed at Elizabeth Newson Centre for another opinion (the Elizabeth Newson Centre in Nottingham, United Kingdom is a specialised centre for the assessment and diagnosis of autism and pathological demand avoidance). Eventually Jenny managed to secure the funding for the assessment and her daughter was eventually diagnosed with autism spectrum disorder and aspects of pathological demand avoidance.

However, this was not the end of the story. Not long after her daughter's diagnoses Jenny had to once again seek support from the CAMHS team, due to her daughter's mental health problems and self-harming. Fortunately, the CAMHS team did now accept that Jenny's daughter had autism and not an attachment disorder and, at the age of 16, they also diagnosed her with an anxiety disorder. They also now accept that the approach that Jenny had been trying to take with her daughter for several years was the right one.

However, Jenny still feels the upset and hurt caused when her daughter was diagnosed with an attachment disorder and felt blamed for causing her difficulties, whilst all the time she was simply trying really hard to understand her daughter. In her heart she knew she hadn't done anything to cause her behaviour but it was still hard.

BETH'S STORY

Beth also has a daughter with serious pathological demand avoidance, anxiety and several other co-existing disorders. As Beth's daughter was born in 1975, Beth reported a long history of misunderstanding and 'blunders' in terms of accessing professional support and advice for her daughter. Over the years she reported having had to go out of her way to 'learn all about autism in order to be able to tell other people about her condition – doctors, consultants, social workers, behavioural nurses and school staff of course'. She reported that it had often been 'hideous' and that it frequently resembled a Stephen King story.

SARAH'S STORY

Sarah has a daughter with autism and pathological demand avoidance and eloquently explains the impact of her daughter's difficulties on the family and for her particularly as a mother. She stated that the biggest impact upon her overall is probably the strain on her brain/mind. This is mainly because every aspect of life has to be thought through in advance and every eventuality has to be carefully planned for 'so you end up having to have a plan A, B and C for any time you might want to leave the house'.

She said that she also has to be prepared for the fact that something might not be available at the time it is wanted, and that she has to try to help her child to understand why this might be. She explained that having a child with autism and pathological demand avoidance forces you to have a whole array of options on hand.

Sarah also reported that she has constant feelings of guilt, which just is not there with her other (neuro-typical) daughter. She acknowledges that all parenting involves guilt, but this is guilt on a completely different level. When your child needs time to unwind and de-stress, and prefers their own company, you feel guilty that you are not spending time with them and helping them learn, guilty that they are having too much screen time. Guilty that they are not eating a variety of healthy food and that you've given up (for now) the added stress of trying to introduce new food to their plate because it is outright refused every time. Guilty that they are not socialising and making friends in the way you know other children can, and guilty because you know that playdates are ten times as hard at this age (9) than they are for other people's children, because your child doesn't share the same social interests or the ability to chat freely and share evenly, which the others in her mainstream class can. So you end up feeling guilty for organising playdates infrequently if at all.

Sarah also reports that she often feels guilty for having to take up the time of the teaching staff by repeating every small action which may eventually lead to a meltdown, and guilty for asking them to be flexible and bend the rules — because you know if they don't, then attendance is not likely to happen at all. For Sarah the 'guilty' thing is quite a big theme!

Sarah also bravely admitted that having a child with autism and pathological demand avoidance can lead to parents feeling isolated. When her child was younger, she could barely leave the house with her, and certainly couldn't join in with the usual 'mums and toddler' groups as her daughter wasn't the least bit interested in being there. More than that, she would actively try to leave. She always wanted Sarah's full attention, so she couldn't even go and have a coffee and a chat with other mums with young children – if there was nothing to hold her daughter's attention, she would actively insist on leaving.

As her daughter has got older, Sarah reports a different type of isolation. She found that because her daughter was invited to fewer events because she may not be able to cope with them, this led to Sarah being invited to fewer social events too. Other people's friendships grew stronger and she reported feeling very much on the outside of them and left out, even though she knew it was not ill-intentioned.

Sarah said she would have liked to have become more involved with Parent Teacher Association (PTA) events, school fairs, and so on, but it has always been difficult to get cover for her daughter, and she definitely wouldn't let Sarah be there and do her own thing.

Sarah reflects that she feels lucky that she is a 'fairly happy person' and none of this has led to mental health issues for her, but she acknowledges that she can clearly see how it might for others. She did say that it is not all bad and was keen to share some of the positives. She said that she has found it very rewarding getting to know how her girl 'ticks'. She also reports that she has been on a 'a pretty steep learning curve with autism and pathological demand avoidance' and that it does feel like she has achieved something – a fairly happy and stable home life for one thing. Through writing a blog, she has received comments about how sharing her story has helped others, and it feels good for her to know that. Life is good, just very fast-paced and full on *all* the time. But one of her favourite sayings is 'there's never a dull moment' with her girl around – even when, some days, it feels dull because she won't agree to leave the house to go anywhere!

MIRIAM'S STORY

Miriam was kind enough to respond to a request for parents to come forward to share their stories of obtaining an autism diagnosis and accessing support in the United States. Miriam lives with her children (including Lucy who has a diagnosis of autism) in New York. One of her sons has a diagnosis of ADHD.

Miriam describes how when her daughter was 13 years old and in the eighth grade at a private school, she was extensively bullied by the other girls. She reported how the other girls took her e-reader (which she used to take to keep herself occupied during break times) from her and held it over the garbage can. Another girl recorded Lucy being bullied and posted it online. She began making excuses not to attend school and did not enter tenth grade. Her mood spiralled and she became increasingly depressed. The crisis intervention team provided her with an ABA therapist but ultimately Lucy was voluntarily hospitalised because she was experiencing suicidal ideation. Miriam recalls her distress when having to take her to the emergency room and being asked to leave her there. She stated it was difficult not being able to speak to her or comfort her. She did acknowledge, though, that she felt fortunate because she could afford to pay for good care for her daughter and stated that for parents without funding, the care may not have been so good.

At this time, Lucy also became increasingly 'picky' about the type and variety of food she was willing to eat.

Miriam again acknowledged that she felt that she was fortunate when Lucy was discharged from hospital as she was very unsure at that time as to what might be the most appropriate next step to support her. She got good support from the Board of Education in her local area who subsequently agreed to fund her place at a residential facility where she is currently placed. Miriam did again acknowledge that she 'got lucky' in this respect as provision does vary greatly from state to state in America. She also stated that knowledge amongst professionals about girls with autism is very variable and that she is currently searching for information to help her team to support her appropriately.

HELEN'S STORY

Helen's story explains so clearly how it felt when her daughter with autism became suicidal.

Helen stated that she knew what was being said about me in the meeting called to discuss her daughter, because her friend was sitting there, not as my friend but in her role as a teacher from another school. She told the attendees at the meeting that she knew me socially and she had already asked me if it was okay to stay in the room whilst Helen and her family were being discussed by the meeting. Helen had agreed for her friend be there – she knew it all anyway and looking back now with hindsight, she is so glad that she had one person there believing what she said was true. She also knew that this meant she had one person who was brave enough to tell her what was truly said at the meeting. At least she would know what they really thought.

Helen recalled, 'The funny thing is, at the point when those words were spoken about me (in a meeting when I wasn't present), I wasn't an over-anxious person. I was a worried and concerned person and this was the appropriate response given the distress I was witnessing in my daughter each morning as I struggled to persuade her to get up and leave the safety of her bed; the daily battle, trying to get her dressed for school, eventually her body giving in and letting me dress her, as her spirit was slowly breaking down.' Each day, as Helen's daughter walked into school she blended in, like a switch clicked in her head, and so Helen believes that her request for help meant she must be the problem as her daughter was reported to be 'just fine' as soon as she got into school.

Helen recalls that it wasn't until much later, years later in fact, that she was so traumatised by each day and each battle that she developed an anxiety disorder. She strongly suspects that she has PTSD now. Every missed call from school, every email from a professional, every letter from the local authority sets it off, she starts shaking and has to sit and breathe, and allow the waves of panic to pass by, until her brain can start to function again. She reported that she has read research that suggests the level of stress parents of children with autism have to live with is similar to that of war veterans suffering from PTSD. She can totally believe this.

Helen recalls the day she 'broke' was the day her beautiful girl asked her to smother her in her sleep. 'It was bedtime and she looked at me with eyes full of pain. "If you do it when I'm asleep then I won't feel it and I won't have to go to school any more." I'm screaming inside, where did it go so badly wrong? I didn't bring you into the world to do this to you. Looking back now, I want to say that was the lowest point, but it wasn't.

'What I didn't know then was I would be faced with my lovely daughter on suicide watch (medicines locked in suitcases and knives in the safe) and that the anxiety would stop her eating and at that point I had to do anything to just get calories into her to keep her living in the world.

'It had been bad in primary school, but as she moved to secondary school our entire world collapsed. By the October, she wasn't "fine" in school any more. The school refusal only home could see became the school refusal that everyone could see as we stood in the car park trying to talk her out of the car, sat in my house witnessing her crying like a wounded animal in her bed, heard her in the background as I rang school each day.'

By the January, Helen recalls sitting in a CAMHS appointment with her, being told that her 11-year-old needed antidepressant medication and listening in horror as her daughter struggled to tell the professionals that she wanted to be smothered so she didn't have to go to school.

At the end of that appointment, Helen recalls the psychiatrist observing her daughter and was not aware that she too was being watched as the psychiatrist packed her bag of notes. In her later letter, the psychiatrist commented that in her opinion Helen had only managed to get her daughter into school so far because of the approach she had taken, but that in her view Helen couldn't do this much longer and her daughter's school placement would eventually fail.

Helen describes her feelings at that time: 'Even now, I realise those words meant so much because just one professional had looked and not found me to be at fault – I wasn't just an over-anxious or a failing parent. I was trying everything I could and on that one occasion I was met with compassion and understanding and not judgement. It is one of the very few moments when that happened.'

Helen said that she 'wasn't broken' when her story started but watching her beautiful girl break, and being judged by many professionals, battling for even the basic support for her, let alone the eventual specialist package of support, broke her too. She didn't need more judgement. As she puts it herself, 'I judge myself at every turn... could I have done it differently...should I have stopped earlier...asked for help in a better way...made someone understand...tried harder...not looked so anxious...not allowed myself to break?

'So I'm sharing this as a plea to professionals. If Mum is anxious it doesn't mean Mum is the problem...it means *there is a problem* and it is through listening, and understanding, that you will support the child, Mum and the whole family. Please don't stand back and judge us whilst we break.'

References

American Psychiatric Association (2013) *Diagnostic and Statistical Manual of Mental Disorders, 5th Edition: DSM-5.* Arlington, VA: American Psychiatric Association.

Eaton, J. (2015) The Psychological Needs of Children and Adults with Neurodevelopmental Conditions Including Autism. In B. Williams, E. Peart, R. Young *et al. Capacity to Change : Understanding and Assessing a Parent's Capacity to Change within the Timescales of the Child.* Bristol: Jordan Publishing.

Prowse, A. (2016) *The Food of Love.* Seattle, WA: Lake Union Publishing.

Useful Resources for Clinicians and Parents

Publications

Attwood, Tony (2016) *Exploring Depression and Beating the Blues.* London: Jessica Kingsley Publishers.

Bridge, Emma Louise and Bridge, Penelope (2016) *Autism, Anxiety and Me: A Diary in Even Numbers.* London: Jessica Kingsley Publishers.

Christie, Phil and Duncan, Margot (2011) *Understanding Pathological Demand Avoidance Syndrome in Children: A Guide for Parents, Teachers and Other Professionals.* London: Jessica Kingsley Publishers.

Dunn Buron, Kari and Curtis, Mitzi (2012) *The Incredible 5-Point Scale: The Significantly Improved and Expanded Second Edition.* Shawnee Mission, KS: AAPC Publishing.

Fidler, Ruth and Christie, Phil (2015) *Can I tell you about Pathological Demand Avoidance?* London: Jessica Kingsley Publishers.

Henault, Isabelle (2005) *Asperger's Syndrome and Sexuality: From Adolescence Through Adulthood.* London: Jessica Kingsley Publishers.

Kershaw, Penny (2011) *The ASD Workbook: Understanding Your Autism Spectrum Disorder.* London: Jessica Kingsley Publishers.

Legge, Brenda (2008) *Can't Eat, Won't Eat: Dietary Difficulties and Autism Spectrum Disorders.* London: Jessica Kingsley Publishers.

Levine, Karen (2015) *Attacking Anxiety.* London: Jessica Kingsley Publishers.

Linehan, Marsha M. (2014) *DBT Skills Training Handouts and Worksheets*. London: Guildford Press.

Lipsey, Deborah (2011) *From Anxiety to Meltdown: How Individuals on the Autistic Spectrum Deal with Anxiety, Experience Meltdowns, Manifest Tantrums and How You Can Intervene Effectively.* London: Jessica Kingsley Publishers.

PBS Academy and The Challenging Behaviour Foundation (2016) *Positive Behavioural Support Information Pack for Family Carers: Resource 5.* Accessed on 9 May 2017 at http://pbsacademy. org.uk/wp-content/uploads/2016/03/Final-Resource-5-PBS-Academy-family-pack.pdf.

Rathus, Jill and Miller, Alec (2015) *DBT Skills Manual for Adolescents.* London: Guildford Press.

Rowe, Alis (2014) *Asperger's Syndrome and Anxiety: Looking at Anxiety in People with Autism Spectrum Disorders.* The Visual Guides, vol. 1. London: Lonely Mind Books.

Rowe, Alis (2015) *Asperger's Syndrome: Meltdowns and Shutdowns. Reactions to Stress and Anxiety in Autism Spectrum Disorders.* The Visual Guides, vol. 3. London: Lonely Mind Books.

Seiler, Laurie (2008) *Cool Connections with Cognitive Behavioural Therapy: Encouraging Self-Esteem, Resilience and Well-Being in Children Using CBT Approaches.* London: Jessica Kingsley Publishers.

Shapiro, Lawrence (2008) *Let's Be Friends: A Workbook to Help Kids Learn Social Skills and Make Great Friends, second edition.* Oakland, CA: New Harbinger.

Sherwin, Jane (2015) *My Daughter is Not Naughty.* London: Jessica Kingsley Publishers.

Stallard, Paul (2002) *Think Good – Feel Good: A Cognitive Behaviour Therapy Workbook for Children and Young People.* Chichester: Wiley-Blackwood.

Stock Kranowitz, Carol (*2001*) *The Out-of-Sync Child.* London: Jessica Kingsley Publishers.

Tadat-Rugeri, Lynn, Langurand, Mary and Caruso, John (2014) *The Thinking Skills Workbook: A Cognitive Skills Remediation Manual for Adults.* Springfield, IL: Charles C. Thomas.

Tchanturia, Kate (2014) *Cognitive Remediation Therapy (CRT) for Eating and Weight Disorders*. London: Routledge.

Whitehouse, Elaine and Pudney, Warwick (1998) *A Volcano in My Tummy: Helping Children to Handle Anger: A Resource Book for Parents, Caregivers and Teachers, first edition*. Gabriola Island, BC: New Society Publishers.

Wilkinson, Lee (2015) *Overcoming Anxiety and Depression on the Autism Spectrum: A Self-Help Guide Using CBT*. London: Jessica Kingsley Publishers.

Useful websites

Autism Canada

Autism Canada was established in 1976 and aims to share best practice in order to support individuals with autism and their families.

www.autismcanada.org

Autism East Midlands (formerly NORSACA)

Autism East Midlands is an autism charity in the United Kingdom which was originally founded in the late 1960s by a group of concerned parents in the Nottinghamshire area who felt that their children with autism were not able to access appropriate schooling. This led to the establishment of Sutherland House, a specialist autism school. Autism East Midlands provide services, information and support for both adults and children with autism.

www.autismeastmidlands.org.uk

Autism New Zealand

Autism New Zealand is a charitable organisation which provides support, education and training for individuals with autism and their families.

www.autismnz.org.nz

Autism Society America

Autism Society America is described as the nation's leading autism organisation, and aims to assist individuals with autism by providing information about treatment, education and current research.

www.autism-society.org

Autism South Africa

Autism South Africa is an organisation that aims to raise awareness of autism throughout South Africa and promotes education, therapy and advocacy.

www.aut2know.co.za

Autism Spectrum Australia (ASPECT)

Autism Spectrum Australia is a non-profit-making service which supports children and adults with autism and their families.

www.autismspectrum.org.au

Carol Gray: Social Stories™

Social Stories are a useful way of introducing ideas to children with autism and helping them to learn social skills and appropriate behaviour.

http://carolgraysocialstories.com/social-stories

Child Exploitation and Online Protection (United Kingdom)

The Child Exploitation and Online Protection Agency is run by the National Crime Agency in the United Kingdom and is focused upon preventing child abuse. It can also provide useful advice to parents and carers who are concerned about protecting their children whilst they are online.

www.ceop.police.uk

National Autistic Society (United Kingdom)

The National Autistic Society (NAS) is a charitable organisation in the United Kingdom which offers support and advice to individuals who have autism and their families.

www.autism.org.uk

PDA Society

The PDA (Pathological Demand Avoidance) Society is a registered charity which has been set up to provide support, advice and training to both parents of children who display extreme demand avoidance and those working with them clinically or in school.

www.pdasociety.org.uk

Subject Index

Author Index